# Courageous Leaders
## TRANSFORMING THEIR WORLD

*"Be strong and courageous. Do not be afraid or terrified because of them, for the LORD your God goes with you; he will never leave you nor forsake you."*

Deuteronomy 31:6

*"Be strong and courageous, because you will lead these people to inherit the land I swore to their forefathers to give them. Be strong and very courageous."*

Joshua 1:6-7

# COURAGEOUS LEADERS

## TRANSFORMING THEIR WORLD

JAMES HALCOMB • DAVID HAMILTON • HOWARD MALMSTADT

PUBLISHING
P.O. BOX 55787 SEATTLE, WA 98155

YWAM Publishing is the publishing ministry of Youth With A Mission. Youth With A Mission (YWAM) is an international missionary organization of Christians from many denominations dedicated to presenting Jesus Christ to this generation. To this end, YWAM has focused its efforts in three main areas: 1) Training and equipping believers for their part in fulfilling the Great Commission (Matthew 28:19). 2) Personal evangelism. 3) Mercy ministry (medical and relief work).

For a free catalog of books and materials write or call:
YWAM Publishing
P.O. Box 55787, Seattle, WA 98155
(425) 771-1153 or (800) 922-2143
www.ywampublishing.com

**Courageous Leaders Transforming Their World**

Published by Youth With A Mission Publishing
P.O. Box 55787
Seattle, WA 98155

ISBN 1-57658-171-3

**Printed in the United States of America.**

# CONTENTS

PART B

# A God-Led Plan—Doing Things Right

PART C

## God-Motivated Action—Doing the Right Things Right

# ACKNOWLEDGMENT

We, the authors, have been immensely blessed and awed by the many exciting occasions when the Holy Spirit opened our hearts and minds to receive our Lord's thoughts, words, and encouragement for this book. Our Creator God has given us an opportunity to collaborate with Him. We acknowledge that without His input from start to finish there would be no reason for writing this book. He is the Alpha and the Omega, the focus at the beginning, throughout, and at the end.

We bow down and give praise, honor, and heartfelt thanks to our God, the God who is so very personal and yet infinite, the God who millennia ago initiated an awesome, life-changing, world-transforming project through His courageous Son, Jesus Christ. We thank You, Father, Son, and Holy Spirit, for Your life-transforming work, which continues through the ages and has impacted our lives. We pray that those who read this book will be inspired to be courageous leaders who will collaborate with You to transform their worlds and bring honor and glory to You.

# Why Another
# Book on Leadership

In frustration, and often in desperation, or even in rage, the cries echo through the ages. Where are we headed? When will it happen? What can we do? Why doesn't someone do something? Who will lead us?

Yes, who will lead? The needs are overwhelming—to accomplish many urgent or worthwhile things, to head in the right direction, to make good things happen now, to transform your community, to overcome evil, to do the right things. Has God inspired you with thoughts, a dream, a hope, a vision for transforming your world? Do you desire to overcome fears and step out courageously to transform your world with God-motivated action?

For many years we have heard about wonderful visions from our brothers and sisters in Christ. Usually these visions remain only as hopes and dreams, gradually fading away. Why? In his book *The Leader of the Future*, highly respected management authority Peter Drucker wrote, "Leadership must be learned and can be learned." We agree. We have seen it happen. The purpose of this book is to inspire, encourage, and prepare many to become leaders—or better leaders—courageous leaders, who will move from a God-inspired vision to a God-led plan and into God-motivated action.

We have been thrilled to watch young and not-so-young leaders and potential leaders invest heartfelt efforts in learning the leadership principles and methods presented in this book. Part A emphasizes the vision, your hopes and dreams, and the importance of knowing God's will and seeking His guidance to *do the right things*. Part B presents a powerful 5-step process for developing the God-led Leaders Plan that helps you to *do things right*, even for complex projects and programs. The Leaders Plan can be developed for the largest of projects and programs, such as discipling a nation, or for the less-extensive projects and programs in your church, home, or office. Part C guides you into God-motivated action so that *the right things are done right* as you implement the plan and reach for the goal set before you.

This book can serve as a road map or flight plan so that you can remain on a true course and reach your goal. It can help prevent many aborted starts, wrong directions, and breakdowns along the way to reaching your goal. How exciting to see God-inspired visions converted to God-led plans and God-motivated actions that bring honor and glory to our Lord. The overall approach and methods presented in this book are readily applicable for any project or program, including any ministry or mission, whether discipling a community, designing and developing an educational complex, launching a relief and development program, developing and distributing worldwide a Christian curriculum, establishing a business, or even building a house.

The three parts of this book provide a seamless transition from vision to plan to action so that the overall objective of a project or program is accomplished effectively and efficiently. This seamless and integrated approach to leadership spans the divide between principle and practice, physical reality and spiritual concept, heart and mind, people and project, the why and the how, goal-oriented and process-sensitive. Those who apply the principles and methods in this book will learn to collaborate with God as they build on the foundation of hearing God's voice and living in wholehearted commitment to doing His will in spirit and in truth. We trust that many will be encouraged to embrace their God-inspired vision, translate it into a God-led plan, and move courageously into God-motivated action with follow-through to complete the overall objective—to see the mission accomplished.

# God Inspired Vision— Doing the Right Thing

# Preparing to be Courageous Leaders

*Do not conform any longer to the pattern of this world, but be transformed by the renewing of your mind. Then you will be able to test and approve what God's will is— his good, pleasing and perfect will"* (Romans 12:2).

O ur Creator inspires us with vision to transform the world with Him—to do His will—to do the right thing. He leads us in preparing God-inspired plans that guide us into doing things right. With the right plans in hand we can move into action to do the right things right. God's plans done in God's ways give us exciting opportunities to collaborate with Him.

It all sounds so obvious, so straightforward. We know that there are many subtle temptations to do things that are not inspired by God. He allows us freedom to do things that are contrary to His will. Even with an inspired vision or purpose we can jump into making plans that, because they are not God's plans, are loaded with our own ideas and fail or result in many detours and delays. Even with God-inspired plans we tend to set about doing things our own way. We follow the world's ways and not the Master's ways.

Part A of this book focuses on the foundational leadership characteristics essential for staying on the right path and doing the right things so that the right thing will be done right. Chapter 1 emphasizes that all leaders bring about change, but only godly leaders bring about godly change. For God's purposes to be accomplished, we must know and seek the God who can cleanse us and transform us to be more like Him. We must grow intimate with our Creator God.

To do that which is right, we must have God as our constant reference point. God is the standard of rightness, as presented in Chapter 2. As we become intimate with the creative God of the Bible, we realize that seeking to do what is right opens up a myriad of possibilities—opportunities for developing, with God, new realities that shape the course of history. As God-led courageous leaders, we can pioneer new things that will benefit our world.

Chapter 3 explores some of the key ingredients of a courageous leader. It presents examples of people who are committed to the goals set before them and demonstrate the qualities of God-inspired leadership.

The final chapter in Part A focuses on courageous leaders who have a passion for accomplishing specific goals. It emphasizes that the callings, goals, or projects can take many different forms as the Lord leads. Thus, a courageous leader might not be in a position to directly guide or conduct the activities of a specific group but could be a leader who points the way for others—even millions of people—through writing, the arts, or other skills that are not connected to any official leadership position. Chapter 4 closes with suggestions on how to document your thoughts on a preplanning form before starting a new project or program. It encourages you to pray and meditate on God's ways and character, especially as related to the vision He gives to you, before you launch into plans and actions.

We trust that Part A will provide a foundation for a seamless transition from vision into plans and from plans into action—concepts and plans that will help you to prepare plans in Part B and plans that will provide a road map for transforming your world. We believe that the principles and examples presented in Part A can provide new insight and encouragement for being agents of godly change. A review or in-depth study of the truths presented in Part A can help you to co-create with God by doing His perfect will.

# CHAPTER 1

# Knowing What Is Right

*The vision concerning Judah and Jerusalem that Isaiah*
*son of Amoz saw during the reigns of Uzziah, Jotham,*
*Ahaz and Hezekiah, kings of Judah* (Isaiah 1:1).

Isaiah played a prolonged leadership role spanning some sixty years during the reigns of four prominent Judean kings. During those tumultuous times, leaders made critical decisions that impacted the destiny of nations for generations. Political turmoil, wars, and shifting military realities, economic booms and disasters, the breakdown of the moral fibre of society and family, and challenges to cultural identity and continuity reared their heads in the form of old dangers and new threats. Amidst the backdrop of this raging turmoil, some of the monarchs failed the test of history, while others excelled even amidst the most adverse of circumstances. Uzziah (792–740) began his reign well; Judah prospered, and hope prevailed in the land. Uzziah inspired hope and confidence. The nation enjoyed the fruit of political, military, and economic ascendancy until Uzziah fatefully compromised principle, bringing a disastrous conclusion to this once laudable reign. Uzziah's lack of integrity overshadowed earlier victories, dashing hope, destroying confidence. His son Jotham (750–732) was not a bad man. Although he did the right thing, he did so with mediocrity. He lacked the vision and courage to challenge the status quo, and under his reign, social deterioration continued its devastating toll. Jotham's son Ahaz (735–715) was a total failure; he neither did the right thing nor did things right. His corrupt leadership undermined the well-being of his nation. In contrast, Ahaz's son Hezekiah (715–686) was one of the more righteous and courageous leaders of the Judean monarchy. Under his leadership, Judah staved off certain military defeat and experienced a cultural and spiritual renaissance. Throughout all their reigns, Isaiah kept addressing the issues necessary for them to embrace so that they could become the courageous leaders that each of them had the potential to be. From the start of his writings, he urged rulers to abandon the corrupt, self-serving leadership standards of the status quo. In a scathing exposé, he declared to the nation:

> *Your rulers are rebels, companions of thieves; they all love bribes and chase after gifts. They do not defend the cause of the fatherless; the widow's case does not come before them* (Isaiah 1:23).

Faced with such a sad reality, Isaiah described the ultimate leadership ideal, pointing the way forward: *"See, a king will reign in righteousness and rulers will rule with justice"* (Isaiah 32:1). In this way, Isaiah expressed a longing that is as contemporary as today's newspaper: a cry for men and women who have such internal integrity and courage that they will rise to the challenge of the time and transform the hurting world into a place that reflects the character of a good and just God.

## SETTING YOUR SIGHTS HIGH / RELATING TO GOD

How are such leaders produced? For Isaiah it all began with a vision, a vision that arrested him in the daily course of events, a vision that drew his eyes heavenward to consider the Most High God. That changed focus marked Isaiah's life and leadership forever. What occupies the focus of your attention? Where are your eyes fixed? The courageous leader must first get the vision right by

16

looking to the ultimate Leader for the necessary perspective to make a positive impact on his or her world. To do the right things right in this world, the courageous leader must first look heavenward and, like Isaiah, begin with a right relationship with the right leader.

> *In the year that King Uzziah died, I saw the Lord seated on a throne, high and exalted, and the train of his robe filled the temple. Above him were seraphs, each with six wings: With two wings they covered their faces, with two they covered their feet, and with two they were flying. And they were calling to one another: "Holy, holy, holy is the LORD Almighty; the whole earth is full of his glory." At the sound of their voices the doorposts and thresholds shook and the temple was filled with smoke. "Woe to me!" I cried. "I am ruined! For I am a man of unclean lips, and I live among a people of unclean lips, and my eyes have seen the King, the LORD Almighty." Then one of the seraphs flew to me with a live coal in his hand, which he had taken with tongs from the altar. With it he touched my mouth and said, "See, this has touched your lips; your guilt is taken away and your sin atoned for." Then I heard the voice of the Lord saying, "Whom shall I send? And who will go for us?" And I said, "Here am I. Send me!"* (Isaiah 6:1–8).

Isaiah's leadership role in the nation was rooted in vision: a vision of God. No other starting point gives sufficient foundation to sustain leaders through the challenges of fulfilling their leadership responsibility. The courageous leader is inspired and driven by vision. To endure, a leader's vision must begin as a vision of God. As Oswald Chambers wrote, "A man with a vision from God is not devoted simply to a cause or a particular issue, but to God Himself."

Sometimes this passage is called "Isaiah's call," although a careful look makes it clear that nowhere does God directly call Isaiah. God does not issue an imperative: "Isaiah, go! I am sending you!"

Isaiah is not conscripted to obligatory service. Rather, God poses a question—thinking aloud, as it were—in the triune Godhead: *"Whom shall I send. And who will go for us?"* Because Isaiah had seen God for who He is, he eagerly and wholeheartedly volunteered his services. On that day in hearing that divine question, Isaiah gained insight into the yearnings and longings of God's heart. He sensed God's passion. He glimpsed God's dream. He understood God's desire. Therefore, he committed himself to do God's will.

When we speak of God's will, we must realize that we're not speaking of a mere philosophical abstraction or a nebulous theological doctrine. We are speaking most essentially of the driving desires of the most awesome Person in the universe. There are many images of God in the world, but only the God of the Bible is both infinite and personal. He's so vast in his natural attributes that *"the heavens, even the highest heavens cannot contain him"* (1 Kings 8:27, 2 Chronicles 2:6) and yet so personal that He dwells *"with him who is contrite and lowly in spirit"* (Isaiah 57:15).

When we speak of God as being personal, it does not mean that we can each shape Him into our subjective, personal image of the divine, molding it according to our own imagination. Rather, it means that He has certain attributes that distinguish Him from nonpersonal life forms and that we share those attributes with Him to some degree only because He, as the loving Creator, decided to shape us according to His image. These attributes include reason, volition, emotion. Therefore, God shares His will with us much like a friend shares the deepest desires of his or her heart with a close companion. This sharing is an expression of proffered friendship, and it is hoped that it is reciprocated with understanding and collaboration. God shares His will with us because He treats us as friends and enlists our collaboration as partners so that together we can make this world a better place.

## SETTING YOUR SIGHTS BROAD / RELATING TO YOUR WORLD

Leadership is not for the mystical isolationist cloistered away in a hermitage. The gaze heavenward to know God more intimately leads us to gaze around us at the reality of a hurting and needy world. When we begin by looking to God, we end up looking to the world, *"For the eyes of the LORD range throughout the earth"* (2 Chronicles 16:9). As we get to know Him, our gaze follows His gaze. We allow His concerns to become ours. Because He's concerned about the state of affairs of the world, we too become concerned. Time spent in His presence teaches us to think His thoughts, to feel His emotions, to choose His will, to speak His words, and to do His acts.

If we truly love the Creator, we cannot be indifferent to the status of His creation. Leadership means service, and if we are to be servants, we must look outward to those in need of our service. We need to focus on the issues of the hurting world and be compassion-driven. We must have that attitude that was so evident in Jesus: *"When he saw the crowds, he had compassion on them, because they were harassed and helpless, like sheep without a shepherd"* (Matthew 9:36). Like Jesus, the courageous leader must allow his heart to break with the things that break God's heart and reach out to the needy world.

## A FOUNDATION FOR CHANGE AND CONTINUITY

The majestic revelation of the holy character of the ultimate Leader, the King of kings, was the foundation for Isaiah's leadership role, defining his life's mission. Indeed, the revealed character and nature of God is the only solid foundation for leadership. It is that which guides, corrects, inspires, and teaches us regarding true leadership. God is the ultimate leadership paradigm, the standard by which all leadership is measured. The more the character of the leader approximates the revealed characteristics of God, the better the leader's service will be, effecting the much-needed change in today's world.

Whole books could be written on the character and nature of God that draw key principles and illustrate useful lessons for the courageous leader. Here we wish to highlight a few essential items and urge you to a lifetime pursuit of the continual discovery of the full richness of the person of God. For our purposes we will consider only the initial things God chose to reveal about Himself in the opening verses of the Bible. We will look at the first three verbs associated with God in the biblical text and reflect on the implications they have for our leadership.

## • The God Who Creates

The first statement we have in Genesis about God is *"In the beginning God created the heavens and the earth"* (Genesis 1:1). God is a creator, an innovator, an entrepreneur who does new things, producing beneficial change, breaking new ground, pioneering new realities. God is not a once-upon-a-time creator, His innovative abilities relegated to the distant past before the beginning of time. Time and time again the Scriptures refer to the ongoing creative character of God. God is a contemporary creator, innovating as surely today as He has in the past, always on the cutting edge. He is no has-been in this area; rather, He leads the field in His incomparable creative skills. Isaiah surely understood this, for God told him, *"You have heard these things; look at them all. Will you not admit them? From now on I will tell you of new things, of hidden things unknown to you. They are created now, and not long ago; you have not heard of them before today"* (Isaiah 48:6-7). Isaiah realized that the creative attribute of God was essential to divine leadership and thus speaks of God as the Creator King (Isaiah 43:15).

Because the new things God does are always done in conformity with His constant and faithful character, His innovations never produce a haphazard zigzagging of cross-purposes and changing goals. Rather, since His creative genius is always consistent with His character, there is always the perfect blend of change and continuity that most enhances life.

When we speak of God as a creator, we recognize that God is not a god of the status quo. He's a change maker. He does not look upon the current state of affairs of the world and lightly accept it as normal. On the contrary, God is sorely distressed by the condition of the world and is about the business of effecting change. He wants this globe to be a different, better place for His creatures and has acted accordingly to transform the world. The tragedies and horrors of this world are not of His making, and He does not passively sit by and indifferently observe the sorrows of a hurting humanity. God does not hopelessly shrug His shoulders and wash His hands of the whole mess while He fatalistically laments, "Oh, well, *que será será*—whatever will be will be." God is at work to turn this world around and enlists us to work together with Him to this end.

20

If we are genuinely to be God's people, we need to adopt His nonconformist attitude. We cannot consider the things that are amiss in the world and shrug them off with a helpless, "Well, that's just the way things are." When we hear of situations that do not reflect the good and loving character of a just and true God, we must not accept them as a fact of life, but we must devise ways to see God's transforming power released to change them forever. In a world that is continually bombarded by satellite images of bad news from every corner, we must not be desensitized by tragedy. Rather, we must be moved deeply by the discrepancy between the current reality and God's will to such an extent that we will live our lives to bring about godly change, exhibiting the good news by serving a hurting world.

Another realization that we have as we consider God's awesome creative abilities is that God is a visionary. He states, *"I make known the end from the beginning, from ancient times, what is still to come"* (Isaiah 46:10). He is forward-looking in His thinking, anticipating the future and acting to make the future better than the present. He does not merely consider today's reality; He dreams of tomorrow's possibilities. Throughout Scripture we are given glimpses into His dream. We are told in 1 Timothy, *"God our Savior...wants all men to be saved and to come to a knowledge of the truth"* (1 Timothy 2:3-4). Similarly, we read in 2 Peter that the Lord does not want *"anyone to perish, but everyone to come to repentance"* (2 Peter 3:9). These poignant declarations describe the desires of God's heart—His vision. Our God is not stuck in the quagmire of a visionless today. He's actively engaged, creatively at work, transforming today's vision into tomorrow's reality.

To become the best of leaders we must get to know Him so intimately that His dreams become our dreams; His vision, our vision; His will, our will. In this way we are not working at cross-purposes with God but are acting as His collaborators. His agenda should shape our agenda; His priorities should impact ours. God's dreams—not just our needs—should be the major influence in defining our vision.

There is an intrinsic sense of hope in modeling your leadership after the creative God of the Bible—the hope that the creative innovations dreamed about today can make for a better tomorrow.

We are not confined to the present. Change is possible as we follow our Creator God. Like God, courageous leaders harness all of their energy toward the fulfillment of their visions for the future, thus creating new realities.

## • The God Who Is With Us

The second statement in Genesis about God is this: *"Now the earth was formless and empty, darkness was over the surface of the deep, and the Spirit of God was hovering over the waters"* (Genesis 1:2). What is meant by "hovering"? This rare Hebrew verb is used only once in conjunction with God. It usually describes the act of a bird incubating an egg—the warm and intimate presence of the parent providing the environment in which life can emerge. Even so, God's presence transforms the inanimate into animate, the potential into actual, chaos into order, darkness into light, despair into hope. Whereas "God the creator" speaks of God's doing, "God the hoverer" speaks of God's being. The leader both does and is. Leadership is both an action for life and a quality of life. God's presence—His "Immanuelness"—with His creation is significant. As a leader He's not distant or removed. He's involved. His presence creates an environment that enhances the life of all around Him. This should be the goal of the courageous leader.

Isaiah understood the importance of the presence of the leader among those the leader serves. He prophesied that God's coming leader would be named *"Immanuel, which means, God with us"* (Matthew 1:23; see Isaiah 7:14, 8:8-10), a prophecy that had its fulfillment in Jesus, who according to John *"made his dwelling among us"* (John 1:14). Isaiah assigns to the coming Immanuel the highest leadership qualifications, saying that *"the government will be on his shoulders. And he will be called Wonderful Counselor, Mighty God, Everlasting Father, Prince of Peace. Of the increase of his government and peace there will be no end"* (Isaiah 9:6-7).

It is comforting to know that God did not just wind up the universe and let it go, observing our history from a comfortable detached distance. God is involved even amidst the chaos of the world. He's committed in personal, practical ways. Identification is costly, but God was willing to pay the price of presence. His identification with our humanity eventually led Him to pay the ultimate price on the cross, where the greatest of all leaders gave His life so that our lives might be transformed. Similarly, the courageous leader's personal involvement with his or her team should inspire hope, confidence, courage, and life. You cannot lead as an armchair theoretician; you must wade in amidst the mess and accompany your team in the process of change. This will require that you, too, will lay down your life in practical, daily servanthood.

Great leaders understand that they cannot lead if they are disengaged relationally from the people they lead. For this reason, George Washington lived with the cold and hungry revolutionary troops through the difficult winter in Valley Forge. His presence amidst them in these difficult circumstances forged this hodge-podge of citizens into a victorious army. Elitism on his part would have bred discouragement among the troops, but his personal commitment and practical involvement won their hearts and loyalty. Likewise, David, even as a young leader, understood that being with the people he led was crucial to his leadership, so *"he went out and came in before the people"* (1 Samuel 18:13 KJV). His greatest failure as a leader occurred when he *"remained in Jerusalem"* (2 Samuel 11:1) and tried to lead his troops from afar. Jesus, our supreme leadership model, practiced the principle of presence. When He formed His leadership team of twelve, He told them that the primary purpose was *"that they might be with him"* (Mark 3:14). Only as this relationship was established could He give them the rest of their mandate: *"that he might send them out to preach and to have authority to drive out demons"* (Mark 3:14-15). Relationship is the necessary context for task. Task is the outgrowth of relationship. Thus, courageous leaders must give of themselves both to the relationship and to the task. Being and doing cannot be dichotomized in us, because they are not dichotomized in God.

Because God walks among us, He's connected to us in a very realistic way. Because He's in touch, He's not deluded about the present state of affairs. He's fully aware of changing situations and is not caught off guard by shifting scenarios. Although God has defined, nonchanging goals, He's incredibly patient and flexible in the ways of achieving them because He dwells in our midst. He does not impose His solution without considering and evaluating our contribution to history. He's the consummate team player, always taking into account all of our decisions and ready with several contingency plans. The biblical prophets based their ministry on the understanding of this principle. God communicated this principle through Jeremiah:

> *"If at any time I announce that a nation or kingdom is to be uprooted, torn down and destroyed, and if that nation I warned repents of its evil, then I will relent and not inflict on it the disaster I had planned. And if at another time I announce that a nation or kingdom is to be built up and planted, and if it does evil in my sight and does not obey me, then I will reconsider the good I had intended to do for it"* (Jeremiah 18:7–10).

Because God is genuinely engaged with us in space and time, He's the ultimate realist. Because He's so in touch with reality, He is never caught fighting straw men or grappling with never-to-happen hypothetical problems. At the same time, He's extraordinarily sensitive to changing realities and can adjust His strategies always to be current. There is no inflexible rigidity in this constantly faithful and ever-present God who deals with certainties as certainties and contingencies as contingencies. Since God is dynamically involved with us, taking into consideration our decisions as He makes His, His leadership of us is always appropriate both for the moment and for the long haul. Thus, God's will is not a static, impersonal concept but it is the volitional expression of a constantly faithful, living God engaged in authentic relationship with His creation. Our choices are significant. God respects them, even when they are contrary to His will. God takes them seriously. This illustrates His tremendous humility as a leader, for He does not merely impose His will but considers ours as together we shape the future.

In a similar way, the courageous leader must endeavor to remain in touch with his or her team so as to be able to modify present strategies to ensure long-term progress toward making the vision reality. This is possible only as close relationships and communication are maintained. Likewise, the courageous leader must respect the decisions of those on the team and work to bring about enthusiastic and voluntary collaboration on the part of all.

## • The God Who Communicates

The third statement in Genesis about God is *"And God said, 'Let there be light,' and there was light"* (Genesis 1:3). God is not silent. He speaks. In fact, He is a communicator par excellence. It is of His very essence to communicate—so much so that throughout all of Scripture this is the most repeated concept regarding God: He said, He spoke, He communicated. Because He is such a superbly skilled and artful communicator, we can be confident that He will make His will known to us. We do not have to guess about the nature of God's dreams: Although they undoubtedly exceed human capability of comprehension as to their vastness, they have been made known to us as to their essence. God is not a withholder of information but a revealer of truth. The 31,175 verses, 1,189 chapters, and 66 books of the Bible bear ample testimony to this. He is the God *"who forms the mountains, creates the wind, and reveals his thoughts to man"* (Amos 4:13).

God's will is not a mystery for the honest seeker. For this reason, King David says to the crown prince as he passes on to him the leadership responsibility over the nation, *"And you, my son Solomon, acknowledge the God of your father, and serve him with wholehearted devotion and with a willing mind, for the LORD searches every heart and understands every motive behind the thoughts. If you seek him, he will be found by you..."* (1 Chronicles 28:9).

God's will is knowable to the courageous leader because God does not hide Himself from us nor does He cloak Himself in a shroud of silence. He communicates as fully as possible because He understands that communication is an act of loving servanthood. The sharing of information empowers the other members of the team. We do not live in an information vacuum with God, nor should we with those whom we lead.

Now, as courageous leaders seeking to do God's will, we must realize that God's will is not a fait accompli. People can and do resist God's will. In fact, many do that which is totally contrary to His will. The biblical text does not support a worldview of fatalistic determinism. Too often people helplessly shrug their shoulders in the midst of adverse circumstances, saying, "It must be God's will..." Not so the courageous leader who understands God's will and who understands that many things in our present experience stand in opposition to God's will. Therefore, the courageous leader prepares himself or herself as if for battle, knowing that the outcome is not fixed, that change is possible, that hindrances can be overcome, that reality can be transformed—but only as obstacles are overcome. This is where courage must be exercised!

The story of the God who creates, who presences Himself, and who communicates, is ultimately the story of redemption, of transformation, of change. This is a story in which we can collaborate with God so that His dreams—and ours—may become reality.

## Transformed to Bring Transformation

As Isaiah was confronted with the vision of the Most High King, fear gripped his heart. He realized as he heard the angelic hosts sing that God is most awesomely holy. That means that every decision that God has ever made has been pure, upright, good, just, loving, merciful, true, righteous, compassionate, wise, kind, honest, noble, gracious. God has proven Himself faithful and trustworthy in every act. Never has He acted deceitfully, shamefully, selfishly, unkindly. His incomparable moral integrity is without blemish. Isaiah feared because he knew that the same could not be said about his own life. How could he be associated with one so good and just when these elements were missing or inadequate in his own life?

Isaiah realized that it was not sufficient to know God's will; he must also learn to walk in God's ways. If he were to carry out God's vision, he must do so by reflecting God's character. Before the outward task could be accomplished, an inner transformation was necessary. Isaiah could not do God's thing in his own way. He would have to learn how to do it God's way. This is what is meant by doing the right things right. So before he could become an agent of transformation, Isaiah needed to be transformed from within.

We live in a world of dissonance, coverup, and hype. Leaders appear to be what they are not. We have dichotomized public and private life. This is not the way of the courageous leader. This leader, like Isaiah, is willing to face the need within as well as the need without and cry out to God for His transforming help. The courageous leader seeks to imitate the moral integrity of Jesus, whose public life was in total harmony with His private life. Like Isaiah, we must ask God to work in us if we ever hope for Him to work through us. All leaders bring about change. Only godly leaders bring about godly change. Therefore, we must seek a new standard of inner integrity and godliness in our lives. To achieve that, we must seek the God who can cleanse and transform us to be more like Him.

# CHAPTER 2

# Doing What Is Right

To do that which is right, we must have God as our constant reference point. God is the standard of rightness, the measure of goodness. Oftentimes we think of that which is right in the most narrow of terms. But the God of the Bible is not a one-dimensional deity. At times, that which is right is understood only in terms of a limited list of "thou shalt nots" and "thou shalts." But the God of the Bible has limitless creative abilities. He is one who opens incredible doors of possibilities to innumerable good and right actions. The world is not a binary cosmos of harshly contrasting points and counterpoints, where every right thing stands in rigid opposition to an equally paired wrong. In the biblical understanding of the world there is indeed a conflict between right and wrong, good and evil, although there is no yin-yang symmetry between the two. God's goodness far outweighs all evil. The options for those who wish to do right far exceed the options for those who do wrong. Goodness releases creativity; evil restricts potential. The pursuit of God opens limitless opportunities; the embracing of anything less limits life.

The God of the Bible is good not just in a moral sense. His rightness has to do not just with ethics. His goodness breaks out

of the constraints of narrowly defined traditional boxes of morality, for God's rightness encompasses aesthetics as well as ethics.
For Him, doing things right has to do not only with doing them
correctly but also with doing them elegantly. For Him, doing
things right means that both the process and the end result reflect
the integrity, wisdom, and beauty of His character. Sometimes we
think that a commitment to that which is right leads to a restricted
life—a black-and-white life in which choices are often limited to a
hopeless array of dismal grays. Nothing is further from the truth,
for the God of the Bible is an unsurpassed artist who has filled the
world with incredible color and beauty. Doing the right thing is so
much more than following a prescribed list of rules that can be
checked off in successive steps or fulfilling a mere moral transac-
tion. It must embody a radical life transformation. It is the ardent
pursuit of the One who does all things with unsurpassed excellence. The things that the courageous leader does that are the most
right are precisely those things that most closely display the excellent beauty of the character and ways of the One who is right.

God's goodness impacts every sphere of life, every expression of
thought, word, or action. Pursuing His goodness has both individual and societal implications, transforming both the person and
every aspect of the world in which he or she lives. God's goodness
is to be seen on the sports field as well as in the church pew, in corporate business deals as well as in family relationships, in areas of
scientific research and technological applications as well as in areas
of personal integrity and morality. When we understand that this
good God is Lord of all of life we must live in full realization that
for the courageous leader there can be no public/private dichotomy.
There is no corporate/personal divide. The courageous leader
understands that horribly destructive things occur to both individual human beings and entire societies when the God of the Bible is
not looked to as the standard of rightness. Without an absolute reference point, humanity is cut loose from an objective moral anchor
and drifts aimlessly in the shifting tides of relativistic, situational,
privatized rightness. This is not a syndrome unique to our times; it
has been true of every generation. Indeed, the Bible relates with
graphic horror the tragedies that took place when "*every man did
that which was right in his own eyes*" (Judges 21:25 KJV).

Even the best human efforts, the grandest enterprises, the noblest schemes, the highest aspirations, fall short if they are not undertaken in a way that reflects the character and nature of the One who is right. Many promising projects have begun well but ended poorly because God was not kept as the unswerving reference point. The record of the leadership of Israel's kings recounts the tragic tale of promising beginnings and disappointing endings of leader after leader who drifted away from God. But one need not look way back in Scripture to see this—it is sufficient to look at today's newspaper to see examples of leaders who have promised much but produced little for the betterment of the world.

Why do so many leaders so often go astray and end up in the quagmire of mediocrity—or worse? To stay on track requires a lifestyle of dependence on God. This habit of regularly consulting God was a hallmark of Israel's most renowned and courageous leader, King David. In the first twelve verses of 1 Samuel 23 we are told of how this great leader repeatedly *"inquired of the LORD, and the LORD answered him"* again and again and again. Evaluating the life of this great military and political leader, God said, *"I have found David son of Jesse a man after my own heart; he will do everything I want him to do"* (Acts 13:22). This was the key of greatness not only for David but also for all those who wish to be courageous leaders through Christlike transformational service.

Everything Jesus did was not only ethically right, it was also elegantly right. Jesus' life is a model of incomparable excellence. His contemporaries said, *"He has done everything well"* (Mark 7:37). Even though He was God incarnate, He lived in such intimate relationship with God the Father that He was able to declare, *"I do nothing on my own but speak just what the Father has taught me"* (John 8:28).

## LEADERS AS FOLLOWERS

The leadership paradigm displayed by Jesus teaches us that before one can lead others, one must first be able to follow God. The leaders who are best known for their skillful leadership abilities are those whose leadership flows from their skillful followership abilities. They know how to wait on God, hear His voice, understand His character, catch His vision, obey His instructions, and implement His plan. They motivate others to follow God's leading to be transformation agents in the world because that is the precept, passion, and practice of their own lives.

The link between being a good follower and a good leader is brought out in a conversation Jesus had with a Roman centurion. *"The centurion replied, 'Lord, I do not deserve to have you come under my roof. But just say the word, and my servant will be healed. For I myself am a man under authority, with soldiers under me. I tell this one, "Go," and he goes; and that one, "Come," and he comes. I say to my servant, "Do this," and he does it"'* (Matthew 8:8-9). The centurion rightly understood that if one is to have authority to lead, one must be under authority. The courageous leader thus must seek to live under the authority of the sovereign God who holds the ultimate authority over all of history.

As leaders, how should we view history? Some people look at history as a continuum of predetermined fixities. Others see history as a spectrum of possibilities. In theological circles this debate is often discussed in terms of the sovereignty of God and the free will of man. Oftentimes these two are pitted against each other as mutually exclusive truths. That is not the case. The Bible clearly speaks both of God's rulership over the cosmos and of the importance of our individual decisions. Therefore, a biblical worldview sees the future as having both fixed and potential realities. All is not predetermined: Our choices are genuinely significant and alter the course of history. On the other hand, all is not up for grabs: God is the sovereign Lord of history.

In this light, to be a follower of God opens up a myriad of possibilities of service in life. Following His lead is not life restricting but life enhancing. Jesus said, *"I have come that they may have life, and have it to the full"* (John 10:10). Because some have a narrow perspective of God's leadership, they think that to follow Him means that one's options in life are restricted. They see obedience as dutifully saying yes to limited options. Following God, in their estimation, does not leave room for much creativity or diversity. For them, obedience is simply aligning oneself with some predetermined plan one must follow in compliant resignation. However, when we understand what a transformational, creative leader the God of the Bible truly is, we must realize that obeying

Him opens up a whole spectrum of creative possibilities. Following is not a passive plodding in His wake but a dynamic relational partnership in which He allows us to be part of His team that shapes the destiny of our world. Under God's sovereign leadership, the destiny of our world is still being determined. Destiny has not been fixed as a series of unchangeable points in a cosmic game of connect the dots. Destiny is something we give form to and help shape as we interact creatively and obediently with God. History is still being made. The future still holds the potential of creativity, of possibilities that are yet to be formed.

## CO-CREATING WITH GOD

In the previous chapter we saw that the first and most foundational revelation of God in the Bible is that He is a creator. Genesis 1:27 tells us that *"God created man in his own image, in the image of God he created him; male and female he created them."* God made us in His image so that we, too, could be creators in relationship with Him. In the Hebrew Scriptures, the verb for "create," *bara,* is used 54 times. While God is the subject of this verb the vast majority of these times, on six occasions this same word is used to describe human action (Joshua 17:15,18; 1 Samuel 2:29; Ezekiel 21:19a,b; 23:47). Of special note are the two occurrences in Ezekiel 19, in which God commanded the prophet to create. What an incredible gift God has given that allows us as finite creatures to participate with Him, the infinite Creator, in shaping the world around us.

Not everything has been determined by God's will, by His choices. The Genesis account tells us how God created the animals and then *"brought them to the man to see what he would name them; and whatever the man called each living creature, that was its name. So the man gave names to all the livestock, the birds of the air and all the beasts of the field"* (Genesis 2:19-20). God gave man a formative responsibility within the created order. What the name of the animals would be was an open-ended, nondetermined issue. God wanted *"to see what [Adam] would name them."* He had not earlier decided what their names should be and manipulated Adam's will into compliance with His own. The choice was Adams's, and God would abide by that choice, respecting the decision of His junior partner. What a phenomenal God this is—who is so willing to involve us in His creative process and respect our decisions that impact the world He fashioned!

God allows us freedom to make decisions not only to shape areas not determined by His will but also in areas where His will is clearly expressed. It is in the latter areas where we can choose to either collaborate with His will or resist His will. Indeed, much of what occurs in the world is not God's will. Many of Jesus' parables illustrate the reality of an individual who *"does not do what his master wants"* (Luke 12:47). God allows us to make decisions that are contrary to His will. Even though our choices are not what His choice might have been, He respects us enough to honor our decisions and let them stand and run their course—even when they counter His will. God releases to us, as individuals created in His image, the authority to make history-shaping decisions. Our choices create new realities. Much of what we see in the world today is the result of this kind of negative creative process: realities brought into being through human decisions that are not made in conformity with the loving character of God.

So, how do we responsibly partner with a sovereign God in co-creating positive new realities in our world? The process begins and is sustained by intentionally seeking the presence of God. This is a rewarding but costly process, demanding our full-hearted devotion. We are told that Nehemiah *"sat down and wept"* (Nehemiah 1:4) upon hearing of the distressing condition in Jerusalem. It took him time in the place of prayer for him to gain God's perspective and be burdened with God's compassion for the situation in Jerusalem. As with Nehemiah, our soul-searching prayer and worship, along with heartfelt meditation and study, should be a transformational experience that enables us to think His thoughts and feel His feelings so that we might then speak His words and do His works. Only then will the courageous leader have the faith and the follow-through that are necessary to be an agent of transformation.

Prayer is not something done only once at the outset of the process. Time and time again throughout the book of Nehemiah we are told of the prayers and worship of Nehemiah and the people (1:5-11; 2:4; 4:4-5; 5:19; 6:9,14; 8:6; 9:5-38; 12:27-43; 13:14,22,29,31). These many passages are not interruptions in the story line. There would be no story line without these passages, for the continuous way in which prayer and praise were integrated into Nehemiah's leadership was key to the success of Nehemiah's action. Indeed, prayer and action are to go hand in hand and be woven together in seamless integration. As Abraham Lincoln said, "You should pray as if it all depended on God and work as if it all depended upon you."

## AN INTEGRATED WORLDVIEW

A gathering of Christian ministers was called together to "blue sky," "green light," or "brainstorm" about the future. They were asked to imagine what they could accomplish in a ten-year time span if they had no budget restrictions and no personnel limitations. For a half hour they worked excitedly in small groups dreaming of all the possibilities. When they came back together in the plenary session and shared their dreams, their enthusiasm grew as they reported of the anticipated planting of a myriad of new churches, of evangelistic thrusts resulting in multiplied thousands of converts, of flourishing discipleship programs and mission outreaches. It seemed as though they had dreamed such a big dream until the moderator asked them to return to their small groups and do the same exercise imagining themselves to be members of the cabinet of their nation's government. Suddenly a hush fell over the room as they realized that all the dreams they had dreamed had to do only with the religious sphere of life. No one had dreamed of health care programs that would reduce infant mortality to half its current rate or of a solution for AIDS. No one had dreamed of a means to clear the nation of its crippling foreign debt or of overhauling the crumbling transportation infrastructure of the land. No one had dreamed of a new standard of integrity and justice in the business circles of the nation or for the development of new technologies that would guarantee potable water for every citizen. No one had dreamed of the eradication of the immoral double standard that had existed among the genders in their culture or for an educational system that would produce a one hundred percent literacy rate. No one had dreamed of the establishment of a godly entertainment system and a means for providing gainful employment and dignified housing for the destitute homeless. Why such a lack of foresight? Why such a narrowness of vision? Did not these ministers care for the nation? Of course they did! Were they not concerned with the human needs around them? Of course they were. But all too often Christians have viewed the world through dichotomized glasses. They have segregated the "spiritual" from the "secular" and have thought that God was very interested in the former and only remotely concerned about the latter.

This is not the picture that the Bible gives us about God. When we read the first five books of the Hebrew Scriptures, we see that in the laws God gives to Moses He instructs him in areas not only of religious worship but also of personal hygiene, agriculture, politics, community health, sexuality, economics, judicial structures, immigration and naturalization laws, educational curriculum, public holidays, music, and the arts—among many other things. Because God is concerned about these things—and every other area of life—we as courageous leaders must likewise adopt an integrated perspective of life that seeks to see the kingdom of God fully expressed in every facet of society. Either God is the Lord of all or He is the Lord not at all. This integrated way of viewing life is absolutely essential for the person who is to be a truly courageous leader, capable of transforming his or her world.

William Carey is known as the father of modern missions, but he had no room in his thinking for narrow-minded religiosity. For him there was no secular/sacred dichotomy. Because he had a nondichotomized biblical worldview, Carey impacted many areas of society in the Indian subcontinent. This British cobbler became not only a world-renowned evangelist and missionary strategist but also

- a botanist who frequently lectured on science
- a publisher who established the first newspaper printed in any Oriental language
- an astronomer who helped free people from the destructive fatalism of astrology
- an entrepreneur who pioneered the first steam engines in India
- an environmentalist who wrote essays on forestry
- an economist who introduced the idea of savings banks to India

- a social reformer who challenged polygamy, female infanticide, and wife burning
- an educator who began dozens of schools
- a linguist who became a professor of Bengali, Sanskrit, and Marathi
- a world citizen who trained India's civil servants
- an artist who wrote gospel ballads in Bengali
- an agriculturist who founded the Agri-Horticultural Society

This indeed is the profile of a courageous leader committed to transforming the world! Carey's integrated perspective of the world should be embraced by all who desire to be courageous leaders. The breadth of impact of Carey's life illustrates the wide variety of ventures in which courageous leaders can be involved. No area of life is to be excluded from God's transforming influence.

Another example of a courageous leader is George Washington Carver. Born to a black woman as a slave during the U.S. Civil War, Carver faced many seemingly insurmountable obstacles in his life. He not only had to live with the prejudice of a society that restricted the educational opportunities for those of his race but also had to overcome debilitating health and economic deprivation that would have discouraged a less courageous leader. Carver's strong faith in God enabled him to conquer these difficulties and become a renowned scientist whose tirelessly creative service transformed the southern region of the United States.

For generations, the economy of the South had been dependent almost exclusively upon cotton. The continuous cultivation of this crop had seriously depleted the soil of nutrients and was destroying the productivity of the land. Carver sought to introduce other crops that would revitalize the soil and free the economy of its perilous dependence on cotton. In the face of economic disaster from the boll weevil plague that wiped out the cotton production, farmers began to follow Carver's advice and switch to peanuts and sweet potatoes. However, there was no ready market for these products. To serve the needy farmers of his region, Carver went to his laboratory and began creating solutions that would transform the lives of millions of people. Carver's scientific discoveries and practical inventions were not divorced from his life of faith. In fact, they were an extension of it. Carver would begin every morning in a devotional walk through his laboratory gardens, communing with God and asking the Creator to unlock the secrets of His creation. As a result of his diligent pursuit of God, among his many other accomplishments, Carver developed over three hundred uses for the peanut (ranging from cheese to soap and from cosmetics to linoleum) and over one hundred new products derived from the sweet potato. Carver demonstrates for us the almost endlessly creative opportunities of doing good if one's worldview is not dichotomized. Because his faith was integrated into every aspect of his life, Carver was able to overcome life's obstacles and co-create with God new solutions that served the needy farmers of his day and transformed the world in which he lived.

Carver's life shows us that you cannot put leadership in a box. His was an unlikely story. His transformational impact on society came in unexpected ways. Because God's creativity is so vast we cannot point to only one model of leadership. There is no one human style, no one human paradigm that is sufficient to describe all the possible ways in which one can be a courageous leader. Leaders are as varied as the people God has created. However, the courageous leader must be able to see the big picture in an integrated way to maximize his or her transformational service in the world. In practical terms, this means that the courageous leader must embrace the following.

## • People/Project

At times, teachings on leadership have falsely dichotomized being and doing, relationships and tasks, people and projects. To pit one side of any of these pairs against the other not only is unwise but also undermines courageous leadership, for the courageous leader must always balance both elements. This is clearly seen in Nehemiah's leadership. Nehemiah had a twofold agenda that encompassed both the people and the project.

The people made possible the accomplishment of the project of rebuilding the walls of Jerusalem, while the project was intended to further the welfare of the people. The people served the project, but the goal of the project was always the well-being of the people. Indeed this is evident in Nehemiah's words to the elders, "Come, let us rebuild the wall of Jerusalem, and we will no longer be in disgrace" (Nehemiah 2:17). Because Nehemiah was committed to both the people and the project, he made adjustments in the way the project was being managed to care for the people, which facilitated motivation of the people for the task. (Nehemiah 4:7-23). Indeed the very structure of the book demonstrates the back and forth balancing interplay between people and project by Nehemiah. Note the literary interchange that underscores this important principle as shown in figure A-1:

| Focus on the people | 1:4-11 | | 4:7-15 | | 5:1-19 | | 7:1–12:26 | | 13:1-31 |
|---|---|---|---|---|---|---|---|---|---|
| Focus on the project | | 2:1–4:6 | | 4:16-23 | | 6:1-19 | | 12:27-47 | |

**Figure A-1**

Indeed, the book culminates with the dedication of both people and walls to God (Nehemiah 12:30), once again underscoring the interrelatedness of people and project.

Jesus' selection of the first disciples likewise illustrates the importance of both being and doing, relationship and task. We are told that *"He appointed twelve designating them apostles that they might be with him* (relationship) *and that he might send them out to preach and to have authority to drive out demons* (task)*"* (Mark 3:14-15, parenthetical comments added). The courageous leader creates an environment where the team can thrive relationally and be productive functionally. Both the people and the project are enhanced by good leadership.

## • Goal-oriented/Process-sensitive

In a similar way, courageous leaders must develop skills to balance both the goal and process of their leadership. Some leadership systems only emphasize the goal. All that counts is the bottom-line, the productivity at the end of the day, the accomplishment of the desired goals. For them the ends justify the means. The pages of history are filled with examples of those left in the wake of this kind of goal-driven/process-insensitive leadership.

However to correct process-insensitive leadership we must not throw out the importance of goal-orientation. If there are no goals, there is no reason for leadership. Unfortunately, it is in vogue in some circles to emphasize the process so much that it is hard to see any goal ever accomplished. If the team has great interpersonal dynamics but does not get the task done, this too is a major leadership failure. The courageous leader must be capable of both things: of motivating people towards the right goal in a right way, a process in which all members of the team are served and God's ways honored. How you get there is just as important as getting there—not more so, nor less so.

2 Kings 5 tells us the story of Naaman, the commander of the Syrian army. He contracted leprosy and set out to find a cure. This goal eventually led him to Elisha who instructed him to bathe in the Jordan seven times. Offended by such ridiculous advice, Naaman stormed off in a huff. In his eyes it was not the right process of achieving the desired goal. Because he was not willing to go through with the process, he nearly missed out on the accomplishment of his goal. However, he had fortunately learned to listen to his subordinates and when one of his maidservants reasoned with him, he followed the recommended instructions. Because he honored the process he accomplished the goal. Oftentimes a leader will miss the God-ordained process of achieving the goal if he or she is not willing to listen to others on their team. Listening to others and to the Lord is key to keep the balance of being goal-oriented and process-sensitive. After all, Jesus is *"the way and the truth and the life"* (John 14:6)—the divine embodiment of both the means and the end.

## • Principle/Practice

The courageous leader must develop skills as an implicational and applicational thinker; always keeping before him or herself the questions of why and how. Considering why something is done develops implicational thinking. It leads one to consider core values and foundational presuppositions. Understanding and communicating the why, the principle behind the action is essential for the leader to be able to multiply other leaders. At the same time the leader must develop an ability to think through many creative strategies of how to practically apply the principles. It is not sufficient to understand all the concepts of leadership in theoretical terms; the courageous leader must be able to lead the charge on the ground.

Some people will naturally tend to think more implicationally, focusing on the concepts, while others will lean toward applicational thinking, emphasizing the practice of leadership. If you have the skills without the understanding or the understanding without the skills you will be limited in your leadership. So, the courageous leader will dedicate energy to enhance his or her natural strengths and strengthen natural weaknesses. Recognizing their limitations, courageous leaders will staff their weakness and lean into other team members who compliment them in their gifting. As the complimentary gifts of others are called forth and honored by making space for them, the leadership team will be strengthened so that all can grasp the why and how of their corporate project.

We see this balance of principle and practice in the way Paul mentored Titus into leadership. In the short 46 verses of Titus, Paul gives his protégé 14 imperatives (1:13; 2:1,6,15a,15b,15c,15d; 3:1,9,10,12,13,14,15)—there is a task to be done and Paul gives him very practical instructions on how he is to go about getting it done. But Paul does not stop there. He knows that if Titus is going to lead he must understand not only what he is supposed to do, but the rationale behind the actions. For this reason, Paul repeatedly explains the why. He uses phrases like *"so that"* (Titus 1:9,13; 2:5,8,10; 3:7,8), *"in order that"* (Titus 3:14), *"because"* (Titus 1:11; 2:8; 3:5a,5b,9,12), *"therefore"* (Titus 1:13), etc. in order to help Titus think through the leadership principles behind the instructions and draw out the implications. Paul served by helping him develop the capacity to think implicationally. This skill is of paramount importance to those who are in key decision-making positions because every leadership decision carries implications that reflect or negate the ways of God.

Thinking implicationally and applicationally must become a way of life for the courageous leader. How does one develop this skill until it becomes second nature, a habit that permeates the thinking and communicating processes? One key is to develop the discipline of asking complex questions. Once again, Jesus is our example. In the Gospels He asks 315 questions. Of these, 115 are binary questions that can be answered with a simple yes or no response. But 200 (nearly two-thirds) are complex or open-ended questions which require more probing thought on the part of one being questioned. 45 of these questions were "why" questions requiring—and indeed facilitating—implicational thinking. Jesus' skillful use of these open-ended, probing questions was one of the hallmarks of His leadership. It should likewise be a part of every leader who realizes the importance of implicational thinking.

Of course it is of great importance that the courageous leader learns not only to ask questions of fellow team members and others related to the project, but also of the Lord. When we do not know the answer to the applicational question (What do I do next? How do I do that?) or the implicational question (Why should it be done this way? What will be the result of this line of action or train of thought?)—we will ask God. God does not fear our questions. Indeed, He welcomes them, for through the asking of questions we sharpen our skills as learners. And above all else we are called to be learners, disciples.

Jesus encourages us, *"Ask and it will be given to you; seek and you will find; knock and the door will be opened to you"* (Luke 11:9). There are so many things you could ask of Him, but make it a top priority to ask Him for wisdom and insight. Ask Him to teach you and lead you. Ask Him to lead you and show you the way in which to go. *"Get wisdom, get understanding; do not forget my words or swerve from them. Do not forsake wisdom, and she will protect you; love her, and she will watch over you. Wisdom is supreme; therefore get wisdom. Though it cost all you have, get understanding. Esteem her, and she will exalt you; embrace her, and she will honor you. She will set a garland of grace on your head and present you with a crown of splendor"* (Proverbs 4:5-9).

## • Heart/Mind

Courageous leaders do not dichotomize the heart and mind, valuing one while devaluing the other. On the contrary, the courageous leader seeks to develop both intellectual prowess and emotional sensitivity. Reason and intuition are both valued. Again the wise leader staffs his or her weakness and leans into the complimentary gifts of others.

We see in Jesus the perfect balance of heart and mind. He was one who was moved to tears over the death of His friend Lazarus as well as over the spiritual insensitivity of the inhabitants of Jerusalem. He was not inhibited emotionally and yet He was very sharp intellectually, debating the best minds in his society, astonishing them with His insight and wisdom. For Him faith is never a blind emotional leap, but a reasonable response to revealed truth. He tears down the heart/mind divide when He says, *"God is spirit, and his worshipers must worship in spirit and in truth"* (John 4:24, emphasis added). Likewise He commands us, *"Love the Lord your God with all your heart and with all your soul and with all your mind"* (Matthew 22:37). Either/or is not an option. Our love for God must be expressed by both/and. An integrated, holistic worldview is the biblical way for the courageous leader.

## • Big Picture Understanding/Detailed Awareness

One of the areas courageous leaders must balance is that of too much or too little detail. Too much detail and the leader gets bogged down in unproductive micro-management. Too little detail and the leader will lose touch with the needs and potential of the team and likewise lose effectiveness. The leader needs to be able to see both the forest and the trees.

It is not enough for the leader to have the balance between these two, he or she must continuously communicate with everyone on the team, so that each has a clear understanding of the corporate big picture, and understands the significance of his or her individual contributions to the whole. This keeping the vision before the people is essential for team unity and motivation. Therefore one of the key ways in which the courageous leader serves the team is by communicating, communicating, communicating. Information is power and the courageous leader shares it as broadly and fully as possible to empower all the members of the team.

## CONCLUSION/SUMMARY

That which enables us to do right as courageous leaders is the pursuit of the One who is Right. As we come to know the creative God of the Bible we realize that seeking to do what is right opens up myriads of opportunities for co-creating with God new realities that shape the course of history. As we seek to follow Him, we recognize that He is Lord over all of life and so we must abandon any distorted, narrow, dichotomized worldview that limits the kingdom of God in any sphere of society. As courageous leaders we can pioneer new things that will benefit and serve our world. In order to do so we must champion people and promote projects. Similarly we must be goal-oriented, while also being process-sensitive. We must learn to think implicationally and applicationally by cultivating the attitude of a learner and by developing the skillful use of asking questions. We must not dichotomize between our heart and mind, rather we should love God with all our being. And finally we must walk in the balance between big picture understanding and detailed awareness, so that we can serve our team with abundant communication. With these things developing in our lives we are on the way to becoming strong and courageous leaders.

# CHAPTER 3

# Strong and Courageous Leaders

The Lord has our attention through one of His many ways of communicating. We have set our sights high by relating to God, our awesome Creator. We have set our sights broad as time spent in His presence results in thinking His thoughts and feeling His emotions for the world. By seeking to do the right thing, we recognize that we want to commit to the goals that He has set before us. He does not force us. We are free to choose, but the Lord says, *"If you love me, you will obey what I command"* (John 14:15).

The Lord said to Joshua, *"Be strong and courageous, because you will lead these people to inherit the land I swore to their forefathers to give to them. Be strong and very courageous. Be careful to obey all the law my servant Moses gave you; do not turn from it to the right or to the left, that you may be successful wherever you go....Have I not commanded you? Be strong and courageous. Do not be terrified; do not be discouraged, for the LORD your God will be with you wherever you go"* (Joshua 1:6-7,9).

As you look at the goal set before you, perhaps you feel overwhelmed and certainly not very strong and courageous. But the Lord reminds you that He will be with you wherever you go. The disciples were not very courageous before the resurrection of

Jesus, but after Jesus rose they were filled with the Holy Spirit and were no longer terrified or discouraged. They reached out with great boldness to speak the Lord's word, to heal, and to perform miraculous signs and wonders through the name of Jesus (Acts 4:28-31).

Peter and John were jailed and later brought before the Sanhedrin because of their strong and courageous teaching and actions.

> *Then Peter, filled with the Holy Spirit, said to them: "Rulers and elders of the people! If we are being called to account today for an act of kindness shown to a cripple and are asked how he was healed, then know this, you and all the people of Israel: It is by the name of Jesus Christ of Nazareth, whom you crucified but whom God raised from the dead, that this man stands before you healed...." When they saw the courage of Peter and John and realized that they were unschooled, ordinary men, they were astonished, and they took note that these men had been with Jesus* (Acts 4:8-10,13).

This chapter will explore some of the key ingredients of a strong and courageous leader. It will point to Jesus, our ultimate Leader, who possessed all these ingredients. It will also present examples of other leaders who were committed to the goals set before them and demonstrated God-inspired, strong, and courageous leadership. Strong implies physical, moral, and/or intellectual power—forceful, cogent, ardent, firm, stalwart, tenacious power to endure stress or pain. Courageous implies bravery that ventures forth and perseveres in the face of danger, fear, or extreme difficulty; firm determination to achieve the goal; keeping up morale when opposed or threatened; meeting strain or difficulty with fortitude and resilience. Even as God said, *"Take courage!"* to Paul (Acts 23:11), so He says the same to those who want to be godly leaders today. We are told to *"hold on to our courage and the hope of which we boast"* (Hebrews 3:6). Therefore, *"Be on your guard; stand firm in the faith, be men of courage; be strong. Do everything in love"* (1 Corinthians 16:13-14).

## LEADERS AS ENABLERS AND ENCOURAGERS

Leaders should be enablers and encouragers who can make it possible for teams, groups, organizations, or nations to accomplish righteous goals. God-inspired leaders enable and encourage people groups to stay focused on God's plans and priorities. The Lord enables some of the most unlikely leaders. Two centuries ago, a 25-year-old farmer went out into a field and had a profound experience with the Lord. The young man wrote:

> I was working out in the open one day, singing the hymn "Jesus, Taster of Sweet Communion." After I had sung the second verse, "Strengthen me powerfully in my soul so that I can find out what the Spirit can do. Take me prisoner in my speech and mind. Lead me, strengthen me, so weakly I walk. Gladly I would lose myself and all that is mine, if You alone will live in my soul. Then that which disturbs my inner peace must finally creep out of the door," I almost lost consciousness.

As the young man entered into the presence of the Lord, he had a vision of the world submersed in evil. He saw himself with a passion to commit his life to the Lord. Then he heard a voice echoing within him, telling him, "You shall confess My Name before the people. Exhort them to repent and seek Me while I can be found. They should call on Me, while I am near, to touch their hearts—that they can turn from darkness to light."

Dr. Alv Magnus of Norway, in his plenary lecture at the University of the Nations 1995 biennial international workshop in Sweden, told of his research on how this young man, Hans Hauge, was used mightily by the Lord to transform the nation of Norway. After his encounter with the Lord, Hans started almost immediately to testify to others about Jesus. Within days, his whole family was converted, and then the people in his neighborhood. When Hans talked to them about God, the people wept because the presence of Jesus was so strong.

Hans believed the Scriptures to be the authoritative and unchangeable Word of God. He preached repentance, emphasizing the need for renewed minds and for hearts committed to Jesus

Christ. But he didn't stop there. Hans wanted his converts to be disciples of Christ. He emphasized strongly the call to follow Jesus. To those who accused him of exaggerating the importance of a life that demonstrates love for God and neighbor, Hans said, "Anyone who carefully considers Christ's teaching and that of His apostles will find that following Christ's footsteps in godly practices is more emphasized than the doctrine of reconciliation. Therefore, this must be practiced and not neglected."

Hans Hauge emphasized not only a personal relationship with the Lord Jesus but also stewardship. Everything should be made available to the Lord and used diligently in His service. Hans looked upon good deeds as being light and witness to men in the world. In his writings he states, "We shall seek, here, to shine for the world by our actions."

As Hans went beyond his own region, he gave advice on new methods of efficient farming. Because he was of their kind, reaching them on their level, the people found new life in God through his preaching. Then they would assimilate the new ideas and methods in their work. Hans not only provided improvements in agriculture but also saw how to start companies that would help the people. He started mills, mines, and factories around which many Christian communities sprang up. These communities took in the poor and became spiritual lights and strongholds throughout the country. Hans wrote hundreds of letters of encouragement as well as books that were widely distributed throughout the country. Although the conversions to dynamic Christian commitment were not massive, the new Christians did become the new standard bearers in society. The result was Norway's gradual transformation from a poor, backward nation with starving people and moral decay into a nation that was wealthy both spiritually and economically. Today, even Marxist economists and historians would agree that the Hauge revival changed the face of Norway.

In the early stages of the Hauge revival, the authorities in the existing power structure met Hans with fierce opposition. They used coercive means to stop him. After only eight years of ministry, Hans was arrested for the eleventh time and put in jail. His friends were not allowed to see him, his Bible was taken from him, and the government even went into villages to remove the books he had written.

Dr. Magnus concluded his plenary lecture about his research, "The Economic Effects of Revival," by saying that during his studies he suddenly saw himself in the prison cell with Hans, who was 33 years old with his ministry of eight years behind him. Alv imagined the devil taunting Hans and telling him, "Hans, you are an idiot. Why are you sitting here rotting in this prison? You cannot be serving a good God. Why serve Him? Look at how you're being treated. Look at how your God rewards your ministry. Throw away the faith and come out in freedom." Then Alv imagined another voice, very soft saying, "Hans, do you remember the song you sang? Do you remember that line, 'Me and what is mine I will gladly lose if only You will dwell in my soul?' Well, you've lost your ministry, your property, your health, your friends, and your freedom. Do you still mean it? Am I worth more than all of these?" Hans answered, "Yes, Lord."

Because Hans Hauge was transformed and had committed his life completely to the goal of being a faithful servant of the Lord, God used him powerfully in the transformation of a nation. Hans was an enabler and an encourager. He empowered the people not only through his preaching and teaching but also through starting companies, bookstores, and factories. He was a catalyst that sparked economic as well as spiritual growth. He demonstrated love for God and for his neighbor. Hans produced much fruit. He was a strong and courageous leader. *"If you remain in me and my words remain in you, ask whatever you wish, and it will be given you"* (John 15:7).

Regardless of our leadership roles, *"let us consider how we may spur one another on toward love and good deeds. Let us not give up meeting together, as some are in the habit of doing, but let us encourage one another"* (Hebrews 10: 24-25).

## LEADERS AS COMMUNICATORS

Jesus often communicated by telling vivid parables to the crowds and His disciples. Following one occasion of listening to Jesus describe the kingdom of heaven by speaking to the people in parables, the disciples asked Jesus, *"Explain to us the parable of the weeds in the field"* (Matthew 13:36). Jesus answered and then explained several other parables. He then asked the disciples, *"Have you understood all these things?"* (Matthew 13:51).

49

Understanding is an essential part of communication. If understanding or grasping the meaning does not take place, there is no true communication. Jesus was the ideal communicator and teacher. During His earthly ministry, crowds of people eagerly followed Him to hear and learn from Him. Some understood, and some did not. *"Coming to his hometown, he began teaching in their synagogue, and they were amazed. 'Where did this man get this wisdom and these miraculous powers?' they asked"* (Matthew 13:54). Regrettably, in many situations the rulers and authorities had hardened their hearts and would not hear His message. They failed to understand what Jesus was saying and doing. There was no communication.

When the disciples came to Jesus and asked Him why He spoke in parables, He replied:

> *"This is why I speak to them in parables: Though seeing, they do not see; though hearing, they do not hear or understand. In them is fulfilled the prophecy of Isaiah: 'You will be ever hearing but never understanding; you will be ever seeing but never perceiving. For this people's heart has become calloused; they hardly hear with their ears, and they have closed their eyes. Otherwise they might see with their eyes, hear with their ears, understand with their hearts and turn, and I would heal them'"* (Matthew 13:13-15).

In speaking to the church in Corinth, Paul emphasized: *"We do, however, speak a message of wisdom among the mature, but not the wisdom of this age or of the rulers of this age, who are coming to nothing. No, we speak of God's secret wisdom, a wisdom that has been hidden and that God destined for our glory before time began. None of the rulers of this age understood it, for if they had, they would not have crucified the Lord of glory"* (1 Corinthians 2:6-8).

A God-inspired leader must be an effective communicator but not necessarily an eloquent orator. The apostle Paul wrote, *"My message and my preaching were not with wise and persuasive words, but with a demonstration of the Spirit's power, so that your faith might not rest on men's wisdom, but on God's power"* (1 Corinthians 2:4-5). Paul demonstrates that the leader God uses is one who is an open channel for the Holy Spirit to instruct and inspire so that his or her words and actions are understood as intended by the Lord.

Spirit-inspired communication is an essential asset for leaders who are guiding persons called to work together. Good communicators release creativity in team members and facilitate teamwork and a spirit of unity and enthusiastic commitment toward reaching the goal. These team members truly hear the leader and understand. Of course, the opposite is true for leaders who are poor communicators, who do not focus on the vision, and who are not attentive to the questions and needs of the team members. Such leaders assume that the people in the group understand the vision, the goals, the guidelines, and the expectations. Poor communication typically results in misunderstandings, confusion, grumbling, frustration, loss of creativity, and distortion of the vision and goal.

Project plans and action needed to fulfill many visions require various gifts and anointings of the leaders who are involved. Some leaders are called to be apostolic leaders who initiate Spirit-inspired plans and help lead the teams into Spirit-inspired implementation of these plans. Some are to be prophetic leaders who keep the team members aware of the vision and God's words to them. Some are to be evangelistic leaders who regularly reach out to others with the gospel. Some are to be pastors and teachers who regularly nurture, educate, and train the teams. Whatever their giftings, God's courageous leaders must be effective communicators. The apostle Paul reminded the church in Corinth:

> *We have not received the spirit of the world but the Spirit who is from God, that we may understand what God has freely given us. This is what we speak, not in words taught us by human wisdom but in words taught by the Spirit, expressing spiritual truths in spiritual words. The man without the Spirit does not accept the things that come from the Spirit of God, for they are foolishness to him, and he cannot understand them, because they are spiritually discerned* (1 Corinthians 2:12-14).

During the past century, the methods for conveying information have increased explosively. Writers often refer to the present era as the "Information Age." Computers, the internet, videos, CD-ROMs, DVDs, remote education, TV, radio, and other media permeate our culture. All of them can be used for communication. The information conveyed can be understood using any of the methods. We must keep in mind, however, that the information can be either for good or for evil.

Christians have been blessed with Spirit-filled messages and Spirit-inspired books that have drawn them closer to the living God. Christian radio and television have impacted millions of people worldwide with information that is understood. It has taken courageous leaders to prepare the excellent materials that are available. But compared to the unrighteous information that is communicated in all forms of the media, only a very small portion of information is Spirit-filled and life transforming. If courageous Christian leaders are to transform their world, they must focus on producing and conveying Spirit-inspired information.

In the nineteenth century, the United States of America was engaged in a gruesome civil war that almost split the union. The president of the USA was Abraham Lincoln. Today, historians rank Lincoln as one of the greatest, if not the greatest, of all American presidents. Seldom has the head of a nation used the power of words more effectively than Abraham Lincoln. Volumes have been written about one of his shortest speeches, lasting less than three minutes and consisting of only 272 words. Lincoln's brief speech was given at the site of the Gettysburg battleground, where only months before tens of thousands of soldiers—both from the North and from the South—had died.

Some say that Lincoln's few words gave the nation a new birth of freedom, effected an intellectual revolution, and changed the world. Although each of the phrases in his address has been dissected, analyzed, and praised by literary critics and scholars, what was most significant was that the speech was Spirit-inspired and impacted a nation. The words have been memorized by millions of American schoolchildren over the years and have withstood the test of time. They are repeated here with the hope that the Spirit of the living God will again speak through these words as they did to a nation in 1863 and to countless others since that time. Especially important in the context of this book is to focus on how communicating the right words at the right time can impact the world.

Lincoln's address delivered at the dedication of the cemetery at Gettysburg (November 19, 1863)

> Fourscore and seven years ago our fathers brought forth on this continent, a new nation, conceived in Liberty, and dedicated to the proposition that all men are created equal.
>
> Now we are engaged in a great civil war, testing whether that nation, or any nation so conceived and so dedicated, can long endure. We are met on a great battle-field of that war. We have come to dedicate a portion of that field, as a final resting-place for those who here gave their lives that that nation might live. It is altogether fitting and proper that we should do this.
>
> But, in a larger sense, we can not dedicate—we can not consecrate—we can not hallow—this ground. The brave men, living and dead, who struggled here, have consecrated it, far above our poor power to add or detract. The world will little note, nor long remember what we say here, but it can never forget what they did here. It is for us the living, rather, to be dedicated here to the unfinished work which they who fought here have thus far so nobly advanced. It is rather for us to be here dedicated to the great task remaining before us—that from these honored dead we take increased devotion to that cause for which they gave the last full measure of devotion—that we here highly resolve that these dead shall not have died in vain—that this nation, under God, shall have a new birth of freedom—and that government of the people, by the people, for the people, shall not perish from the earth.

## LEADERS AS AGENTS OF UNITY

Millions of people worldwide enjoy team sports, whether as players or as spectators. Teams that exhibit exceptional teamwork are especially exciting to watch. Also, it is exhilarating to be a player on such a team. When all team members play together in perfect unity, an integrity of playing the game exists that communicates completeness and perfection of the whole. The players radiate team spirit. Solidarity enables the team to manifest its strength.

Unity is a key to success in any team endeavor. The coaches, managers, and on-field leaders need to instill in all the players the concepts of unity, the importance of each player, and each player's function. They must communicate that each member is part of the whole as well as how they are to work together. Team unity requires leaders who are effective communicators and are committed to a common goal. Teams need three essential components: commitment, communication, and unity. With these they can accomplish goals that are impossible to achieve by the same number of individuals who are not committed to the same goal or do not communicate with one another. *"Just as each of us has one body with many members, and these members do not all have the same function, so in Christ we who are many form one body, and each member belongs to all the others. We have different gifts, according to the grace given us"* (Romans 12:4-6). By working together as a team, people can most effectively use their skills, interests, and strengths.

Part B of this book emphasizes using planning methods that lead to team unity for developing God-inspired plans. The relationships that lead to unity are crucial for any type of project. Leaders must be the agents for ensuring unity. The planning process should use steps that when followed will be pleasing to the Lord. Jesus prayed to the Father for all believers just before His arrest and crucifixion: *"I have given them the glory that you gave me, that they may be one as we are one: I in them and you in me. May they be brought to complete unity to let the world know that you sent me and have loved them even as you have loved me"* (John 17:22-23).

New personnel who are added to a group or team must understand the God-inspired vision and be committed to the group. Leaders must repeatedly communicate the vision and ensure complete unity in the group. When leaders are diligent in this, creativity flows throughout the team and the personnel radiate dynamic energy, synergy, and enthusiasm to reach the goal.

## LEADERS AS PROTECTORS AND DEFENDERS

Violence, assault, child abuse, murder, riots, genocide, and other atrocious acts occur daily throughout the world. Righteous protectors and defenders are needed to provide shields and safeguards for the people. A major responsibility of government leaders should be to maintain reliable protection groups and systems to deter criminals and prosecute perpetrators. In war a nation's military is the usual defender used to drive away enemy attacks or ward off threats from an aggressor.

Wars have courageous leaders—those who risk and often lose their lives while repelling an enemy. For their courage and heroism, these leaders are honored, sometimes posthumously, with a nation's highest medal of honor. In civilian situations, courageous leaders risk their careers and even their lives while standing up for what is right—for the truth, religious freedom, opposition to cruel, inhuman, and oppressive policies. Some leaders establish programs that help the poor and starving or provide protection and love for the abandoned and dying. Mother Teresa's Sisters of Charity have been publicly recognized worldwide for their compassion and love for the poor and dying. However, seldom are these civilian heroic and courageous efforts noticed, understood, or appreciated. They might even result in unjust attacks against those serving the needs of the people.

There are always those who resist change and would maintain a cruel status quo rather than rock the boat. As we described earlier in the chapter, such was the case for the opponents of Hans Hauge. By committing his life completely to God and allowing God's power to flow through him, Hans was the living channel used to transform Norway from a backward, poor, and unjust nation into one of the wealthiest nations economically and spiritually. The authorities during his ministry did not want change. They jailed him, tortured him, and kept him imprisoned under inhuman conditions until his health broke. The impact of Hans Hauge's courageous life was recognized only after his death.

Regrettably, a nation's government leaders—who should be protectors of the people—can be the perpetrators of injustice, as they were for Hans Hauge. Such leaders use their power to establish and interpret or change laws so they can use the law to enforce unrighteousness and strip away personal freedoms from those of opposing views. They use military forces to start wars against peaceful neighbors. But as injustice and oppression increase within a nation, God enables courageous protectors and defenders to arise. Such was the case in the Soviet Union. Aleksandr Solzhenitsyn, later proclaimed a literary genius, was able to let the world know through his brilliant writing about the pain, suffering, and inhuman treatment inflicted by the communist government on many citizens in his nation. Solzhenitsyn, a young Soviet army officer during World War II, had been schooled and indoctrinated in Marxist and Leninist theories. Suddenly he became a political prisoner for being outspoken about his disdain for Stalin and the evil he saw happening in the Soviet Union. There followed many years of transfers to a series of prisons, labor camps, and penal institutes known as the "Gulag Archipelago."

In prison, Solzhenitsyn heard the stories of other political prisoners undergoing inhuman treatment. These stories and subsequent observations of Soviet life changed his perspective and shaped his strong convictions and character. These difficult years formed his new worldview that recognized the destructive and evil aspects of communism and Marxism. Through amazing circumstances, Solzhenitsyn secretly wrote several books that surprisingly he was able to microfilm and get into Western Europe and America, where they were printed. These books greatly influenced world opinion and understanding about the Soviet Union's internal oppression and contributed greatly to the collapse of the Soviet system. A brilliant writer who was shaped by many years of hardship became a powerful force in the transformation of a so-called superpower nation.

The biblical account of Esther in the fifth century B.C. is an exciting story filled with intrigue. Esther was an orphaned Jewish girl who became a beautiful young woman who was chosen by King Xerxes, ruler of the Persian kingdom, to be his queen. This placed her in a position to be used by God to rescue the Jews, who were dispersed and scattered among the people of Persia in all one hundred twenty-seven provinces of the kingdom. Through the cunning of Haman, a highly ranked but evil nobleman, an edict was issued for the Jews in all provinces to be killed. But God had raised up Esther *"for such a time as this"* (Esther 4:14) to be the channel for God to do the impossible while she did the possible. Through fasting and prayer, both by the Jews throughout Persia and by Queen Esther and her inner group, God guided her with an ingenious strategy, which she put into action. The result was that the edict was reversed and the Jews were delivered from the death sentence. Subsequently, the Jews received much favor under King Xerxes.

These examples illustrate that our God can deliver us from seemingly impossible situations. His ways are the right ways.

> *For though we live in the world, we do not wage war as the world does. The weapons we fight with are not the weapons of the world. On the contrary, they have divine power to demolish strongholds. We demolish arguments and every pretension that sets itself up against the knowledge of God, and we take captive every thought to make it obedient to Christ* (2 Corinthians 10:3-5).

## LEADERS AS SERVANTS OR SERVANTS AS LEADERS

For the past three decades, an increasing number of for-profit corporations, nonprofit organizations, and even some government-related institutions have adopted the Greenleaf concepts of servant leadership. These ideas were presented by Robert K. Greenleaf in a 1970 essay, "The Servant as Leader." This essay was the first of many essays and books that Greenleaf wrote on the subject. Greenleaf's Judeo-Christian background, his long and outstanding career at AT&T, and his teaching experience at Harvard, MIT, and other institutions on organizational management had prepared him for a deeper understanding of leadership. A key event, which built upon his vast experiences, occurred in the mid-1960s when he read Herman Hesse's novel *Journey to the East*. New understanding gained in reading the book convinced Greenleaf that true leadership originates from those who have a deep desire and commitment to serve others.

After that first essay in 1970, Greenleaf pursued the servant-leader theme and wrote a series of essays dealing with the nature of leadership, the structure of academic institutions, businesses, trusteeships, seminaries, and other organizations. Hundreds of thousands of copies of his essays and books can be found around the world. They have been food for thought to those concerned with issues of leadership, service, and a more caring society.

So what is servant leadership? Greenleaf wrote in his 1970 essay that a servant leader is one who is a servant first. He states, "[Servant leadership] begins with the natural feeling that one wants to serve, to serve first. Then conscious choice brings one to aspire to lead. The difference manifests itself in the care taken by the servant—first to make sure that other people's highest priority needs are being served. The best test is: Do those served grow as persons; do they, while being served, become healthier, wiser, freer, more autonomous, more likely themselves to become servants?"

The concepts of servant leadership are profound, and they are not readily grasped. They must be lived. Present and past generations of people have lived primarily in hierarchical systems in which leaders were leaders first and servants second. Although these leaders often served their people very well, the priority was not the well-being of those being served. It is a blessing that Greenleaf and his followers have influenced corporate and institutional leaders to think seriously in terms of servant leadership. The many positive attributes of Greenleaf's essays must be instilled in all leaders as they assemble people to work on any goal or project.

The principles of servant leadership are biblical. They originate in the character of God. Jesus spent considerable time teaching the concepts to His disciples, who had difficulty grasping the ideas. Jesus had to repeatedly emphasize, *"The greatest among you will be your servant"* (Matthew 23:11). *"The kings of the Gentiles lord it over them; and those who exercise authority over them call themselves Benefactors. But you are not to be like that. Instead, the greatest among you should be like the youngest, and the one who rules like the one who serves"* (Luke 22:25-26). *"Whoever wants to become great among you must be your servant"* (Matthew 20:26). When the disciples came to Jesus and asked, *"Who is the greatest in the kingdom of heaven?"* (Matthew 18:1), Jesus responded, *"Unless you change and become like little children, you will never enter the kingdom of heaven. Therefore, whoever humbles himself like this child is the greatest in the kingdom of heaven"* (Matthew 18:3-4). Humility is essential for the servant leader, and this emphasis on humility is repeated frequently in the Bible.

Jesus is the ultimate model of the servant leader. Matthew wrote that Jesus *"did not come to be served, but to serve, and to give his life as a ransom for many"* (Matthew 20:28).To the Christians at Philippi, Paul wrote:

> *Each of you should look not only to your own interests, but also to the interests of others. Your attitude should be the same as that of Christ Jesus: Who, being in very nature God, did not consider equality with God something to be grasped, but made himself nothing, taking the very nature of a servant, being made in human likeness. And being found in appearance as a man, he humbled himself and became obedient to death—even death on a cross!* (Philippians 2:4-8).

One of the most dramatic illustrations of the servant as leader is Jesus washing the feet of His disciples. *"It was just before the Passover Feast. Jesus knew that the time had come for him to leave this world and go to the Father. Having loved his own who were in the world, he now showed them the full extent of his love"* (John 13:1). Jesus *"got up from the evening meal, took off his outer clothing, and wrapped a towel around his waist. After that, he poured water into a basin and began to wash the disciples' feet, drying them with the towel that was wrapped around him"* (John 13:4-5). When Jesus finished washing their feet, He proceeded to instruct them: *"I have set you an example that you should do as I have done for you. I tell you the truth, no servant is greater than his master, nor is a messenger greater than the one who sent him"* (John 13:15-16).

Jesus, the ultimate servant leader, had emptied Himself of all divine power and privilege to be born as a baby to be a member of a despised minority; He became flesh and dwelt among us; He shared His life with His disciples and lived in the same conditions with them; He demonstrated excellence as He astonished the teachers of the law, healed the sick, fed the multitudes, and had compassion. He made the ultimate sacrifice of being executed on the cross so that we might be saved. Then He provided hope for the future with His resurrection. In the process, He gave us the example of a servant leader and told us to follow His example.

A name that became known to countless millions of people worldwide during the latter part of the twentieth century is that of Mother Teresa. Born in Albania in 1910, Mother Teresa became a nun and served the poor and dying in India for most of her life. Certainly not the kind of career to which the world usually pays attention. But Mother Teresa's life touched the hearts of people. Her spirit of love and compassion and her commitment to identify with the poor and dying and to serve them with all her strength gave to the world a living example of a servant leader.

Mother Teresa demonstrated those special characteristics and sacrifice that provide hope for the future. Deservedly, in 1979 she was awarded the Nobel Peace Prize, the most prestigious award given in human recognition of attainment. In introducing Mother Teresa at the Nobel award ceremony, Professor John Sannes of the Norwegian Nobel Committee described what it was about the "spirit of Mother Teresa" that marked her "better than anyone else." He concluded his introduction saying, "With her message she is able to reach through to something innate in every human being—if for no other purpose than to create a potential, a seed for good. If this were not the case, the world would be deprived of hope, and work for peace would have little meaning."

Dr. David Aikman, former senior correspondent for *Time* magazine, includes Mother Teresa in his excellent book *Great Souls: Six Who Changed the Century*. At the end of his section on this strong and courageous servant leader, Aikman wrote:

> Against the weightlessness of so much modernity, Mother Teresa laid out a plumb line—God's plumb line, to be precise—of what the human virtue of compassion really means. More precisely, she lived out the total significance of the New Testament Greek word, *agape*—the deepest meaning has to do not with feeling,

but with the giving up of one's life. One person's life, of course, is never a sufficient source of light to disperse the darkness threatening to engulf entire cultures. But in our twentieth century, with its frequent inability to distinguish true light from mere glitter, Mother Teresa not only demonstrated what true light is. To her dying day, she pointed the way for millions and millions of others to find it too.

# CHAPTER 4

# Transforming Your World

*Do not conform any longer to the pattern of this world,
but be transformed by the renewing of your mind. Then
you will be able to test and approve what God's will is—
his good, pleasing and perfect will* (Romans 12:2).

This scripture includes and encapsulates an amazing truth.
When people turn away from following the crowd in the ways
of the world and truly seek to know God, their lives are transformed. The changes in their thinking and direction in life are profound. Having been transformed by the renewing of their minds
and completely committed to the Lord, they have an inner peace
and joy. God empowers them to act according to His perfect will.

The preceding chapter gave some examples of persons whose
lives were transformed by the renewing of their minds. Recall Hans
Hauge, the 25-year-old Norwegian farmer who was transformed
when he was out in the field and opened his heart and mind to God
as he sang a hymn: "Strengthen me powerfully in my soul so that I
can find out what the Spirit can do...Gladly I would lose myself and
all that is mine, if You alone will live in my soul." God dramatically
transformed and empowered Hans. In obedience he immediately

embarked on a dynamic eight-year ministry that impacted an entire nation. God used Hans to transform the nation of Norway.

Likewise, recall Mother Teresa, another servant leader. She was transformed by our Creator God, who gave her an intense passion for demonstrating His love in a hurting world. Visualize the process—a baby girl is born in Albania, grows up, is called and transformed by Jesus, prepares and becomes a nun, goes to India, and works amongst the rejected, the destitute, and the dying. Her passion to serve the Lord in her calling leads to many heartbreaks but also to inner peace, joy, and strength. The result? She radiated the love of Jesus. Her influence increased, and her light shone increasingly brighter. Many others caught the vision.

Mother Teresa's light not only resulted in thousands of others becoming involved directly in Sisters of Charity ministries worldwide but also demonstrated what true light is. To millions of people, Mother Teresa pointed the way to the light. She became a symbol and glowing example of a transformed life transforming her world. Hans Hauge and Mother Teresa both had passion for their calling. They were obedient to do God's perfect will in their lives.

This chapter continues the focus on courageous leaders who have a passion to accomplish specific goals. We want to emphasize that the callings, goals, or projects can take many different forms as the Lord leads. Thus, a courageous leader might not be in a position to directly guide or conduct the activities of a specific group but could be a leader who points the way for others through writing, the arts, actions, or other skills that are not connected to any official leadership position.

The first section of this chapter focuses on a passion to disciple your world. Subsequent sections focus on a passion for truth and a passion to know God and make Him known. A passion to be transformed and obey God's plan is the thrust of the final section. We trust that this chapter will help you evaluate your zeal, fervor, passion, and intense devotion for your calling and inspire you toward the goal set before you.

## A PASSION TO DISCIPLE YOUR WORLD

All Christians are called to be disciples of Jesus Christ. They are also called to make disciples in their spheres of influence, "their world." Your world could be your family, your school, your place of work, your neighborhood, or your church. Or you may be someone whom the Lord calls to disciple an organization, a community, or even a nation. The people group and area of society for which you have been given a vision from the Lord is the world you are called to disciple. The Holy Spirit empowers you as you live and lead courageously with passion to attain the goal set before you. Reflection on some true-life stories of those who have gone before—with a passion to disciple their world—gives us hope and inspiration.

Abraham Kuyper was a famous Dutch reformer in the late 1800s and early 1900s. Early in his career he was a pastor of a small country church. In 1880 he founded a university, the Free University of Amsterdam, which took the Bible as the unconditional basis on which to rear the whole structure of human knowledge in every area of life. Kuyper became a writer and an editor. From 1901–1905 he served the nation of Holland as an outstanding prime minister. He is credited with transforming the nation to the glory of God. Feel his passion as he spoke at a reception in his honor:

> One desire has been the ruling *passion* of my life. One high motive has acted like a spur upon my mind and soul. And sooner than that I should seek escape from the sacred necessity that is laid upon me, let the breath of life fail me. It is this: that in spite of all worldly opposition, God's holy ordinances shall be established again in the home, in the school, and in the State for the good of the people; to carve as it were into the conscience of the nation the ordinances of the Lord, to which the Bible and Creation bear witness, until the nation pays homage again to God.

Kuyper's perseverance, fervor, and passion were rooted in his close walk with Jesus. In his devotional classic *To Be Near Unto God,* Kuyper writes, "The fellowship of being near unto God must become reality in the full and vigorous prosecution of our life. It must permeate and give color to our feeling, our perceptions, our sensations, our thinking, our imagining, our willing, our acting, and our speaking. It must not stand as a foreign factor in our life, but it must be the *passion* throughout our whole existence."

Abraham Kuyper's world expanded throughout his life—from pastor of a small country church to founding and nurturing a Bible-based university to a myriad of community and national services, including being prime minister of his nation and author of books that bore witness to Christ worldwide. Kuyper's actions were spurred by the burning conviction that Jesus Christ rules by a living power which He exercises over lands and nations, generations, families, and individuals. Kuyper maintained a passion to disciple his world to the very end of his life in 1920. If we embrace the intimate fellowship with God that marked the life of Abraham Kuyper, we will know and rely on *"the love God has for us"* (1 John 4:16). Jesus told His disciples, *"A new command I give you: Love one another. As I have loved you, so you must love one another. By this all men will know that you are my disciples, if you love one another"* (John 13:34-35). To disciple our worlds, we need to maintain an intimate fellowship with God—to understand in great depth that *"God is love, and he who abides in love abides in God, and God abides in him"* (1 John 4:16 RSV). The apostle Paul prayed for the Ephesians that they would be *"rooted and grounded in love"* so they would *"know the love of Christ which surpasses knowledge"* and *"be filled with all the fullness of God"* (Ephesians 3:14-19 RSV).

One of the teachers of the law asked Jesus, *"Of all the commandments, which is the most important?"* Jesus answered him, *"Love the Lord your God with all your heart and with all your soul and with all your mind and with all your strength. The second is this: 'Love your neighbor as yourself.' There is no commandment greater than these"* (Mark 12:28,30-31).

In response to the first and greatest commandment from our Lord, it seems fitting that we obey His final commandment—to *"go and make disciples of all nations, baptizing them in the name of the Father and of the Son and of the Holy Spirit, and teaching them to obey everything I have commanded you. And surely I am with you always, to the very end of the age"* (Matthew 28:19-20).

As you seek to disciple your world, it is important to check regularly with the apostle Paul's reminder to the church in Corinth:

*If I speak in the tongues of men and of angels, but have not love, I am only a resounding gong or a clanging cymbal. If I have the gift of prophecy and can fathom all mysteries and all knowledge, and if I have a faith that can move mountains, but have not love, I am nothing. If I give all I possess to the poor and surrender my body to the flames, but have not love, I gain nothing. Love is patient, love is kind. It does not envy, it does not boast, it is not proud. It is not rude, it is not self-seeking, it is not easily angered, it keeps no record of wrongs. Love does not delight in evil but rejoices with the truth. It always protects, always trusts, always hopes, always perseveres* (1 Corinthians 13:1-7).

Many, like Abraham Kuyper, have gone before and abided in close fellowship with God in order to disciple their worlds. Now we have the same opportunity to be in such close fellowship that the love of Christ lives in us, and He has promised to be with us always as we reach out to disciple our worlds.

## A PASSION FOR TRUTH

To promise to tell the truth, the whole truth, and nothing but the truth is a promise that witnesses must swear to when they testify in a court of law in many nations that have effective legal systems. To violate this oath by swearing to what is untrue is perjury, which is considered a major crime. Without truth, the legal system fails. Without truth in a governing system and among its officials, deception, corruption, rampant injustices, and eventually collapse of the nation or organization ensue.

Jesus said, *"I am the way and the truth and the life"* (John 14:6). As recorded in the gospels, Jesus said seventy-nine times, *"I tell you the truth."* For example, He said, *"I tell you the truth, whatever you bind on earth will be bound in heaven"* (Matthew 18:18); *"I tell you the truth, wherever the gospel is preached throughout the world, what she has done will also be told, in memory of her"* (Mark 14:9); *"I tell you the truth, anyone who will not receive the kingdom of God like a little child will never enter it"* (Luke 18:17); *"I tell you the truth, no one can enter the kingdom of God unless he is born of water and the Spirit"* (John 3:5). Over and over again Jesus underlined the fact that He was telling the truth—that His statements were accurate and exactly what they purported to be and in accord with facts.

Jesus promised His disciples that when He left He would *"ask the Father, and he will give you another Counselor to be with you forever—the Spirit of truth. The world cannot accept him, because it neither sees him nor knows him. But you know him, for he lives with you and will be in you"* (John 14:16-17). The Spirit of truth, the Holy Spirit, will not force Himself on us. He guides our lives only as we allow Him. To walk in the Spirit is to walk in the truth and to be near to God. As parents we can identify with the apostle John when he said, *"I have no greater joy than to hear that my children are walking in the truth"* (3 John 4). The Spirit is the protector of truth itself. Jesus told His disciples that *"when he, the Spirit of truth, comes, he will guide you into all truth"* (John 16:13).

The previous section of this chapter pointed out that the importance of knowing and relying on God's love is related to passion for discipling your world. Likewise, a commitment to truth is critical as you reach out passionately to disciple your world. A direct link exists between truth and love. Without truth there can be no genuine love. *"Love does not delight in evil but rejoices with the truth"* (1 Corinthians 13:6). The apostle John wrote a note to Christians who were exposed to false teachers with the hope that his communication would renew their commitment to truth. In his opening words, he related truth with love: *"To the chosen lady and her children, whom I love in truth—and not I only, but also all who know the truth—because of the truth, which lives in us and will be with us forever: Grace, mercy and peace from God the Father and from Jesus Christ, the Father's Son, will be with us in truth and love"* (2 John 1-3).

In his letter to the believers scattered throughout the regions of Asia Minor, the apostle Peter wrote, *"Now that you have purified yourselves by obeying the truth so that you have sincere love for your brothers, love one another deeply, from the heart"* (1 Peter 1:22). A world that is not open to the Spirit of truth is not open to true love. Worldly people passionately seek love but cannot and do not receive truth. Therefore they find neither true love nor truth. Truth and love cannot be separated.

In listening to impeachment proceedings because of misdeeds of an American president, it became apparent that there was a clash of kingdoms—those who believed in pursuing truth versus those who were willing to cover up or gloss over the sins with a barrage of lies or half-truths. The seriousness of lies is illustrated in Luke's account of Ananias and his wife Sapphira, who sold a piece of property and kept back part of the money for themselves, bringing the rest to the apostles. What they had done was commendable up to this point; so far so good. But then they misrepresented the facts in what they told the others. Then Peter, discerning their deception, said, *"Ananias, how is it that Satan has so filled your heart that you have lied to the Holy Spirit... What made you think of doing such a thing? You have not lied to men but to God"* (Acts 5:3-4). Both Ananias and his wife died as a result of their falsehood.

In Revelation, all liars are listed among those evil sinners sentenced to eternal punishment:

> *He who was seated on the throne said, "I am making everything new!" Then he said, "Write this down, for these words are trustworthy and true." 'He said to me: "It is done. I am the Alpha and the Omega, the Beginning and the End. To him who is thirsty I will give to drink without cost from the spring of the water of life. He who overcomes will inherit all this, and I will be his God and he will be my son. But the cowardly, the unbelieving, the vile, the murderers, the sexually immoral, those who practice magic arts, the idolaters and all liars—their place will be in the fiery lake of burning sulfur"'* (Revelation 21:5-8).

God is passionate about truth. He is truth and the Spirit of truth. In the latter half of the twentieth century, He raised up a man whose strong and courageous commitment to truth sparked a major transformation in the world. Aleksandr Solzhenitsyn became a man with passion for truth—truth that through his vivid writing uncovered and made known to the world the lies, the deception and inhuman treatment of the people in the Soviet Union, a people held in bondage under a repressive, atheistic, communist system. Solzhenitsyn's intense devotion to truth and freedom was a major factor in toppling the communist regime in the Soviet world and cast dark clouds of suspicion worldwide over all Marxist philosophy. In effect, this one writer took on the entire Soviet superpower, and his passion for truth unveiled to the world an empire ruled by an evil governmental system.

Solzhenitsyn's strong convictions and character were shaped through years of suffering and hardships in Soviet prisons and penal camps. When asked by Dr. David Aikman whether his life under difficult and cruel conditions in the camps was something that he cherished—as part of his calling—rather than regretted, Solzhenitsyn answered "Yes!" adding that "in those circumstances human nature becomes much more visible. I was very lucky to have been in the camps—and especially to have survived." Aikman concluded his chapter on Solzhenitsyn in his excellent book *Great Souls: Six Who Changed the Century* with the powerful statement, "For that imprisonment, for his survival and for Aleksandr Solzhenitsyn's unwavering commitment to speaking the truth at all costs, the entire world should be grateful."

By the grace of God, Solzhenitsyn survived many years of imprisonment in labor camps and penal institutions. It was this period of suffering that gave him the opportunities to meet and talk with other political prisoners and gain a perspective on what was happening throughout the Soviet empire. It was this period that gave him opportunities to seek answers and reflect on what was happening in his nation. It was this period that enabled him to gain insight and understanding of the fundamental evils within communism and Marxist philosophy. It was this period that gave him stamina, courage, and passion for truth and the moral authority to write his award-winning vivid books that exposed those evils.

Through his books, the seeds for action against oppression and bondage in the nation began to grow. The seeds would be nurtured and grow both inside and outside the country. What a tremendous transformation! A young Soviet army officer during WWII was transformed by the renewing of his mind through years of imprisonment in labor camps. He was guided by the Spirit of truth and enabled by the Holy Spirit to make the truth known throughout the world. The transformation that occurred in nations amazed the world.

## A PASSION TO KNOW GOD AND MAKE HIM KNOWN

Recently at a memorial service for a beloved pastor, the pastor's son, who was conducting the service, asked if any persons in attendance would like to comment on his dad's life. Dozens of people responded: "He was a man of God"..."He spoke as a man who knew God"..."When he gave a sermon it was as though God spoke through him"..."I came to know God through him"..."The love of Jesus was expressed through his life"..."Jesus Christ was his best friend"..."He arose every morning at 4 A.M. to talk with the Lord and seek His guidance." Testimony after testimony spoke of a life lived by a man who had a passion to know God and to make Him known.

This pastor's sixty years of ministry on this earth continue to live following his departure for life eternal in heaven. The Jesus who was introduced to thousands of people through the life of this pastor now lives in them. Several pastors who came from far and near to honor their departed friend mentioned that the pastor they were now honoring was their role model. They recognized that he was a man who knew God, a man who had a natural grace and winsome passion to make God known to his congregations and all his acquaintances. As a pastor, his project, his program, was to make God known. His son concluded the sharing time describing how his dad worked on this project throughout his life, how he continued to seek to know more and more about his God, his infinite, all powerful yet personal God—his best friend. All who knew this beloved pastor exclaimed that he was a true and faithful servant of the Lord. He was a courageous leader who transformed his world wherever the Lord led him.

The apostle Paul passionately exclaimed, *"I want to know Christ and the power of his resurrection"* and *"I consider everything a loss compared to the surpassing greatness of knowing Christ Jesus my Lord"* (Philippians 3:10,8). Paul's intimacy with God empowered him to communicate the good news of Jesus

Christ with great wisdom, compassion, and authority. His God-inspired letters to the Romans, Corinthians, Galatians, Ephesians, Philippians, Colossians, and Thessalonians attest to Paul's passion to know God and to make Him known.

Through his intimacy with Jesus Christ, Paul was given a holy love for all of God's people, and he became a mighty ambassador who transformed his world. His transformed life illustrates a basic Christian leadership principle. When our first priority in life is an intimate, personal, and dynamic fellowship with our Creator God, He directs His power, guidance, and wisdom into and through us. He enables us to co-create with Him. As we *"put on the new self, created to be like God in true righteousness and holiness"* (Ephesians 4:24), we can be used by Him to transform our world according to His perfect will.

The extraordinary *Christian Growth Study Bible* (Zondervan Publishing House) contains a unique thirty-path study guide. The thirty paths have been arranged to help us to know God more intimately (paths 1–24) and to make Him known (paths 25–30) as we allow the Holy Spirit to guide us along the paths. The articles and biblical passages related to each study path are outlined in sequence throughout the books of the Bible from Genesis to Revelation. All of us can benefit immensely by frequently seeking the Holy Spirit's guidance to lead us through the paths outlined in the *Christian Growth Study Bible.* These regular times of reflection and meditation will keep us on the right paths as we proceed to develop God-led plans. As we draw close to God, He shows us how to collaborate with Him, not only to develop God-inspired plans but also to implement them with God-motivated action, action that brings joy to God's heart, action that makes God known in our world.

## A PASSION TO BE TRANSFORMED AND OBEY GOD'S PLAN

Earlier chapters have presented examples of leaders who followed God's ways and cocreated with Him. These leaders offered their *"bodies as living sacrifices, holy and pleasing to God."* They did not conform *"to the pattern of this world."* They were *"transformed by the renewing"* of their minds and were able to do God's will...

*"his good, pleasing, and perfect will"* (Romans 12:1–2). Hans Hauge offered himself as a living sacrifice if only the Spirit of the living God would dwell in him. He was transformed, and the power of the Lord dwelt in him. Hans was used by the Lord to transform and reform the nation of Norway. Abraham Kuyper had a passion to be transformed and was used by the Lord to reform the nation of Holland. Mother Teresa's transformation changed darkness to light for the poorest of the poor and those dying in the streets of India. She said, "I am God's pencil; a tiny bit of pencil with which He writes what He likes." In the hand of Jesus that bit of pencil wrote for the world a modern-day story of the meaning of compassion. The list goes on and on through the years of those who became living sacrifices, who opened their hearts and minds so that the living God could dwell in and work through them.

Today, the world needs servant leaders who will courageously lay down their lives at the cross of Jesus, leaders who have a passion to be transformed by Him, leaders who want their hearts and minds to be opened to God's perspective, His perfect will, His plans. *"Surely the Sovereign LORD does nothing without revealing his plan to his servants the prophets"* (Amos 3:7).

When the Lord reveals plans to a transformed leader, the leader must take action to obey. God's revelation requires an inspired response that you know would bring joy to His heart. Perhaps this could be an innovative program or project in your family or your church or even throughout your community or nation that focuses on God's awesome greatness, His creation, His character, His love. Jesus taught, *"You are the light of the world. A city on a hill cannot be hidden....In the same way, let your light shine before men, that they may see your good deeds and praise your Father in heaven"* (Matthew 5:14,16).

The apostle Peter wrote, *"But you are a chosen people, a royal priesthood, a holy nation, a people belonging to God, that you may declare the praises of him who called you out of darkness into his wonderful light....Live such good lives among the pagans that, though they accuse you of doing wrong, they may see your good deeds and glorify God on the day he visits us"* (1 Peter 2:9,12). There are many ways to praise God and bring joy to God's heart. We can praise Him through excellence in persevering from a

God-inspired vision to God-led plans and into God-motivated action so as to reach the goals set before us. As we seek and obey Him, we are given strength in His joy: *"for the joy of the LORD is your strength"* (Nehemiah 8:10). Those who are gifted in the arts often praise the Lord beautifully through inspired music, dance, or the fine arts. Others who are gifted in writing, designing, composing, acting, preaching, teaching, scientific research, or technical skills can offer inspired praise and joy through books, plays, videos, speaking, opening minds of children to the gospel, giving new insight on God's creation, or helping the people with technical services that enable, protect, and heal. Obedience and perseverance in whatever God calls you to will bring glory and joy to Him.

The Lord might impress on you a situation that breaks His heart…a situation that is vicious, corrupt, and depraved and needs to be corrected or profoundly reformed. God has frequently expressed in the Bible His heartfelt grief and pain as people and nations have turned away and rejected Him and have been consumed by wickedness. When we feel God's pain and grief with the evil all around us, we have the basis to pray and seek Him to understand whether He is calling us into action to correct a heartbreaking situation. Is the Lord giving you the passion to right the wrong and to present your body as a living sacrifice to reform a situation and change grief to joy?

Before launching into major plans and action, pray and meditate on God's ways and character, especially as related to the vision He gives. Record the situation that God impresses on you, whether an existing situation that breaks His heart, or a future situation that will bring joy to His heart.

It is helpful to use a pre-planning form (Figure A-2) to record the things that the Lord impresses on you. Record on the form a brief description of the situation that breaks God's heart and the situation that brings joy to God's heart. To do this well may require deliberate research, diligent prayer, thoughtful reflection, and concerted discussion by and among members of the leadership team. In the bottom section of the form, record those thoughts and words that you believe God has spoken concerning the situation and your involvement. The pre-planning form will be important for developing a

God-led plan. The form in Figure A-2 was filled out by a leader who works in one of the nations in Eastern Europe. A blank pre-planning form of the type shown in Figure A-3 can be used as you seek God's purposes for you as a courageous leader.

**✝ Pre-Planning Form**
**Preparing to Co-Create with God**

### Understanding God's Ways and Character

| Brief description of the **existing situation**\* which breaks God's heart | Brief description of the **future situation**\* which would bring joy to God's heart |
|---|---|
| Poverty of thought & stifled creativity | Biblical worldview restored in church and proclaimed/taught through books, arts, in clubs, TV, universities, schools, preschools, businesses |
| Orphans live in poverty and are treated as animals | Orphans being lovingly cared for and nurtured as well as trained and released into their callings and giftings |
| Elderly in old folks homes dying in inhuman situations with little care | Elderly being cared for with love and dying in dignity |
| Mentally ill living in institutions like prison wards | Mentally ill being respectfully treated and cared for |
| Broken families due to alcoholism, divorce, inequality of man and woman | Restoration of the family unit as the most basic unit in society |
| Disunity in churches | Unity that results in churches reaching their communities with love and compassion |
| Unreached who die without knowledge and hope of eternity with God | Church-planting and discipleship programs that meet people's needs and reflect God's intentions for man |
| Injustice and corruption in laws and politics | New laws being written and enforced according to God's laws |
| Economic disaster, where the poor are getting poorer | New businesses being established that create jobs, generate quality products and respect man with his creativity and bless the poor as well as other nations |
| Ecological devastation of the air, land and environment | Stewardship being taught and restored and responsible programs undertaken that bring long-lasting change |
| Youth are unreached | Church planting among the young people through relevant means, s.a. music |

### \*Hearing God's Word (Brief documentation of things God has spoken concerning the situation)

| |
|---|
| Ezekiel 34: godly models for leadership are lacking and Biblical leadership, i.e. servant-leadership must be taught and modeled |
| Genesis 1:28-29 Man made in the image of God. Man is an image bearer and therefore has value, purpose, and creativity and is called to be a co-laborer with God and a steward of all that God entrusted to him. |
| Isaiah 61: God wants to set the captives free and bring justice |
| James 1:27 pure and undefiled religion in God's sight to visit orphans and widows and keep oneself unstained by the world |
| Matthew 25:35-46 feed, drink, visit, etc. our responsibility to respond with compassion in practical, physical ways to those in need and distress |
| Luke 2:52 God's intentions for all of man's needs and all of life; social, physical, spiritual and wisdom (application of knowledge) |
| Matthew 28:18-20 make disciples of all nations to obey all that I commanded you |
| Jeremiah 29: seek the welfare of the city (nation) |
| Jeremiah 5:1 Run to and fro through the streets of Jerusalem, look and take note! Search her squares to see if you can find a man, one who does justice and seeks truth; that I may pardon her. |

Figure A-2

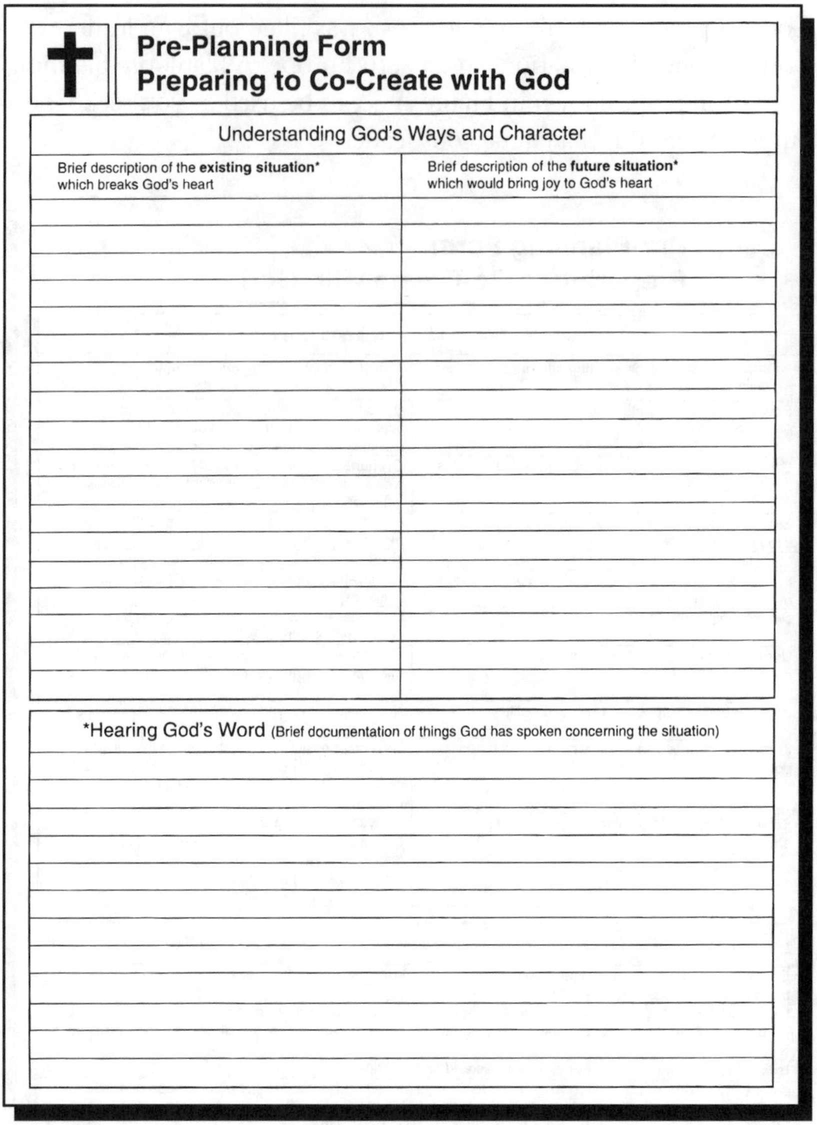

| ✝ | **Pre-Planning Form**<br>**Preparing to Co-Create with God** |
| --- | --- |

Understanding God's Ways and Character

| Brief description of the **existing situation**\*<br>which breaks God's heart | Brief description of the **future situation**\*<br>which would bring joy to God's heart |
| --- | --- |
| | |

\*Hearing God's Word (Brief documentation of things God has spoken concerning the situation)

Figure A-3

Now let's proceed to Part B and learn about the 5-step planning method for doing things right. We call it the Leaders Plan.

# A God-Led Plan—
# Doing Things Right

# The 5-Step Leaders Plan

*"'For I know the plans I have for you,' declares the Lord, 'plans to prosper you and not to harm you, plans to give you hope and a future'"* (Jeremiah 29:11).

In Part A we discussed knowing God's will and developing a courageous vision based on the knowledge of His character and the needs of the world. In Part B you will move from vision into seeking and knowing God's plan for your project. The unique 5-step planning process presented in the following chapters can give you a powerful plan, which we are calling a Leaders Plan, that can be readily shown to others.

*"And the Lord answered me: 'Write the vision; make it plain upon tablets, so he may run who reads it. For still the vision awaits its time; it hastens to the end—it will not lie. If it seem slow, wait for it; it will surely come, it will not delay'"* (Habakkuk 2:2-3 RSV).

God's nature and character are to be the foundation for our leadership. We have seen in Part A that God is visionary. Since we are created in His image, we too can be visionary. Now we will see that He is also a planner, and He likewise encourages us to be planners. When we develop our vision in unity with Him our vision will be right. Likewise, when we develop our plan in unity with Him, our plan will be right. Both our vision and our plan should flow out of our obedient relationship with God as we seek to know His will and act courageously to transform our world. As diagrammed in Figure B-1, this book is about obediently moving from a God-inspired vision (Part A) to a God-led plan (Part B) to a God-motivated action (Part C).

Figure B-1

## GOD'S INSPIRATION FOR A LEADERS PLAN

Part B shows how to obediently develop the God-inspired Leaders Plan through proven principles of leadership and management that are found throughout the Bible. Nehemiah is an outstanding example of a courageous leader as he set out to rebuild Jerusalem's wall to protect his people from the enemy. However, before any work began on the wall, Nehemiah had to present his plan to the king, a plan that was inspired by God. From the time the vision began to be formulated in his heart and mind in November-December 446 B.C. (Nehemiah 1:1) to March-April 445 B.C. (Nehemiah 2:1), Nehemiah obviously gave a lot of time and effort to elaborate a Leaders Plan. Much research and reflection must have gone on during these four months. His plan gave him a basis for clear communication. When questioned by the king regarding his Overall Objective, he was able to answer him: *"If it pleases the king and if your servant has found favor in his sight, let him send me to the city in Judah where my fathers are buried so that I can rebuild it"* (Nehemiah 2:5). Likewise, when the king questioned him about the needed time frame to complete his project, Nehemiah had a ready answer (Nehemiah 2:6) because he had with due diligence done his homework and developed a useful Leaders Plan.

## BIBLICAL PRINCIPLES AND TODAY'S TECHNOLOGY

The biblically-based process of developing a Leaders Plan will train you in a vital 5-Step sequence that has been used to plan industrial and governmental projects as well as church and mission projects. It is our hope that the planning process presented in Part B will encourage you to seek and chart God's plan for your project, whether it be a local outreach program, a church ministry complex, a community development project or the discipling of a nation.

Effective planning focuses on the skillful use of the right approach to do the right thing. Planning excellence does not happen automatically. It results from the application of the right planning process that we will be explaining over the next five chapters. This process begins by deciding on an Overall Objective and continues by making a thorough list of the desired End Items. To reach these we will then learn how to lay out Milestones and identify Supertasks that are logically related in a time sequence. Then we will be equipped to estimate the needed resources (personnel, time, materials and finances) to implement the vision.

The process of developing the Leaders Plan has resulted from years of research and development and experience on a wide variety of programs. Although many of these concepts were actually demonstrated by Nehemiah, they have been combined with God-given modern technology and utilized by NASA for putting man on the moon. One of the most valuable by-products of the Apollo Program was not only microcircuitry and metallurgy products, but also the way to plan and manage programs. The Leaders Plan described here has resulted out of a need to get the right things done right.

You do not, however, have to be involved in a huge project to apply biblical principles of planning and the practical information provided in this book. We trust that you will be encouraged as you seek to prepare God's plan for your project, whether it is designing a training curriculum for preschool children or taking on a major international project. By following this proven planning process you will discover ways to release creativity and develop team spirit as you seek to please God and courageously co-create with Him.

## WHAT IS A LEADERS PLAN?

A Leaders Plan is the documented record of a team's commitment to certain objectives and actions that enables them to accomplish a corporate goal in a specific time period in accordance with God's will. It is a covenant of the team's planned actions to achieve God's revealed destination and purpose for the future.

## WHO PREPARES A LEADERS PLAN?

Planning should not be a solo effort. It is the responsibility of the whole leadership team to prepare the Leaders Plan. This is not a task to be delegated to consultants and specialists. All the key persons involved in the implementing of the plan can and should contribute to the development of the plan. King Solomon, whose world-renowned wisdom is proverbial, gives us many God-inspired planning principles. He wrote, *"Plans fail for lack of counsel, but with many advisers they succeed"* (Proverbs 15:22).

Team leadership is one of the best ways to reap the benefits described in Proverbs 15:22. All on the team must have the attitude of servant-leaders. One on the team would serve as coordinator, but all contribute with their various gifts and expertise. It may be important to include appropriate specialists in several categories. Everyone on the leadership planning team must be willing to accept specific responsibilities for the implementation of the corporate Leaders Plan. For greater effectiveness, each team member should be trained and oriented in the process of preparing a Leaders Plan before the actual preparation of the Leaders Plan. Each member will participate in the exciting process of the multiple authorship of one unified plan. The practice of multiple authorship of a corporate plan is a strategic method of obtaining the benefits of a Proverbs 15:22 council.

The Declaration of Independence set the course for the creation of a new nation, the United States of America. It traced out a plan that would impact the world. However, this important historical document was not the creation of any one individual. Though such prestigious men as Thomas Jefferson and Benjamin Franklin contributed to it, it was created through a process of multiple authorship. When it was elaborated to everyone's satisfaction, all 56 delegates signed it, committing themselves and those they represented to the implementation of the plan they had co-authored. Many of them feared God and courageously laid down their lives and fortunes to see their vision for freedom and their plan for a new nation become a reality. The image of the group responsible for the multiple authorship of this important document appears on the back of the US two-dollar bill, shown in Figure B-2.

Figure B-2

## THE RIGHT PROCESS FOR PREPARING A LEADERS PLAN

If you have ever planned a trip, you know the many steps involved in the process. Consider this example and then transfer the elements of the trip-planning process to that of preparing a Leaders Plan, which is, in effect, a plan for a trip into the future. When planning a long trip, you often begin by marking up a road map with all the points or places at which you want to stop or visit. You do this before trying to figure out the exact travel routes that will take you to your desired destinations, as illustrated in Figure B-3.

Next, you develop a sequential pattern of arrows representing travel between each of these points along the planned route, as shown in Figure B-4.

As with travel planning, a Leaders Plan basically consists of:

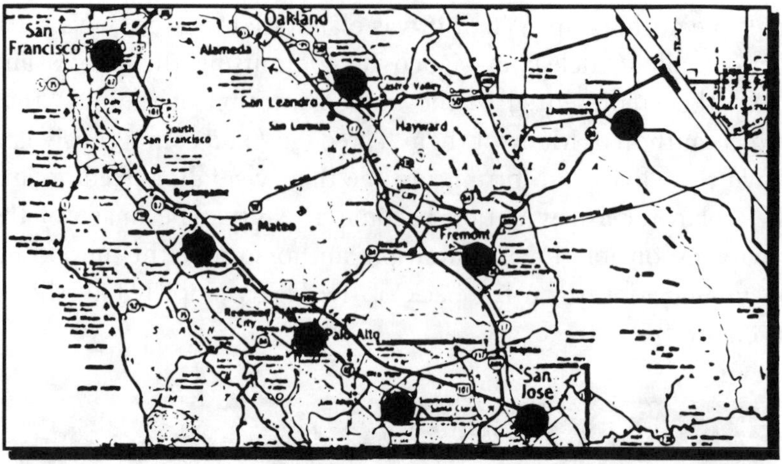

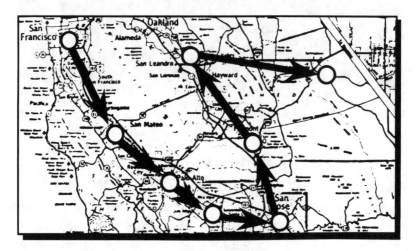

Figure B-3

Figure B-4

- A charted layout of Milestones you want to reach along the pathway of time leading to the attainment of the desired objective.
- A determination of the main tasks needed to reach each Milestone, the duration time required for each task, and the total calculated time for reaching the objective.

This completed chart becomes the leadership team's basic "road map" for time travelling into the future, as illustrated in Figure B-5.

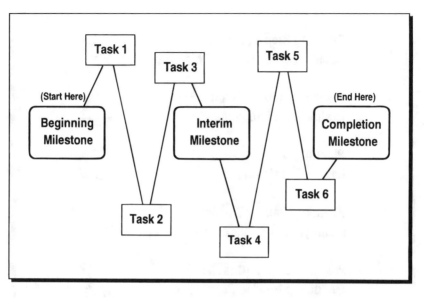

Figure B-5

## THE LEADERS 5-STEP PLANNING PROCESS

The Leaders Plan results from following five sequential steps. This effective and yet simple process can greatly enhance any leader and his or her team in the preparation of a useful plan for intelligently guiding the future actions of an important project or corporate endeavor. Planning is hard work, but in many instances it has become unnecessarily difficult and complex as a result of the lack of an easily understandable and workable process. The worlds of business, government, education, and the church are filled with a potpourri of ambiguous terms such as: *strategic plans, tactical plans, long range plans, short range plans, visions, missions, goals, objectives, purposes, aims, forecasts, budget plans, cash flow projections, budgeted cost of work performed, estimated actuals, scheduled dates, actual dates, earliest dates, latest dates, target dates, drop dead dates.* The process used in the Leaders Plan is designed to simplify the planning process and equip the courageous leader with the knowledge and skills necessary to create the right road map.

A failure to plan is a plan to fail. But how is one to plan correctly? A proven 5-step planning process is discussed in detail in the ensuing chapters, and is outlined in Figure B-6,

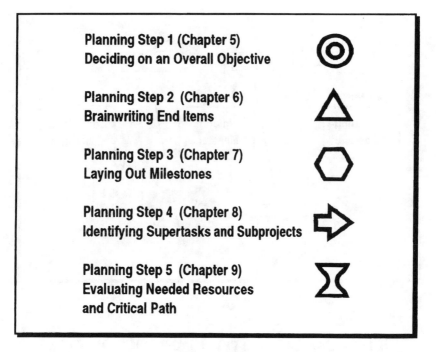

**Planning Step 1 (Chapter 5)**
**Deciding on an Overall Objective**

**Planning Step 2 (Chapter 6)**
**Brainwriting End Items**

**Planning Step 3 (Chapter 7)**
**Laying Out Milestones**

**Planning Step 4 (Chapter 8)**
**Identifying Supertasks and Subprojects**

**Planning Step 5 (Chapter 9)**
**Evaluating Needed Resources**
**and Critical Path**

Figure B-6

Proper planning follows an important progression from Step 1 through to Step 5, as shown in Figure B-7. Skipping intermediate steps can cause delays, frustrations, and confusion. Just as you should not jump from vision straight into action without planning so you should not jump to the fifth step of planning without going through the first four steps. Each step follows the other in a necessary and logical sequence, from the most general to more specific, from the big picture towards ever increasing detail.

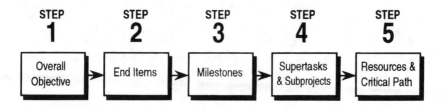

| STEP 1 | STEP 2 | STEP 3 | STEP 4 | STEP 5 |
|---|---|---|---|---|
| Overall Objective | End Items | Milestones | Supertasks & Subprojects | Resources & Critical Path |

Figure B-7

Let us now consider each of these five crucial steps.

## Chapter 5

# Planning Step 1— Deciding on an Overall Objective

The first step in developing a Leaders Plan is deciding on the precise ways to communicate what you and your team believe God desires for you to accomplish. In this chapter you will learn the important elements that make up the Overall Objective and how to establish it properly in terms of both text and graphics. You will learn not only how to describe properly a specific, attainable Overall Objective but also how to identify the challenge of a relatively vague program by analyzing the existing problem, and then describing a desired future solution. A step-by-step demonstration exercise, applicable for individual effort or in a meeting with a team of planners, will lead you through this process.

A hallmark of great leaders is their keen sense of mission. Great leaders are able to communicate clearly the objectives they have a passion to see accomplished, objectives that shape all of their actions and guide all their efforts. This was certainly the case with Jesus, the greatest of all leaders. Time and again in various ways, Jesus stated the Overall Objective of His life. Some of those statements are found in the Gospel of Mark.

*"Let us go somewhere else—to the nearby villages—so I can preach there also. That is why I have come"* (Mark 1:38).

*"It is not the healthy who need a doctor, but the sick. I have not come to call the righteous, but sinners"* (Mark 2:17).

*"You know that those who are regarded as rulers of the Gentiles lord it over them, and their high officials exercise authority over them. Not so with you. Instead, whoever wants to become great among you must be your servant, and whoever wants to be first must be slave of all. For even the Son of Man did not come to be served, but to serve, and to give his life as a ransom for many"* (Mark 10:42-45).

To preach...to call sinners...to serve...to give his life: these are defining statements that impact life. Significant objectives are born out of a desire to make a transforming difference in your world.

Nehemiah was also a man of vision. This vision had been shaped by two factors: He knew his God, and he knew his world, for he had looked both above him and around him. This resulted in unswerving confidence in the trustworthy character of God and profound compassion for his people who had been left destitute and without a homeland because of the ravages of war. Both his confidence and his compassion were the result of thoughtful consideration. The opening words of his prayer (Nehemiah 1:5) echo the words of biblical greats like Abraham (Genesis 24:3,7), Moses (Deuteronomy 4:39; 7:9), Solomon (1 Kings 8:23; 2 Chronicles 6:14) and Daniel (Daniel 9:4). Nehemiah then (Nehemiah 1:8-9) proceeded to quote Moses' understanding of the just and merciful character of God (Leviticus 26:33-42; Deuteronomy 4:27-31; 28:64; 30:1-5). His words are evidence of many hours of searching the Scriptures in an overwhelming desire to know God. But he not only listened to God's word. He also had listened to the words of his brother Hanani and other refugees from Jerusalem regarding the devastation of the city: *"Those who survived the exile and are back in the province are in great trouble and disgrace. The wall of Jerusalem is broken down, and its gates have been burned with fire"* (Nehemiah 1:3). This report drove Nehemiah to heart-searching, career-defining prayer. In the four months that elapsed between verse 1:1 and verse 2:1, a conviction emerged from his having listened to his peers and dialoguing with God. Nehemiah had dedicated himself to do excellent research, and as a result he came to understand both God's perspective and the human need. Therefore he became convinced that two things must occur:

- Jerusalem's walls and gates had to be rebuilt
- Jerusalem's people had to be restored.

This dual conviction became the Overall Objective throughout Nehemiah's life. Nehemiah stated it with conviction in 2:17, *"You see the trouble we are in: Jerusalem lies in ruins, and its gates have been burned with fire. Come, let us rebuild the wall of Jerusalem, and we will no longer be in disgrace."* This Overall Objective became such a defining passion that even the book that bears Nehemiah's name is structured around the twin objectives of restoring the walls and restoring the people (see Figure A-1).

## What Is an Overall Objective?

An Overall Objective is a description of the primary desired accomplishment, the ultimate End Item. The more you and your team understand the Overall Objective, the greater your probability of success.

A target—something at which you specifically shoot, best represents the Overall Objective of any program. Because the sequence of all Supertasks and Milestones in the Leaders Plan eventually leads to the target, a target symbol helps describe the concept of the Overall Objective. A slogan for a program is not an objective. The program itself is not the Overall Objective. These point to the target at which you are aiming. The Overall Objective is a description of the target, the desired future situation, as illustrated in Figure B-8.

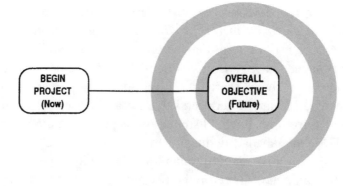

**Figure B-8**

The Overall Objective might be an accomplishment in one or more of the physical, spiritual, intellectual, or societal domains.

In construction, the Overall Objective is usually described in contractual terms, such as completing a given structure (a physical accomplishment) by a certain date and within a given budget.

In a research program, the Overall Objective might be to invent a scientific instrument to measure specific water impurities (an intellectual and physical accomplishment)

In business, the Overall Objective might be described as a twenty-percent improvement in sales or profit per year for the next five years (an intellectual and physical accomplishment).

In an advertising campaign, the Overall Objective might be more difficult to determine. When working with an ad agency, however, it should be described in the most tangible terms possible, such as to achieve an acceptable buyer motivation that will result in capturing twenty-five percent of a prospective market (an intellectual accomplishment).

In missions discipling, the Overall Objective might be to serve in all the major spheres of a specific community in ways that empower the people in every area of society for the kingdom of God (a spiritual and societal accomplishment).

In education, the Overall Objective might be to develop and implement a total capability to make a "A Biblical Foundation For Early Childhood Education" curriculum and associated resources available to one million of the world's preschool children (a spiritual, intellectual, and physical accomplishment).

An outstanding historical instance of setting and reaching a specific Overall Objective occurred when President Kennedy challenged America in his inaugural address to land an astronaut on the moon within ten years (a societal, intellectual, and physical accomplishment). Figure B-9 shows the Apollo program Overall Objective on the Leaders Plan, Step 1 Form.

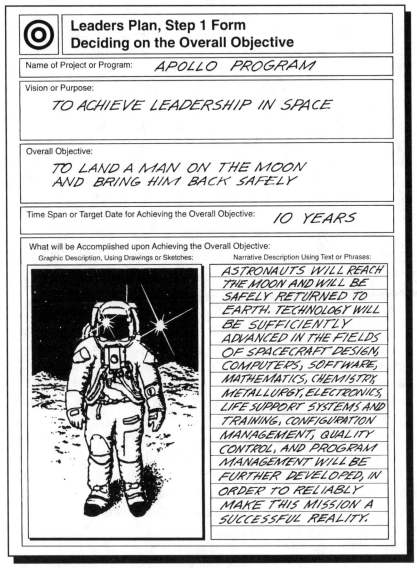

Figure B-9

## How to Decide upon an Overall Objective

Several examples were used in the preceding description of **what** an Overall Objective is. Now we turn to the question of **how** an Overall Objective is decided on. In, general, the wording of the Overall Objective should be established by means of the multiple authorship of a Proverbs 15:22 council. This is a committed leadership team of members of one's community or organization who begin by seeking God and allowing Him to birth a vision to be transformational servants. The team could use the Pre-Planning Form introduced in Chapter 4 (Figure A-3) to do an analysis of what breaks God's heart and could come to recognize the need for a solution to an existing problem or deficient situation. An awareness of God's character and insight into what would bring joy to His heart would open the door to creative ideas that might be translated into an Overall Objective. As together the team members look at both the needs around them and the One who is the solution above them, they define an Overall Objective.

The Overall Objective can be a statement of what one believes the situation should be in the future compared with what it is at present. It is basically a description of a future solution to an existing problem or deficient situation. The initial God-inspired proposal for the Overall Objective can originate from the leaders or any person within the group, but all members of the team should participate in the shaping of it until a consensus is confirmed in prayer.

Arriving at a consensus around the Overall Objective builds unity for the team. In Nehemiah 2:17-18 we see that Nehemiah ratifies the leadership team's assessment of the undesirable predicament of the city (*"Jerusalem lies in ruins and its gates have been burned"*). He then proposes a creative solution to the corporate problem (*"Come, let us rebuild the wall of Jerusalem, and we will no longer be in disgrace"*). The beneficial result of this process of establishing the Overall Objective as a team was that together, *"they committed themselves to the common good."* What marvelous esprit de corps is gained from such a process!

### • Illustrating the Step 1 Procedure

An exciting new early childhood education program illustrates the process of filling out a Step 1 Form. Over the past twenty years the staff in the College/Faculty of Education at the University of the Nations (U of N) Kona campus, has designed, developed, produced, and tested a unique early-childhood education program and curriculum (ages 2-7). Recently, as interest in the program grew internationally, the U of N team set about to implement a big vision—to make the teacher methodology, curriculum, and associated materials available to millions of children worldwide.

A plan was developed using the 5-step planning procedure described here in Chapters 5-9. A Step 1 Form of the type illustrated in Figure B-9 for the Apollo Program helps you to get started right. The form requires that the team documents the name, vision, Overall Objective with time span, and what will be accomplished upon achieving the Overall Objective. As an example of the process, the authors have filled in sequentially in Figures B-10 to B-13 each of the preceding items using available information from the U of N educators who are involved with the project.

## • Deciding on the Name

Naming the project or program is important. After all, as we saw in Chapter 2 the task of naming is the first assignment Adam received from God (Genesis 2:19)! A name for the project may be decided at the start of planning, or the decision may be delayed until the Overall Objective is confirmed. For this project, the U of N team decided on the name "A Biblical Foundation for Early Childhood Education." The name communicates the type of program, and it is documented on a Step 1 Form, as seen in Figure B-10.

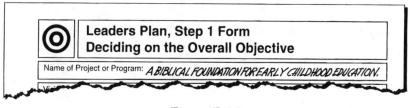

Figure B-10

## • Summarizing the Vision

The God-inspired insight or motivation that ignited interest in pursuing the project or program should be summarized and then recorded on the Step 1 Form. Perhaps the vision was something that was born out of an intense awareness of something that breaks God's heart. Or perhaps the vision began with a vivid image of what would be pleasing to the Lord. Whichever the case, the vision statement describes creative ways to correct the undesirable situation and implement the God-inspired foresight, revelation, hopes, and dreams. For this early childhood education example, the vision is shown on the Step 1 Form, in Figure B-11.

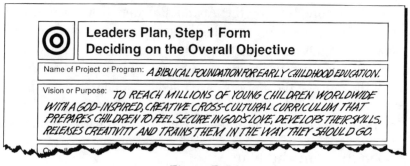

Figure B-11

## • Preparing the Statement of Overall Objective

The leadership team must prepare a statement that clearly communicates the Overall Objective. This statement should be brief but to the point. It should state clearly the target (the what) and should relate to the vision. Also, it might indicate "who does what to whom and with what results." Intentionally asking these questions as a leadership team helps to define the Overall Objective. The team must work together until the statement clearly communicates what all members have in their hearts and minds for the Overall Objective. This process can be challenging and may take a long time. Remember to go back to God frequently in prayer as you seek to understand His heart and mind for the Overall Objective, listening to Him and to one another.

At this point of the process, the leadership team tries to clarify exactly why they are planning to do that which is specified in the Overall Objective. This helps the team hone their understanding of the purpose of the project. Oftentimes the team members will return to their *Pre-Planning Form* and rehearse the things that break God's heart and that bring joy to God's heart in light of this project. They will remind themselves of the words of the Lord they have received as they have waited in His presence for insight and revelation. They may meditate on the character and ways of God or reflect further on the needs of their world. They will bring to the table the fruit of having looked up to God and outward to the world. Then they will summarize in a few brief sentences the result of their deliberations. Their words will be a distilled expression of their passions and convictions that have led them to embark on this project. They express their corporate foundational values that will serve them as a guiding beacon and steady them as a sure anchor throughout the process of developing and implementing the project. The Overall Objective for the project "A Biblical Foundation for Early Childhood Education" is shown on the Step 1 Form in Figure B-12.

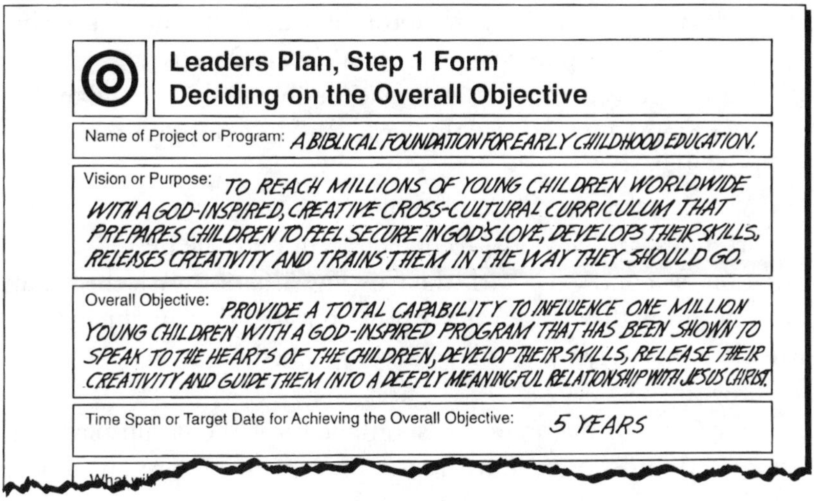

**Leaders Plan, Step 1 Form**
**Deciding on the Overall Objective**

Name of Project or Program: *A BIBLICAL FOUNDATION FOR EARLY CHILDHOOD EDUCATION.*

Vision or Purpose: *TO REACH MILLIONS OF YOUNG CHILDREN WORLDWIDE WITH A GOD-INSPIRED, CREATIVE CROSS-CULTURAL CURRICULUM THAT PREPARES CHILDREN TO FEEL SECURE IN GOD'S LOVE, DEVELOPS THEIR SKILLS, RELEASES CREATIVITY AND TRAINS THEM IN THE WAY THEY SHOULD GO.*

Overall Objective: *PROVIDE A TOTAL CAPABILITY TO INFLUENCE ONE MILLION YOUNG CHILDREN WITH A GOD-INSPIRED PROGRAM THAT HAS BEEN SHOWN TO SPEAK TO THE HEARTS OF THE CHILDREN, DEVELOP THEIR SKILLS, RELEASE THEIR CREATIVITY AND GUIDE THEM INTO A DEEPLY MEANINGFUL RELATIONSHIP WITH JESUS CHRIST.*

Time Span or Target Date for Achieving the Overall Objective: *5 YEARS*

Figure B-12

## • Establishing the Time Span or Target Date

The Overall Objective should always answer the question: What are the time parameters for completing the program? Avoid "ASAP" (as soon as possible). Try to establish true requirements, such as completing the construction of a new school before the students arrive on September 14. It should be clear to all that the completion has to occur before that date.

If the completion date of a new instrument introduction program is not that obvious, look for clues, such as " prototype has to be available prior to the start of a key mission into the Amazon." Even when a date is mentioned, always write out the overall time span allowed. If a drop dead date or target date (latest allowable date) is mentioned, make a quick conversion and insert the estimated time span from beginning to conclusion.

## • Describing What Will be Accomplished upon Achieving the Overall Objective

Describing what will be accomplished should be done in two different ways: graphically and verbally. For some it will be easier to begin with words, for others with images. The most effective result is obtained when both methods are used in combination. The picture of an astronaut standing on the moon, as seen in Figure B-9, is combined with words that describe the impressive accomplishments upon achieving the Overall Objective.

A way of organizing the information obtained by the planning team for Step 1 is shown for the Early Childhood Education Form, in Figure B-13.

When describing the end results of the program/project use powerful descriptive words to depict accurately the desired future situation, as contrasted with the existing situation. Ask the group to come up with a dozen descriptive phrases that might help to articulate precisely what will be accomplished upon completion of the program.

Be careful to maintain the spontaneity of the group planning session. Avoid long, drawn-out preconceived presentations. Otherwise the group of planners will sense that they are not needed, and that this is only a sales pitch for your personal idea. Your role as leader is to bring out the team member's creativity, and help them become committed team players by having them participate in shaping the origins of the program. All should be able to communicate the Overall Objective and how it could alter the future.

## THE IMPORTANCE OF AN OVERALL OBJECTIVE

Establishing and communicating the Overall Objective triggers every aspect of the program, whether it applies to a huge

### Leaders Plan, Step 1 Form
### Deciding on the Overall Objective

Name of Project or Program: *A BIBLICAL FOUNDATION FOR EARLY CHILDHOOD EDUCATION.*

Vision or Purpose: *TO REACH MILLIONS OF YOUNG CHILDREN WORLDWIDE WITH A GOD-INSPIRED, CREATIVE CROSS-CULTURAL CURRICULUM THAT PREPARES CHILDREN TO FEEL SECURE IN GOD'S LOVE, DEVELOPS THEIR SKILLS, RELEASES CREATIVITY AND TRAINS THEM IN THE WAY THEY SHOULD GO.*

Overall Objective: *PROVIDE A TOTAL CAPABILITY TO INFLUENCE ONE MILLION YOUNG CHILDREN WITH A GOD-INSPIRED PROGRAM THAT HAS BEEN SHOWN TO SPEAK TO THE HEARTS OF THE CHILDREN, DEVELOP THEIR SKILLS, RELEASE THEIR CREATIVITY AND GUIDE THEM INTO A DEEPLY MEANINGFUL RELATIONSHIP WITH JESUS CHRIST.*

Time Span or Target Date for Achieving the Overall Objective: *5 YEARS*

What will be Accomplished upon Achieving the Overall Objective:

Graphic Description, Using Drawings or Sketches:

INSTILLING BIBLICAL VALUES

Narrative Description Using Text or Phrases:

*•NURTURES A YOUNG CHILD'S RELATIONSHIP WITH GOD. •INSTILLS BIBLICAL VALUES DEEPLY INTO A CHILD'S HEART. •CREATES AN ENVIRONMENT WHERE CHILDREN ARE LOVED AND VALUED. •TAUGHT TO CHILDREN OF MANY NATIONS AND BACKGROUNDS. •CAN BE ADAPTED FOR USE WITH OLDER CHILDREN, HOME SCHOOLS. •FIELD TESTED IN PRESCHOOLS FOR 15 YEARS WORLDWIDE. •TEACHER-FRIENDLY LESSON FORMAT FULL OF PRACTICAL IDEAS. •42 SCRIPTURES PUT TO LIVELY EASY-TO-LEARN MUSIC. •3 LESSON PLAN MANUALS AND A BIBLICAL FOUNDATION PRECEPT BY PRECEPT. •CHILDREN AND PARENTS COMMIT THEIR LIVES TO THE LORD.*

**Figure B-13**

construction effort such as the Alaska Pipeline or to the planning of an R&D breakthrough in a small electronics firm. Keep in mind that a well-stated Overall Objective provides the rationale for reaching it.

A program or an entire organization will suffer if its Overall Objective is not properly defined. Sometimes a program goes astray

merely because the only existing description of its final accomplishment is a hazy, vague dream. Far too many programs do not
reach a goal or objective simply because none has clearly been set.

Once, a CEO (Chief Executive Officer) of a large company
asked, following a brief description of our planning system, "Can
I use your system to develop a five-year plan for my company?" I
answered with another question: "A five-year plan to do what?"
The CEO was stumped. He had no immediate answer. What a
tragedy that this CEO—like so many of our leaders in business,
industry, government, and non-profit organizations—made major
decisions without ever clearly defining the Overall Objective for
the organization.

One very important lesson learned from the Apollo space program is that when the leadership of a company, an organization,
or an entire country establishes a clearly defined Overall Objective
and makes the planning decisions necessary to reach this Overall
Objective, a much greater chance for success exists. "We can put
an astronaut on the moon, why can't we...?" How many times
have we heard that question when we discover that the office
copier keeps jamming or the VCR defies being programmed for
recording a 9:00 movie?

That's just the point. Behind most great achievements are persons who made decisions to achieve something specific. When
something doesn't work, it often is traceable to the *lack* of a decision to achieve something specific.

All corporate activity happens because key persons make
choices and decisions. When persons with authority and accountability decide to establish an Overall Objective, the goal is eventually met. But without a clear Overall Objective, little is ever
accomplished.

A Leaders Plan is a process of developing a plan of action to
achieve a specific Overall Objective. Therefore it should be evident
that the right Overall Objective must be established clearly before
anything else is attempted.

## CONCLUSION/SUMMARY

Chapter 5 has presented Step 1 of preparing a Leaders Plan
and the procedure for establishing a clear Overall Objective for a

## ◎ Leaders Plan, Step 1 Form
## Deciding on the Overall Objective

Name of Project or Program:

Vision or Purpose:

Overall Objective:

Time Span or Target Date for Achieving the Overall Objective:

What will be Accomplished upon Achieving the Overall Objective:

Graphic Description, Using Drawings or Sketches:

Narrative Description Using Text or Phrases:

**Figure B-14**

specific program. It has illustrated the stepwise application of a Step 1 Form of the type shown in Figure B-14. It has given examples that illustrate WHAT an Overall Objective is. It has described HOW to establish the Overall Objective in terms of a few carefully chosen words and graphics so as to communicate the big picture for any program. Step 1 helps to analyze the existing problematic situation and then articulate a desired contrasting situation in the future. Step 1 also explained WHY a carefully prepared and clearly worded Overall Objective helps determine the success of a project and initiates the development of a powerful Leaders Plan.

We believe that Step 1 will be done right if you do the right thing by knowing God's will and acknowledging His vision. He wants us to work in unity with Him and with each other right from the start. Thus it is very important that the team prays together and seeks His thoughts, His words, and His illustrations for the Overall Objective. An exciting process ensues as He releases synergism and creativity and a special bonding of the team. The results are a planning process and a plan that bring honor and glory to Him.

# CHAPTER 6

# Planning Step 2— Brainwriting End Items

*"Plans fail for lack of counsel, but with many advisers they succeed"* (Proverbs 15:22).

Step 2, as described in this chapter, produces a valuable document, the End Item Table. The End Item Table is a thorough and properly arranged checklist of program elements needed for accomplishing a mission or completing a project, without having to consider timing, sequences or dates. End Items can be physical, such as supporting equipment, supplies, and personnel; or intellectual, such as design drawings and permits; spiritual, such as intercessory prayers, loving God, and spiritual warfare; or societal, such as an evangelized nation and a discipled community.

In this chapter you will learn about the impressive impact of listing End Items using the creative process called "brainwriting." Brainwriting End Items is a powerful concept, an innovation for team members preparing a Leaders Plan. This process infuses creative input into planning without focusing on sequences, timing or dates The End Items produced as a result of disciplined yet freewheeling planning ensures that creative, accurate, and thorough information is obtained. That this occurs even before any logic diagramming or scheduling gets under way in Steps 3, 4 and 5 is very important. End Item planning enables members of the planning team to go to the end of the task to describe the task product. This process encourages a careful look at problems, but more importantly, it describes what the solution is before you get bogged down in the tasks needed to solve the problem.

Consider the sad situation expressed by Nehemiah in the Scriptures. Nehemiah was not happy with the current state of affairs in Jerusalem. He knew that God's heart, even more than his own was broken over the tragic situation in Jerusalem. Nehemiah's sorrow was such that even the king noticed it and asked him about it. In response, Nehemiah told the king of the undesirable situation, *"the city where my fathers are buried lies in ruins, and its gates have been destroyed by fire"* (Nehemiah 2:3). In light of these bad tidings, the king asked, *"What is it you want?"* (Nehemiah 2:4). Nehemiah had done his homework and was prepared to answer the king with a plan. His Overall Objective was to rebuild Jerusalem and deliver its inhabitants from oppression. Although the Overall Objective is also the ultimate End Item, there are many other intermediate End Items between the current situation (the existing problem) and the ultimate End Item (the future solution). Nehemiah's desired End Items are clearly recorded in the Bible, for there we see the contrast between the existing problems and the future solutions as seen in Figure B-15.

Now, what has God put on your heart? Has He given you a vision and desire to transform a bad situation into an inspired solution? You must answer these key questions to realize your ultimate End Item, your Overall Objective, and subsequently to determine the necessary intermediate End Items. The rest of this chapter will also give you insight into brainwriting, the unique method of determining the many End Items essential to developing the Leaders Plan.

## WHAT ARE END ITEMS?

The term End Item may not seem profound, but it represents one of the most helpful concepts you will learn from this book. Read carefully. Determining End Items is a major breakthrough in the planning process because it provides creativity, accuracy, and thoroughness. It also eliminates serious difficulties commonly

| EXISTING PROBLEM | FUTURE SOLUTION |
|---|---|
| Walls of Jerusalem broken down (Neh 1:2) | Walls of Jerusalem rebuilt (Neh 6:15) |
| Old gates of Jerusalem burned (Neh 1:2) | New Gates of Jerusalem in place (Neh 7:5) |
| King Artaxerxes orders Jerusalem's rebuilding stopped (Ezr 4:17-23) | King Artaxerxes reverses his order and Jerusalem's rebuilding resumes (Neh 2:6) |
| Jerusalem's inhabitants living in disgrace before enemies (Neh 2:17) | Jerusalem's inhabitants vindicated before enemies (Neh 6:15) |
| Jerusalem's poor experiencing economic injustice (Neh 5:1-5) | Economic injustices of Jerusalem's poor righted (Neh 5:9-13) |
| God-ordained feasts not being celebrated: a cause of sorrow (Neh 8:17) | God-ordained feasts reinstituted: a cause of joy (Neh 8:13-18) |

Figure B-15

experienced in using most project management programs. The concept of End Items can be readily understood by considering some synonyms.

## • End Items Are Task Products

Everybody knows about tasks. Traditional project planning usually begins by making a list of tasks. The big problem of starting with tasks is that the list often becomes so large and cumbersome that leaders get buried in detail and lose sight of the manageable segments for reaching the Overall Objective.

The initial attempts of a major television network to plan the activation of a complex motion picture production facility resulted in great difficulty for just this reason. The project leader was the controller, who was selected by top management because he had all the computers necessary to do project planning. Like any good executive, the controller sent a memo to all department heads requesting that each submit all the tasks necessary to activate the studio. Like good department heads, each sent back a list of tasks. "Lease cameras," "Build sound stage 21," "Purchase stereo sound mixers," "Hire producers," "Activate fire department," "Purchase fire extinguishers," and so forth. The controller got his tasks—all 37,000 of them. After attempting to place these tasks in sequence on huge wall charts, he gave up.

This common trap can be easily overcome by starting at the end of the task or series of tasks and working backward. The task product of "Design sound stage" and "Build sound stage" is "Sound stage." As a task product, therefore, the End Item is the noun at the end of a verb or a list of verbs in a series of project tasks.

## • End Items Are Solutions

Think about the ten biggest problems you had during the past month or so and write them down. Now describe the name of the solution next to each problem. The solutions are End Items. When you wrote down specific solutions, you were creatively performing the End Item planning of Step 2.

The Australians, for example, were after the America's Cup in the sport of sailboat racing. They used creative End Item planning by first identifying the problem: "Our boat is too slow." They identified the creative End Item solution as "A faster boat." How would they achieve this? Through another End Item: via "keel vanes" to get the boat up out of the water to minimize the effects of friction. The Australians won the America's Cup, which the United States had kept for about a hundred years. The United States later regained the cup by applying an appropriate End Item solution to the same problem.

Having recorded your thoughts about various problem/solution situations on the Pre-Planning Form will be helpful as a reference in establishing the End Item Table.

## • End Items Are Specified Outputs

Computer programming requires that a specified output be described before certain phases of programming get under way. Borrowing from this concept will aid in preparing a Leaders Plan. The End Items of Step 2 can be considered specified outputs.

If you face the tough task of planning research, you may find resistance by some. They may state that research cannot be planned.

They may affirm, "After all, research is innovation, and innovation cannot be pre-planned. Innovation and planning are a contradiction in terms." Although it may be challenging to plan research, each university Ph.D. candidate is living proof that great innovations regularly appear before dissertation time. These research dissertations are excellent examples of End Item planning. The Ph.D. candidate had to come up with a specified output, an important development of knowledge or a breakthrough as the heart of the dissertation. This type of specified output generation will substantially aid in pre-structuring any research plan based on the best available understanding at any given time.

### • End Items Are "Desirements"

An Air Force officer once coined the word desirement as a weapons system procurement term to describe what is really wanted. Small children use the desirement concept to describe what they want when they go to the store with their mom. Indeed moms do the same when they go to the store. They think of their Overall Objective (groceries for our meal). The next step is to make a list of desired End Items—they do not make a list of tasks ("open the door, go out the door, get in the car, start the car, drive to the store, etc."). Their list of End Items consists of all of the things they need to reach their Overall Objective ("milk, flour, eggs, sugar, etc."). This written planning helps them be assured that when they go to the store they will obtain everything they desire to obtain. Not only do Air Force officers and moms understand the concept of "desirements," God does! If He is our ultimate desire and joy then our other desires fall into place. For this reason the psalmist tells us, *Delight yourself in the Lord and he will give you the desires of your heart*" (Psalm 37:4).

Try the desirement approach: Describe the End Item as what you really desire, no matter how difficult it may seem to obtain. This nurtures creativity by escaping the bounds of tradition.

## THE OVERALL OBJECTIVE IS THE PRIMARY END ITEM

The Overall Objective should be described as an accomplishment or achievement in a way that will coincide with the definition of the level 1 deliverable End Item located uppermost on the End Item Table that you will prepare in Step 2 of the planning process.

It is very important to be as specific as possible. "Man on the Moon" is specific. "Significant achievement in outer space technology" is not. Too many assumptions would have to be made, and it would be impossible to plan effectively in Step 2.

## How Brainwriting Yields Creative End Item Information

*"Write the vision; make it plain upon tablets, so he may run who reads it"* (Habakkuk 2:2).

Step 2 of the Leaders Plan enables all of the participants on the planning team to contribute End Items that will be needed to realize the Overall Objective. Following a period of seeking the Lord for revelation the team coordinator asks each participant to write down on paper or on the Leaders Plan Step 2 Form (see Figure B-16) all the End Items that come quickly to mind, usually in a short period of time, about thirty minutes. The items can range in significance from the most to the least important! They may be in any of the End Item categories: physical, intellectual, spiritual, or societal.

All participants are then asked to read their lists to the group. The entire group thus shares in the process, although typically there is some overlap in the participants' lists. Experience shows that in a planning team of twenty to thirty participants each person comes up with items that are unique compared to the others. The total items written down by all of the team members form the basis for the End Item Table. This process is referred to as "brainwriting."

## The End Item Table

Preparation of a Leaders Plan requires a creative, accurate and thorough process. The End Item Table becomes a complete set of ideas, organized by categories. It is the vital link between the Overall Objective and the subsequent steps in the planning

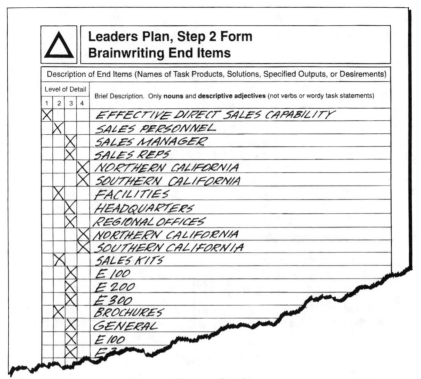

**Figure B-16**

process. Brainwriting End Items is like fishing with a net. When all the team brainwrites their desired End Items, it is like casting the net into the water. When those ideas are shared and compiled it is like pulling the net back into the boat, filled with many fish. There still remains an important step in the process: the caught fish must now be sorted. Similarly, the team must now categorize all of their ideas into logical groupings, establishing sets and subsets of End Items. The End Items must be put in the right taxonomy, distinguishing between the major and minor End Items, just as you would distinguish between a tree's trunk, branches, twigs and leaves.

The information obtained by the brainwriting process should be arranged into logical categories. When portrayed graphically, your chart will have a triangular shape. It should have only one level 1 End Item at the top (which is the Overall Objective), a few major intermediate End Items on level 2, and many End Items on level 3, and so on, as needed. This is like an engineer's portrayal of a given product broken down into its logical assemblies, subassemblies and parts as illustrated in Figure B-17.

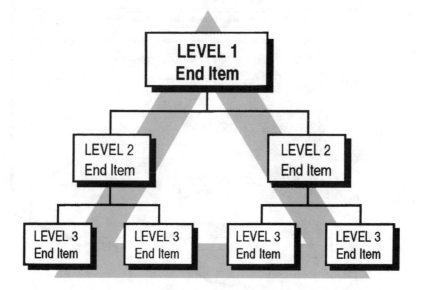

**Figure B-17**

In order to achieve this, the team members are then asked by the team coordinator to rank each item on their lists as a level 2, 3 or 4 level based on its overall significance. This information is correlated by the team so as to arrive at a consensus about the relative importance of each End Item and marked as level 2, 3, or 4. The level 3 or 4 End Items are then listed under appropriate level 2 End Items. The level 2 End Items shown in Figure B-18 are Sales Personnel, Facilities, Sales Kits, and Brochures.

The same information in outline format shown in Figure B-18 can also be put in a graphic format as shown in Figure B-19. The graphic format organizes each End Item as either a highlighted level 2 main heading or several non-highlighted level 3 or level 4 subheadings.

## THE IMPORTANCE OF BRAINWRITING END ITEMS

A primary reason for End Items is to assure that planning will be creative, accurate, and thorough. Bypassing the End Items in

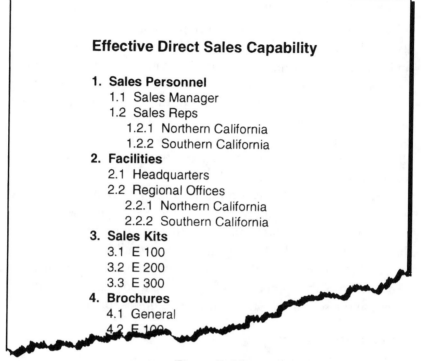

**Effective Direct Sales Capability**

**1. Sales Personnel**
    1.1 Sales Manager
    1.2 Sales Reps
        1.2.1 Northern California
        1.2.2 Southern California
**2. Facilities**
    2.1 Headquarters
    2.2 Regional Offices
        2.2.1 Northern California
        2.2.2 Southern California
**3. Sales Kits**
    3.1 E 100
    3.2 E 200
    3.3 E 300
**4. Brochures**
    4.1 General
    4.2 E 100

Figure B-18

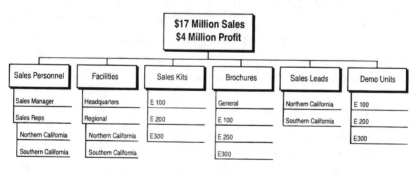

Figure B-19

Step 2 and proceeding directly to Milestones in Step 3 and Supertasks in Step 4 will invariably lead to major difficulties. An adequate End Item Table produced in Step 2 becomes the guide for producing significant Milestones in Step 3 and Supertasks in Step 4.

## • Creative Planning

End Items guarantee that your plans will be developed creatively through use of the process of brainwriting, which you will find exceeds the capabilities of the common "brainstorming" process. This process ensures that you and every member of your team generate specific and often powerful, original ideas for your plans. Both the introverts as well as the extroverts on your team will find brainwriting an effective way to share their ideas. It will allow you to maximize individual creative contributions of each team member and gain unity.

Creativity is always needed but is missing in so many programs. It can, however, be easily applied during Step 2 of the planning process. Creativity is often no more than escaping the bounds of thinking established by formal education or traditions, which often imply that you cannot do this or that. Next time you feel the need to be creative, use the approaches of "desirement" or "specified output" to release the seemingly elusive creative solutions for your program.

## • Accurate Planning

It would be embarrassing to present a plan to a client or your organization's staff, only to discover that the plan is inaccurate. One glaring error can reduce confidence in the overall Leaders Plan. By carefully following Step 2, you can ensure that your plans are reliable because you are freed from the complexities of scheduling, resource allocation, and budgeting. You and your team will be concentrating on requirements, concepts, problems, and solutions.

## • Thorough Planning

Lack of thoroughness in a plan can be disastrous. A major printing company near San Francisco built a new plant near the coastal range that has been the victim of catastrophic flooding from unseasonable rains. The resultant loss of expensive paper in the plant exceeded one million dollars. The manager in charge of planning and activating the new plant had not purchased the right kind of insurance and was promptly invited to resign.

Step 2 has been designed so that a Leaders Plan is thorough. It allows for as much detail as desired by the planning team during the preparation of the End Item Table. All suggestions, regardless of detail (forest, trees, branches, and twigs), are included in this one document, without limitation.

At the close of Step 2, you and the members of the planning team can confidently conclude that the list of End Items is thorough and need only be organized, sequenced, and timed to produce the Leaders Plan.

## • Ensurance That the Leaders Plan Includes Enough Detail

The combination of Steps 2, 3, and 4 determines that the right amount of detail is included in the completed Leaders Plan. By using brainwriting, Step 2 encourages an unlimited amount of detail to ensure thoroughness and adequate details for the Leaders Plan. The subsequent Step 3 is designed so that the many details are organized into a few essential Milestones. The details for each Milestone are retained in a printed outline. The Milestones are sequenced together by Supertasks so that the Leaders Plan remains uncluttered and easy to comprehend.

## • Maximization of Individual Contribution

The procedure for brainwriting used in generating creative ideas in Step 2 guarantees that you maximize the information you will obtain from each individual participating in this important planning effort. You will benefit from the fullest creative capacity and background specialty of each individual based on a proven procedure that motivates voluntary enthusiastic participation on the part of each individual planner.

## • Stimulation of Group Unity

Step 2 builds team input. It discourages the select committee approach and encourages the whole team approach through a disciplined planning procedure that builds camaraderie with proven methods of leadership and team building. The concept of listing and focusing on End Items is a breakthrough for team leadership.

You want to make sure that all the right input is included at this early stage of developing the Leaders Plan. The right input can come only from the right people—those who are committed to the Overall Objective. You will want to include people in the planning sessions who can provide the expertise in each major discipline represented in your program. Even if your planning team seems large, the members can work together effectively.

Brainwriting is a greatly improved version of brainstorming that helps you deal directly and effectively with individual planners in a creative environment. Brainstorming in a planning session may result in one or two individuals dominating the session, even though the Scriptures tell us that *"everyone should be quick to listen [and] slow to speak"* (James 1:19). Such monopoly discourages others, such as quiet geniuses, from contributing even though you would like to have their input. Brainwriting allows all to make a full contribution.

## CONCLUSION/SUMMARY

This chapter has presented the powerful concept and process of brainwriting End Items. The process, which is Step 2 in developing a Leaders Plan, not only generates essential End Item information for Steps 3, 4 and 5, but also yields unique input and creativity from all planning participants. The resulting teamwork and sense of unity among the participants provide a creative environment and a solid information foundation for developing an inspired Leaders Plan.

The what, how and why of brainwriting End Items is one of the unique features of this book. The reader will find this process a major help in all planning efforts. Only brief samples of End Item Tables have been shown in this chapter. Examples of complete End Item lists from several major projects may be viewed at the website www.courageousleaders.com.

A blank Step 2 Form for the Leaders Plan is shown in Figure B-20.

△ **Leaders Plan, Step 2 Form**
**Brainwriting End Items**

Description of End Items (Names of Task Products, Solutions, Specified Outputs, or Desirements)

| Level of Detail | | | | Brief Description. Only **nouns** and **descriptive adjectives** (not verbs or wordy task statements) |
|---|---|---|---|---|
| 1 | 2 | 3 | 4 | |
| | | | | |
| | | | | |
| | | | | |
| | | | | |
| | | | | |
| | | | | |
| | | | | |
| | | | | |
| | | | | |
| | | | | |
| | | | | |
| | | | | |
| | | | | |
| | | | | |
| | | | | |
| | | | | |
| | | | | |
| | | | | |
| | | | | |
| | | | | |
| | | | | |
| | | | | |
| | | | | |
| | | | | |
| | | | | |
| | | | | |
| | | | | |
| | | | | |
| | | | | |
| | | | | |
| | | | | |
| | | | | |
| | | | | |
| | | | | |
| | | | | |
| | | | | |

Figure B-20

113

CHAPTER 7

# Planning Step 3— Laying Out Milestones

In this chapter, you will gain an understanding and appreciation of Milestones and why they are so important to all leaders and others who are responsible and accountable for any important human endeavor. You will learn to become skillful in identifying and naming each important Milestone. You will learn to express an entire Leaders Plan on one graphic display without getting into too much detail. Thus, the graphic plan may be posted on the wall or on a desk to give you a convenient way to quickly follow the progress toward the Overall Objective. By learning how to do this, you will find it easy to make the normally difficult transition from an outline format of the plan to a network chart format.

Step 3 produces Milestones, the important points along the way for reaching the Overall Objective of a Leaders Plan, as well as a Milestone Layout Chart, the initial strategic organization of the plan into a logical sequence. The chart is a network of interconnected rectangles and lines that provides valuable information about the sequential and concurrent relationships of Milestones throughout the Leaders Plan.

Step 3 documents those major events or points along the way to reaching the goal. This is one of the big differences between a Leaders Plan and most other types of plans or schedules. This chapter explains the importance of the Milestone and how it is used, especially at the levels of leadership where decisions are made concerning effective strategy and follow-through to completion of the Overall Objective.

## WHAT ARE MILESTONES?

The term "milestones" originated in the days when the Romans ruled the world. As they built extensive roadways throughout their empire, they placed roadside stone markers every mile to indicate to travelers their progress toward their desired destination. Jesus made reference to these mile markers when He said, *"If someone forces you to go one mile, go with him two miles"* (Matthew 5:41). Such second-mile servanthood would not be possible without the presence of milestones that served as checkpoints measuring one's progress.

So it is that for us Milestones are the important predictable events used as checkpoints in time during the course of tracking the implementation of a plan. A Milestone is depicted graphically as a rectangle that encloses a statement that clearly identifies the Milestone. It is usually located at the beginning or the completion of a task or series of tasks in a project. Also, special Milestones can be located at periodic points in the Leaders Plan for evaluating cumulative resources required.

### • Milestones are End Items Placed in a Logical Time Sequence

Step 2 generates End Items: things, nouns, objects, three-dimensional physical items like "prototype" or intellectual items like "design drawings." Step 3 places these End Items in the fourth dimension of time. For example, if "prototype" is a three-dimensional End Item, "begin building prototype" and "prototype available" are the fourth-dimensional representations of the prototype, as shown in Figure B-21. These would appear as Milestones in the Leaders Plan. The Overall Objective, the ultimate End Item, becomes the final major Milestone.

## 3D End Items Become Milestones in the Dimension of Time

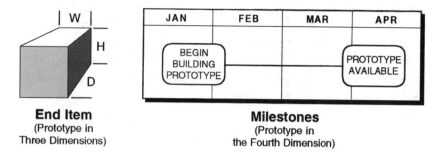

**End Item**
(Prototype in
Three Dimensions)

**Milestones**
(Prototype in
the Fourth Dimension)

Figure B-21

An excellent example of laying out Milestones is documented in chapter 3 of Nehemiah. The goal was to restore Jerusalem's defenses. This required the rebuilding of the walls and the gates of the city. For this reason, when Nehemiah arrived in Jerusalem he made a reconnaissance trip around the city to assess the exact nature of the challenge before him, *"examining the walls of Jerusalem, which had been broken down, and its gates, which had been destroyed by fire"* (Nehemiah 2:13). This thoughtful research enabled Nehemiah to break down the Overall Objective into End Items that could have their progress measured and thus become Milestones. Nehemiah recognized that to rebuild Jerusalem's defenses ten gates would have to be restored. These gates were (clockwise beginning in the North of Jerusalem):

1. The Sheep Gate (3:1)
2. The Fish Gate (3:3)
3. The Jeshanah Gate (3:6)
4. The Valley Gate (3:13)
5. The Dung Gate (3:14)
6. The Fountain Gate (3:15)
7. The Water Gate (3:26)
8. The Horse Gate (3:28)
9. The East Gate (3:29)
10. The Inspection Gate (3:31)

The rebuilding of these gates and the wall sections between adjacent gates became Nehemiah's natural Milestones. The large vision was now being broken down into manageable components, which would allow all the members of his team to find a place to best exercise their respective gifts. With the Milestones defined, communication between all the team members would be enhanced and progress towards the corporate goal could be easily evaluated. Because he had identified his Milestones, Nehemiah could easily track the progress toward their completion. The Scriptures document this for us thus:

1. Reconstruction of walls and gates begun (Nehemiah 2:18)
2. Walls halfway rebuilt (Nehemiah 4:6)
3. Walls totally rebuilt (Nehemiah 6:15)
4. Gates fully rebuilt and doors hung (Nehemiah 7:1)

The establishing of these Milestones released faith in the hearts of all the team members that enabled them to see changed circumstances in their future and to work together in unity to achieve their goal in record time: in just fifty-two days (Nehemiah 6:15)! Despair waned and confidence waxed as Nehemiah courageously helped the team define their Milestones and see how they could make an enduring and beneficial difference in their world.

Jesus undoubtedly had laid out Milestones in collaboration with the Father that guided Him through His earthly life and ministry. The great hymn of Philippians 2:6-11 summarizes Jesus' earthly ministry and details the primary Milestones of his earth-transforming career. Perhaps the major Milestone that Jesus set before Himself was the redemptive act of giving His life for us on the cross (Hebrews 12:2). Because He had clearly defined Milestones, Jesus was able to evaluate what He had accomplished on the cross and declare, "*It is finished*" (John 19:30). The final Milestone, the Overall Objective, had been accomplished and the world would never be the same again. Similarly, all truly transformational projects carry the mark of the cross

## CREATING AND IDENTIFYING MILESTONES

Correctly creating and identifying Milestones can be difficult if certain ground rules are not followed. A common pitfall, for example, is to use a task description to identify a Milestone. Remember that a Milestone is a point in time. It is usually the beginning or end of a Supertask.

In Step 2, you thoroughly planned the project in terms of the needed End Items. Therefore, in order to generate the Milestones needed in Step 3, you first have to select the higher level (level 1 and level 2) End Items, as shown in Figure B-22.

Subsequent figures will show how to convert End Items into Milestones, and how these Milestones are placed into a time and sequence relationship on the Milestone Layout Chart. Note that the level 1 End Item in the Figure B-22 is the Overall Objective and the final major Milestone. It will be placed at the right-hand side of the Milestone Layout Chart.

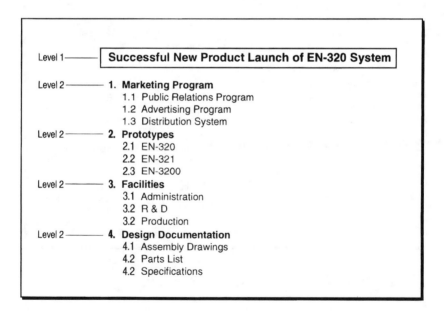

Figure B-22

## • The Precise Language of Milestones

Milestones must be carefully written in a language that is understood and respected by leaders. Beginning Milestones imply the authority to start; completion Milestones measure results. As in good creative writing, the succinct text within Milestone symbols must communicate the intent and meaning of ideas as effectively as possible. Step 2 has produced End Items. Step 3 must now convert End Items to the precise language of Milestones.

## • Converting End Items to Milestones

For every program, each level 2 End Item will initially suggest two Milestones, a beginning and completion point. Interim Milestones are added later. Milestones are formed by combining End Items (nouns) with preferred verbs, as shown in the Figure B-23.

| Level 2 End Item | + | Verb | = | Beginning Milestone | or | Completion Milestone |
|---|---|---|---|---|---|---|
| Marketing Program | | Develop | | Begin Developing Marketing Program | | Marketing Program Developed |
| Prototype | | Build | | Begin Building Prototype | | Prototype Built |
| Facilities | | Acquire | | Begin Acquiring Facilities | | Facilities Acquired |
| Design Documentation | | Prepare | | Begin Preparing Design Documentation | | Design Documentation Prepared |

**Figure B-23**

## • Preferred Verbs are Key

Milestones can convey their meaning better through preferred verbs. Avoid the overuse of the verb "completed," as in "prototype completed" or its incorrect use as in "personnel completed." Use more descriptive and accurate verbs, such as "personnel selected and trained."

## • Preferred Milestone Verb List

Using a preferred verb is the key to create the precise language of Milestones. The following is a sample list of such verbs:

| | | | |
|---|---|---|---|
| Accessed | Concentrated | Fashioned | Obtainable |
| Accomplished | Concluded | Finished | Ordered |
| Accrued | Concocted | Fixed | Organized |
| Accumulated | Constructed | Formalized | Originated |
| Achieved | Consummated | Formed | Overcome |
| Activated | Corrected | Founded | Perfected |
| Advanced | Created | Framed | Polished |
| Altered | Culminated | Fulfilled | Prepared |
| Amended | Delegated | Furthered | Prevailed |
| Amplified | Designed | Gained | Produced |
| Apportioned | Determined | Generated | Promoted |
| Are On Hand | Developed | Graded | Proved |
| Are Ready | Devised | Have In Stock | Realized |
| Arranged | Discharged | Heightened | Reconstructed |
| Attainable | Dispatched | Implemented | Recovered |
| Attained | Disposed | Improved | Refined |
| Augmented | Effected | Improvised | Reformed |
| Authored | Elaborated | Incorporated | Regulated |
| Built | Ended | Increased | Resolved |
| Captured | Enhanced | Installed | Restored |
| Carried | Enlarged | Instituted | Revised |
| Catalogued | Enriched | Intensified | Shaped Up |
| Categorized | Erected | Introduced | Simplified |
| Ceased | Established | Invented | Stopped |
| Classified | Evolved | Is Available | Strengthened |
| Cleaned Up | Exhausted | Is On Job Site | Succeeded |
| Closed | Executed | Manufactured | Systematized |
| Coined | Expanded | Matured | Terminated |
| Completed | Extended | Mended | Untangled |
| Composed | Fabricated | Mobilized | Validated |

## PRODUCING A MILESTONE LAYOUT CHART

The initial graphic time sequence of a Leaders Plan is the Milestone Layout Chart, a refinement of the proven PERT (program evaluation and review technique) charts that emphasize management Milestones and their logical interrelationships. The Milestone Layout Chart serves as a framework for guiding the planning and developing Steps 4 and 5. It can also be very useful in early stages of planning by enabling you to display the strategy and logic sequence for an entire program on one large sheet of paper. This becomes useful to everyone who needs to follow the plan's progress, without getting bogged down into too much detail.

### • Determining a Milestone Layout Format

The initial layout of Milestones in any Leaders Plan should establish a logical sequence of the plan's major beginning and completion points. This layout can use both concurrence and/or sequence. As a general rule, all programs should be laid out in a shape that represents maximum concurrence so that many phases can be conducted simultaneously whenever possible. Nehemiah practiced exemplary maximum concurrence when he enabled 41 different teams to be working simultaneously on different sections of Jerusalem's walls (Nehemiah 3:1-32).

If one Milestone represents the beginning phase and another the completion phase, the Milestone layout could look like the typical hexagon shape, as illustrated in Figure B-24. Thus, the hexagon is used as the symbol for Step 3. It is actually rare that a program could be planned completely this way, because each phase would have to be independent of the other. It is more typical that phases interact, which requires that some sequential interrelationships be shown on the chart.

### • Mandatory Sequence Layout

When resources (personnel, finances, etc.) are uncertain or known to be limited, programs which could otherwise have used a high degree of concurrence may need to be laid out sequentially, as shown in Figure B-25. Even with reasonably unlimited resources, some programs technically require a sequential layout.

122

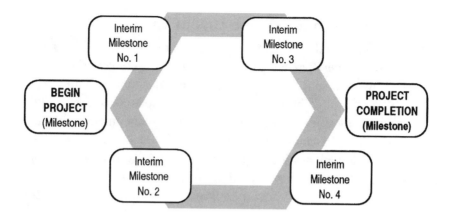

**Figure B-24**

In construction, for example, the foundation must be built first, and then the structure, followed by the interior. The Milestone layout would still have Milestones at the beginning and end of its major phases, but the overall layout would appear as a series of sequential phases, with very little concurrence possible.

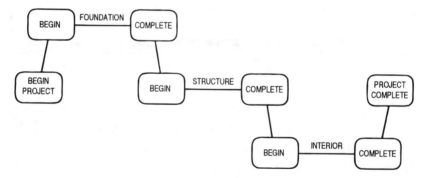

**Figure B-25**

Sequential layout, of course, takes more time than concurrent layout to reach the Overall Objective. Because time can influence the effectiveness of a program, it is very important to look for as many ways as possible to achieve concurrence. Even for a mandatory sequence layout, this can be accomplished with the fast-track method of overlapping partial phases of work or by using lead/lag task relationships, as illustrated in Figure B-46 in Chapter 8.

## • Developing a Milestone Layout Chart

When proceeding with the generation of the Milestone Layout Chart, remember that all you have to do is to convert the level 2 End Items to beginning and completion Milestones. Assume that one of your level 2 End Items was "design documentation." Then create two Milestones: "begin preparing design documentation" and "alpha release design documentation completed." Because the work on design documentation could proceed directly from the "begin program" Milestone, you would draw a sequence line from it to "begin preparing design documentation," as shown in Figure B-26:

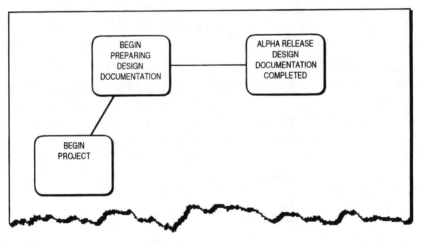

**Figure B-26**

Draw a line from rectangle to rectangle, linking succeeding Milestones. Note that this sequence line always moves toward the right of your chart. This helps you to keep the logic sequence moving forward and not backward, preventing an illogical "catch 22" loop.

Next, you might consider another level 2 End Item, "prototypes." which you realize could be built concurrently. Therefore, you would create two more Milestones: "begin building alpha prototypes" and "alpha prototypes ready for test and evaluation." You decide that this phase of work could also proceed from the "begin program" Milestone. Here is when the value of Milestone layout planning begins to become obvious, as shown in Figure B-27. Remember, at this point you are still not detailing tasks. You are only concentrating on establishing beginning Milestones and completion Milestones.

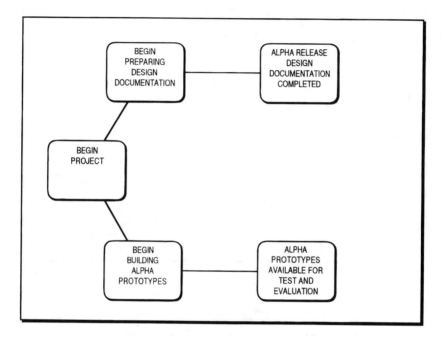

**Figure B-27**

After further reflection, you realize that you cannot begin building the alpha prototypes until the alpha release of design documentation is available, so you now decide to rearrange your layout to reflect this new logical thinking and Milestone interrelationship. Notice how easy it is to make changes as you develop the chart, either by using paper Posts-Its™ or a suitable computer program.

Rearrange the Milestones to show correct sequence, being careful to show the sequence line always angling to the right, as seen in Figure B-28:

Proceed to the next major Milestone in the documentation chain: "beta release design documentation completed." The next logical Milestone would be "begin building beta prototypes," as seen in Figure B-29:

From "begin program" you again believe that the quality analysis program, another level 2 End Item, should get started and

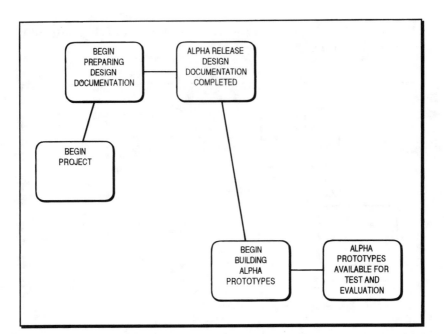

Figure B-28

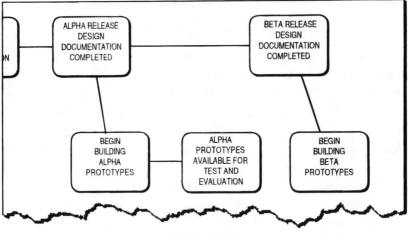

Figure B-29

continue to the point at which it is operational. So, you would create two Milestones "begin preparing quality analysis program" and "quality analysis program ready for operation" and interconnect them with logical sequence lines, as illustrated in Figure B-30:

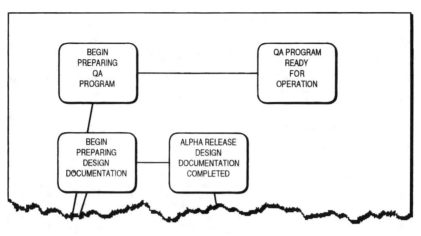

**Figure B-30**

Based on another level 2 End Item, you would also create two Milestones: "begin preparing marketing strategy" and "marketing strategy available," to proceed from the "begin program" Milestone, as shown in Figure B-31:

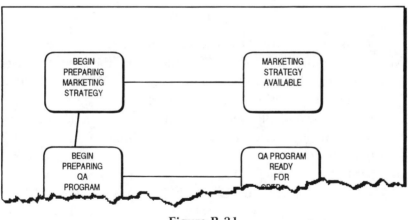

**Figure B-31**

The two Milestones for the level 2 End Item "new facilities" would also proceed from the "begin program" Milestone, because there is little interaction with the other phases. Therefore, this phase could be conducted concurrently with the other items on your Milestone Layout Chart.

Because you then realize that the facilities have to be ready for occupancy before building the alpha prototypes, you would set up this sequence by drawing in the sequence line from "new facilities ready for occupancy" to "begin building alpha prototypes," as shown in Figure B-32:

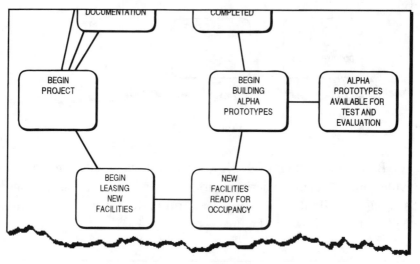

Figure B-32

Continue converting each level 2 End Item into beginning Milestones and completion Milestones, and then interconnect each Milestone logically. You know that your Milestone Layout Chart is near completion when all phases of work in the program are on the chart and all level 2 items on your End Item table have been checked off. Some key additional Milestones from level 3 End Items may have to be added between the existing Milestones in order to make the logical sequence correct.

The Milestone Layout Chart should thus include only the beginning and completion Milestones created from level 2 End Items, and a few important level 3 End Items. Never create a Milestone from End Items at level 4, 5, or farther down the list, as this would invariably put too much detail on the chart.

To draw your Milestone Layout Chart to a close, you will usually create a Milestone such as "begin pilot run production of 200 units" into which all previous parallel sequences will converge. Following that, you might add a series of major sequential

Milestones depicting how the program will be successfully completed. For this new product introduction example, two more Milestones are added to show the major accomplishment, as shown in Figure B-33:

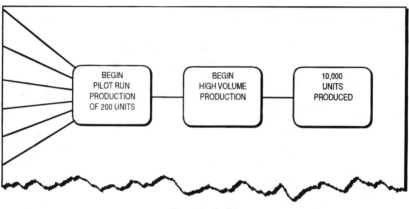

Figure B-33

## • The Hexagon: Symbol of Step 3

As previously mentioned, the pictorial layout of Milestones in step 3 often resembles a hexagon, as shown in Figure 34. This is because the sequential relationships of Milestones causes them to

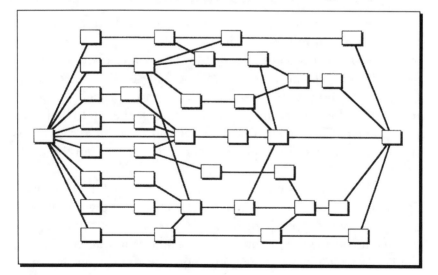

Figure B-34

span from left to right along the center of the Milestone Layout Chart, from the beginning Milestone at the left side of the chart to the completion Milestone at the right side.

Concurrent Milestone relationships diverge from the beginning, continue parallel, and then converge to program completion to approximate the hexagon shape.

## THE IMPORTANCE OF MILESTONES AND RELATED LAYOUT CHARTS

The Milestone Layout Chart produced in Step 3 is primarily designed to depict and communicate an overall strategy for reaching the Overall Objective in one highly visible big picture. Leaders and their teams who are responsible for making major decisions, especially during the critical early phases of developing the Leaders Plan can use the Milestone Layout Chart for viewing, analysis and reference.

Another major purpose for generating the Milestone Layout Chart in Step 3 is to establish a summarized graphic preview of an entire program for use as a guide in further planning steps.

The information of Step 3 will serve as a necessary framework for effectively planning the Supertasks of Step 4 or for planning optional Subprojects when additional subsidiary plans and details are needed for larger programs.

At the start of this chapter you learned that Milestones are End Items placed in a logical time sequence. They are predictable events used as checkpoints during the course of tracking a project. Thus, the primary purpose of evolving Milestones is to concentrate on the points of most interest to those leaders who are responsible for overseeing and monitoring the status of the Leaders Plan. The leader's role, in addition to planning, is to track the plan to successful completion. The leader must plan the work and work the plan.

Milestones are key starting points that depict management decisions and interim "destinations" or challenging goals in program activity for reporting status and accurately tracking accomplishments during the progress of a program. Without Milestones, the Leaders Plan cannot be of any more use to busy leaders than a road map without cities.

- ## Ensurance of Proper Management Decisions

Every program or major phase within a program is always triggered by a decision from someone who has been given related authority. Properly shown as a beginning Milestone, the decision must occur before a program or phase can begin.

- ## Ensurance of Dependability

Without major assessment points at well-spaced intervals, work has a tendency to bog down in the middle of a program which inevitably results in an eleventh-hour, chaos-and-crisis situation. Milestones as interim challenging goals increase the motivation and productivity of all the key players in the program, and therefore are excellent for increasing the likelihood of reaching the final Milestone, the Overall Objective of the program, as illustrated in Figure B-35:

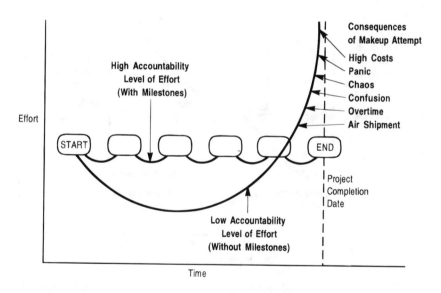

**Figure B-35**

- ## Establishment of the Responsibility/Accountability Loop

The price of being a leader is that of being both responsible and accountable. As described in Part A, Jesus' example as servant leader is our model. Jesus demonstrated perfect accountability to the Father. He acted responsibly in all that He did. This interplay of responsibility and accountability in a leader's life was recognized by a Roman military officer who said to Jesus, "*I myself am a man under authority, with soldiers under me*" (Matthew 8:9). Jesus commended him for his insight in these matters.

Milestones are powerful tools that can help us implement the concepts of responsibility and accountability. Your job description essentially describes your responsibility. You can personally perform all the tasks for which you are responsible, or you may delegate the responsibility to members of your team. If you delegate the responsibility, you will eventually hold that person accountable for completing the task. Thus, you have set up the responsibility/accountability loop, as illustrated in Figure B-36:

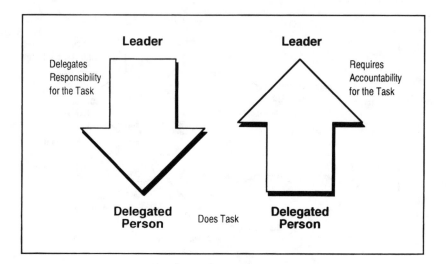

**Figure B-36**

The beginning Milestone formalizes the delegation of responsibility to another person to begin a specific work phase, as shown in Figure B-37:

The completion Milestone closes the loop in the responsibility/accountability cycle by formalizing the precise point in time at which the delegated person responsible for the task will be held accountable for completion of work, as shown in Figure B-38:

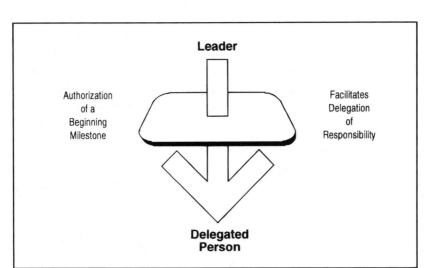

Figure B-37

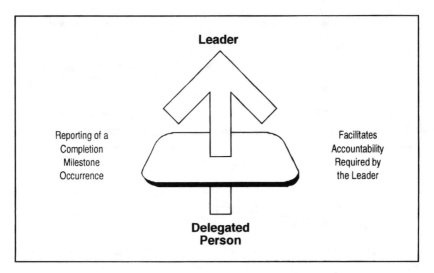

Figure B-38

## • Improvement of Communication

Experienced leaders will agree that one of the biggest problems in organizations is the lack of effective communication between the various departments and often between a leader and his or her team members, or between team members themselves. The Milestone can be an important key in solving this particular problem.

A Milestone in a Leaders Plan is similar to a memo with a delayed-action fuse. A leader could be out of the country when the Milestone occurs, but when that time comes, it is as if the leader was giving a directive to another team member to act precisely according to the instructions printed on the Milestone, as illustrated in Figure B-39:

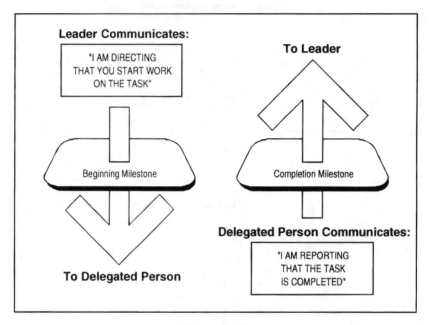

Figure B-39

## • Establishment of a Lateral Interface Between Organizations

Milestones can help overcome the vast gray area of communication and coordination between organizations. For example, a CEO has determined that a production start-up is late for a new product introduction cycle. A check with the Vice President of Production reveals that the pilot production tooling is not ready because engineering never furnished a final set of design drawings for the prototype. A check with the Vice President of Engineering shows that a preliminary set of drawings was sent to production some time ago, but that no one in engineering was aware of the problem until this moment.

All this could have been prevented with the use of two interface Milestones—one in engineering, and one in production—to alert the managers in each department to their precise interface responsibilities, as shown in Figure B-40:

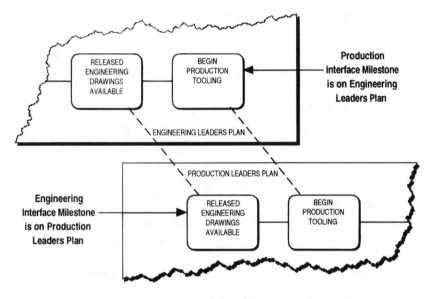

**Figure B-40**

## STEP 3 PERSONNEL

During Step 3, you should always remember that you are generating important Milestones and that they must be identified and arranged by those leaders who are actually responsible and accountable for the occurrence of the Milestones. The whole leadership team should be actively engaged in this process.

Planning a new product introduction involves leadership, wisdom, and insight for making important, on-the-spot planning decisions about marketing, engineering, production, purchasing, and so on. In this case, the CEO and the entire staff representing these functions should be present. One meeting can produce the Milestone Layout Chart. This meeting can pay dividends in eliminating the myriad of costly problems and delays that can occur later without this kind of planning.

## CONCLUSION/SUMMARY

Step 3 provides an effective way to convert the End Items developed in Step 2 directly into major Milestones and, in so doing, to select properly the right amount of detail to be included on the Milestone Layout Chart. Thus the Milestone Layout Chart is not overcrowded with excessive detail and it serves to give leaders the big picture at a glance. As the leadership team develops Step 3 together, they set up the important strategic framework from which the task details of Step 4 will be effectively created and sequenced.

Step 3 shows how to create a Milestone Layout Chart, the first network graphic display in the planning process, by identifying Milestones and sequentially arranging them on one sheet. This chapter has shown the basic concepts of why leaders can relate to Milestones, those points in the Leaders Plan where team members are responsible and accountable.

An example of using a Step 3 Form is shown in Figure B-41, and a complete Step 3 Form is shown in Figure B-42.

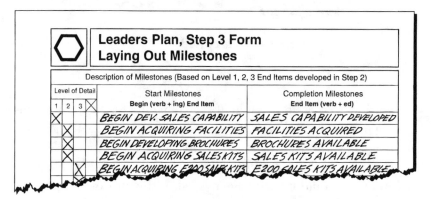

Figure B-41

**Leaders Plan, Step 3 Form**
**Laying Out Milestones**

| Description of Milestones (Based on Level 1, 2, 3 End Items developed in Step 2) | | | |
|---|---|---|---|
| Level of Detail | | Start Milestones<br>Begin (verb + ing) End Item | Completion Milestones<br>End Item (verb + ed) |
| 1  2  3  ✕ | | | |
| | | | |
| | | | |
| | | | |
| | | | |
| | | | |
| | | | |
| | | | |
| | | | |
| | | | |
| | | | |
| | | | |
| | | | |
| | | | |
| | | | |
| | | | |
| | | | |
| | | | |
| | | | |
| | | | |
| | | | |
| | | | |
| | | | |
| | | | |
| | | | |
| | | | |
| | | | |
| | | | |
| | | | |
| | | | |
| | | | |
| | | | |
| | | | |
| | | | |

Figure B-42

137

# CHAPTER 8

# Planning Step 4—
# Identifying Supertasks
# and Subprojects

*"The Lord has assigned to each his task"* (1 Corinthians 3:5).

In the previous chapter you identified the Milestones and produced a Milestone Layout Chart. In this chapter you will identify the Supertasks, the major manageable segments of work that need to be completed to reach a Milestone. You will also learn about developing Subprojects for very complex projects. The Subprojects require complete Leaders Plans that are prepared with the same 5-step planning method described for the overall project's Leaders Plan.

From this chapter, you can learn how to work effectively with the right planning team to obtain understandable technical expressions that describe Supertasks, as well as how to include the optimum amount of task detail in the plan. You will see how to develop the right information platform in Step 4 for making better judgments about evaluating needed resources in Step 5.

If we look again at the biblical example of Nehemiah's courageous leadership we see that many tasks had to be accomplished in order to reach the Milestones of rebuilding the ten sections of

Jerusalem's wall and the corresponding gates. One could attempt to identify every minuscule task involved in a large project, but the result would be detrimental bureaucratic overkill. At this stage, the leadership team needs only to define the largest of tasks, known as Supertasks, each of which could be divided into many smaller tasks.

## WHAT ARE SUPERTASKS AND MILESTONE/SUPERTASK SUMMARY CHARTS?

The main purpose of Step 4 is to show how creative work activity will be performed to cause Milestones to occur. Step 4 identifies Supertasks and the logical relationships between them and Milestones. The new information developed in Step 4 is added to the Milestone Layout Chart to produce a Milestone/Supertask Summary Chart. This chart can be developed for an entire program or for Subprojects within the overall Leaders Plan.

The basic new information produced in Step 4 is tasks suitable for a Leaders Plan. A better description would be "Supertasks," because they are the action items necessary to achieve Milestones. Key people apply them to describe and monitor work activity. The manageable segments of work that must be accomplished in a program to reach a Milestone are the Supertasks. The key word is manageable, because specific persons are responsible and accountable for the execution of all the work. A Supertask is a single uninterrupted segment of work to be performed by an individual or team. A Supertask is a summarized manageable segment of work representing a series of tasks or a whole Subproject.

In planning, Supertasks appear as enhancements on the Milestone/Supertask Summary Chart in the form of rectangular or color code symbols with text descriptions and other surrounding information. They represent the expenditure of resources. Supertasks are represented with the same size rectangle on the Leaders Plan.

## THE MILESTONE/SUPERTASK SUMMARY CHART

When the manageable segments of work called Supertasks are properly combined with the Milestone Layout Chart, a new chart is formed, called the Milestone/Supertask Summary Chart. It is an expression of the program or major phase of the program on a single sheet of paper showing all the information generated in Steps 1 through 4. It is the first chart in the leaders' planning process that shows a total program plan in terms of Milestones, Supertasks, and their logical relationships. It is laid out to show a definite logical sequence from left to right. Only time/resource estimates need to be added to the Supertasks to turn the Milestone/Supertask Summary Chart into a complete Leaders Plan.

## IDENTIFYING SUPERTASKS

Step 4 uses the best creative approach for reaching the challenging Milestones established earlier in Step 3. The planning process determines the right amount of detail for Supertasks. Each Supertask identified in Step 4 will more likely represent the right amount of detail because of the sorting and top-down planning processes done in Steps 2 and 3.

Based on their experience, training, methods of organizing planning materials, and personal preferences, individuals have different approaches to solving problems. Just as in previous planning steps, the brainwriting approach works best because it maximizes individual contribution yet achieves group concurrence as it gets integrated into the plan. In most situations where several disciplines are involved, the planning team must integrate individual creativity into a common plan. The best approach will emerge from the wisdom and counsel of a well-chosen planning team that uses the team planning methods provided by Step 4.

For complex projects, it is always advantageous to develop Milestone/Supertask summaries for the overall program with key leaders and technical specialists who are present in team planning sessions held in a suitable environment. Later more detailed tasks evolve for separate major phases of a program in subcommittee team planning sessions.

## • The Arrow: Symbol of Step 4

An arrow pointing from left to right is the conventional symbol of work activity in diagrams using the classic Critical Path Method. The arrow in both CPM and PERT (program evaluation and review technique) is used as the graphic chart symbol of the task or activity. The beginning of the task is shown at the tail of the arrow and the end of the task is at the head of the arrow, as illustrated in Figure B-43. Note, however, that some project management software programs use a different symbol—the rectangle—to depict the Supertask.

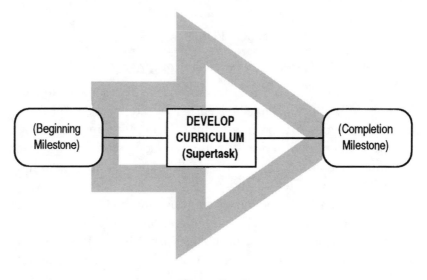

**Figure B-43**

## • A Biblical Example of Supertasks

Chapter 3 of the book of Nehemiah lays out the Supertasks required in the rebuilding of the wall surrounding Jerusalem. As you read through the following record of the Supertasks related to the ten Milestones involved in the reconstruction of Jerusalem's walls, several key things stand out:

First of all, there is no unnecessary or excessive detail. The record doesn't list all the particulars of each Supertask, but gives a sufficiently clear overview so that leadership can be given to the project. This enables the leadership to major on the majors.

Second, note that every Supertask has an individual or a team in charge of its completion. People take ownership over their corresponding responsibilities, allowing for clear communication and accountability.

Third, note that not all the Milestones required the same amount of effort to be achieved. Some Milestones necessitated only one Supertask (e.g. Milestones 4, 5, 7 and 10), while Milestones 3 and 6 required that many Supertasks be accomplished.

Fourth, note that this clear delineation of Supertasks and responsibilities allows for these Supertasks to be accomplished concurrently, greatly hastening the completion of the Overall Objective. Only when Supertasks are clearly determined can it be seen which ones can be done concurrently (at the same time) and which ones must be done sequentially (one after another).

Here is a summary of the Milestones and Supertasks in Nehemiah 3. Take time to read this great chapter on leadership.

## Milestone #1: Wall from the Sheep Gate to the Fish Gate completed (verses 1-2):

1. Supertask #1: led by Eliashib the high priest
2. Supertask #2: led by the men of Jericho
3. Supertask #3: led by Zaccur son of Imri

## Milestone #2: Wall from the Fish Gate to the Jeshanah Gate completed (verses 3-5):

4. Supertask #4: led by the sons of Hassenaah
5. Supertask #5: led by Meremoth son of Uriah
6. Supertask #6: led by Meshullam son of Berekiah,
7. Supertask #7: led by Zadok son of Baana
8. Supertask #8: led by the men of Tekoa

## Milestone #3: Wall from the Jeshanah Gate to the Valley Gate completed (verses 6-12):

9. Supertask #9: led by Joiada and Meshullam
10. Supertask #10: led by Melatiah and Jadon
11. Supertask #11: led by Uzziel son of Harhaiah
12. Supertask #12: led by Hananiah, one of the perfume-makers
13. Supertask #13: led by Rephaiah son of Hur
14. Supertask #14: led by Jedaiah son of Harumaph
15. Supertask #15: led by Hattush son of Hashabneiah
16. Supertask #16: led by Malkijah and Hasshub
17. Supertask #17: led by Shallum son of Hallohesh

## Milestone #4: Wall from the Valley Gate to the Dung Gate completed (verse 13):

18. Supertask #18: led by Hanun and the residents of Zanoah

## Milestone #5: Wall from the Dung Gate to the Fountain Gate completed (verse 14):

19. Supertask #19: led by Malkijah son of Recab

## Milestone #6: Wall from the Fountain Gate to the Water Gate completed (verses 15-26):

20. Supertask #20: led by Shallun son of Col
21. Supertask #21: led by Nehemiah son of Azbuk
22. Supertask #22: led by Rehum son of Bani
23. Supertask #23: led by Hashabiah
24. Supertask #24: led by Binnui son of Henadad
25. Supertask #25: led by Ezer ruler of Mizpah
26. Supertask #26: led by Baruch son of Zabbai
27. Supertask #27: led by Meremoth son of Uriah
28. Supertask #28: led by the priests from the region
29. Supertask #29: led by Benjamin and Hasshub
30. Supertask #30: led by Azariah son of Maaseiah
31. Supertask #31: led by Binnui son of Henadad
32. Supertask #32: led by Palal son of Uzai
33. Supertask #33: led by Pedaiah son of Parosh

## Milestone #7: Wall from the Water Gate to the Horse Gate completed (verse 27)

34. Supertask #34: led by the men of Tekoa

## Milestone #8: Wall from the Horse Gate to the East Gate completed (verses 28-29a):

35. Supertask #35: led by the priests
36. Supertask #36: led by Zadok son of Immer

## Milestone #9: Wall from the East Gate to the Inspection Gate completed (verses 29b-31):

37. Supertask #37: led by Shemaiah son of Shecaniah

38. Supertask #38: led by Hananiah and Hanun
39. Supertask #39: led by Meshullam son of Berekiah
40. Supertask #40: led by Malkijah, one of the goldsmiths

**Milestone #10: Wall from the Inspection Gate to the Sheep Gate completed (verse 32):**

41. Supertask #41: led by the goldsmiths and merchants

## THE IMPORTANCE OF IDENTIFYING SUPERTASKS

Step 3 produced Milestones that show *what* is to be accomplished; Step 4 will identify Supertasks to show *how* it will be accomplished.

Establishing Milestones is the role of leaders who need to oversee the entire project. The role of Supertask generation in Step 4 is for those leaders, technical managers and other professionals, who are trained to know how to accomplish specific Supertasks. The following subsections discuss the importance of carefully determining the Supertasks in the Leaders Plan.

### • Formalizing Specific Job Descriptions

Supertasks reveal how progress will be made in the Leaders Plan. Often this requires one or more highly trained and experienced specialists. Supertasks thus represent the future job descriptions of these specialists.

### • Isolation of Planning from Scheduling

Solving the planning and scheduling problem simultaneously is a difficult, if not impossible task for management, because there are two unknowns at the same time. In mathematics you deal with two or more unknowns by using differential equations. The procedure calls for separately solving each unknown while holding all other unknowns constant. Step 4 uses this same procedure by solving the planning unknown while holding the scheduling function constant—then later dealing with the scheduling unknown in Step 5. Step 4 isolates and concentrates first on solving the unknown element of planning by effectively describing Supertasks and arranging them in the most logical sequence without regard to how long each Supertask will take.

## • Encouragement of Participatory Management

Supertask planning, as provided in Step 4, combines management leadership with a disciplined method of involvement for the entire planning team through a uniform standard and formalized leader planning process. This particularly encourages and motivates voluntary enthusiastic participation by professionals and technical specialists because it allows them to express their own personal methods of accomplishment. In planning, professional and technical specialists are not expected to know each other's specialty, although such knowledge does establish a good working relationship among them all. All this builds a basis of cooperation and coordination between professionals of one or several organizations.

## • Depiction of Manageable Segments of Work

Step 4 builds a viable platform for planning and allocating the use of resources because it divides the Leaders Plan into manageable segments of work. This means that Supertasks are determined whereby effort can be readily estimated in terms of predicted time and resources by those persons responsible and accountable. For the sake of brevity, as illustrated in Figure B-44, it may be necessary to estimate the duration time and cost of building a barn, a Supertask, although it is easier to estimate the cost of building a barn door or a plank in the barn door.

## • Display of Interrelationships and Interdependencies

A graphic portrayal of both Supertasks and Milestones on one chart provides a way to interconnect them in terms of sequence and concurrence. It is usually desirable to plan any program using the concept of maximum concurrence, especially when little interdependency exists between Supertasks.

Step 4 not only describes Supertasks but also sets up their sequence. This is accomplished with sequence lines connected from the end of a preceding Supertask or Milestone to the beginning of the succeeding Supertask or Milestone.

Every line that appears on the chart developed in Step 4 is a sequence line that depicts either a desirable or mandatory

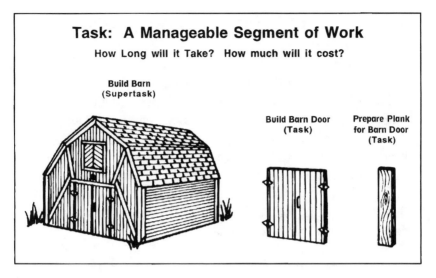

Figure B-44

situation whereby one part of a program (Supertask or Milestone) must be completed before another can start, as shown in Figure B-45:

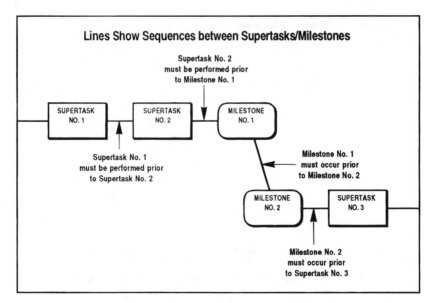

Figure B-45

## • Overlapping of Supertasks for Accelerating the Program

Step 4 offers possibilities for accelerating a program by "fast tracking," a way for identifying and arranging certain Supertasks which can be overlapped effectively, as shown in Figure B-46. For example, it is common to expect that a major shopping center structure will follow traditional planning guidelines for the sequential phases of land acquisition, building design, building construction, fixture installation, and merchandise stocking. The costs for this sequence are tremendous. The interest alone could amount to millions of dollars for land acquisition and construction loans before profits can begin to be realized.

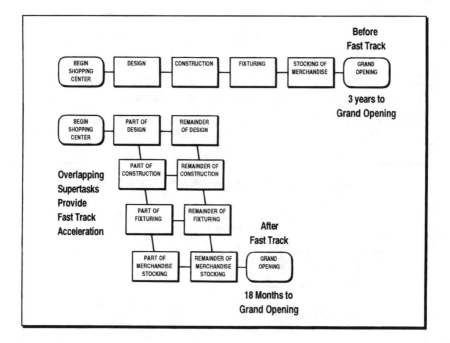

Figure B-46

## • Ensurance of the Right Amount of Detail

One of the biggest problems in traditional project planning is too much detail. Because this process usually calls for (1) setting the project goal and (2) making a task/activity list, thousands of detailed tasks are identified and sequenced on huge charts. The information may be technically correct but is of limited use by the organization's leaders and their teams and their related groups involved in the project. Too much detail is difficult to create, track, and revise and often requires large amounts of computer activity to process the information. Also, the huge hard-copy print-outs are also difficult to include in published proposals and reports. The concept relating to the right amount of detail is illustrated in Figure B-47.

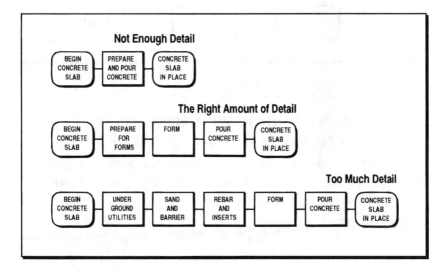

Figure B-47

## • Elimination of Illogical Loops

When a prototype fails a test (it is not supposed to, but it can), it must be redesigned. It has to go back to the drawing board. The problem with the expression "back to the drawing board" is that it implies going back in time. The plan is sometimes drawn with a loop to the design–build–test cycle. This is an impossible and illogical planning concept, because time cannot go backward. As shown in Figure B-48, the correct way to represent the process when the test fails is start a new action sequence of redesigning, rebuilding, and testing the new prototype.

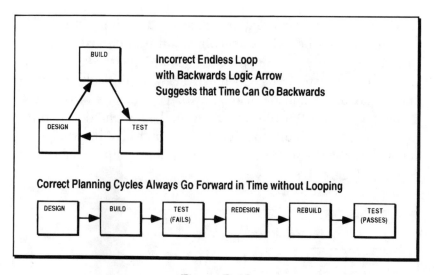

Figure B-48

## CREATING SUBPROJECTS FOR A COMPLEX OVERALL OBJECTIVE

Supertasks best describe the product of Step 4 which, by design, produces summarized manageable segments of work. For most applications, this is very efficient and practical because more than adequate detail is produced in the End Item Tables of Step 2. The 5-step planning process purposely generates an extremely useful family of information, including a highly desirable big picture illustrated in the Milestone/Supertask Summary Chart. However, if the Overall Objective is very complex, it is important to show additional details on separate charts called Subproject Leaders Plans. Each Subproject is analyzed as a separate detailed Leaders Plan with its own End Items, Milestones, Supertasks, logical interconnections, and critical path. When a large complex project requires the development of many Subproject Leaders Plans, then each of these plans is related to the overall Leaders Plan, much in the same way as state or province maps relate to the overall map of a nation. Indeed the map of the nation could itself be seen as a Subproject of the map of the whole globe; which in turn would be a Subproject of the map of our solar system, and so on.

Some of the Supertasks laid out by Nehemiah were of such magnitude that they could have been a Subproject with their own leadership team. Consider Supertask #10 (see page 143). Melatiah and Jadon most likely developed a more detailed Subproject Leaders Plan that would have considered issues like how they would clear the rubble from their construction site, methods for transporting timber and stone, means of providing food and water for their work team, etc. Such detail would not have been appropriate for Nehemiah's overall Leaders Plan, but would have been essential for Melatiah and Jadon's Subproject Leaders Plan in order to complete the Supertask entrusted to them.

Many large projects may require the development of Subprojects. We've referred to the project of sending a man to the moon and bringing him back to earth safely. This complex overall project necessitated many Subprojects, such as the Mercury Subproject, the Gemini Subproject, the Apollo Subproject, and others. Similarly if one's project aimed at discipling a whole nation, the magnitude of the task would require the development of many Subprojects, such as:

- an Evangelism and Church Planting Subproject,
- a Justice and Governmental Issues Subproject,
- a Healthcare and Counseling Subproject;
- an Early Childhood Education Subproject,
- an Environmental Stewardship Subproject,
- an University of the Nations Subproject, etc.

The possibilities are limitless. Subproject charts are a detailed reflection of the equivalent Supertasks on the Leaders Plan. Each Subproject chart becomes a separate related Leaders Plan with its own sequential interconnection of Milestones, Supertasks, time/resource estimates, dates, and critical path. Each has its own unique name to indicate a part of the whole. It is locked in with the same time frame as its equivalent Supertask on the Leaders Plan. The (longest) critical path time duration for each Subproject determines the duration time for its equivalent Supertask.

An illustration of how a Supertask from an overall Leaders Plan may be expanded so as to show details and be interlocked with the corresponding charts of a Subproject Leaders Plan is provided in Figure B-49.

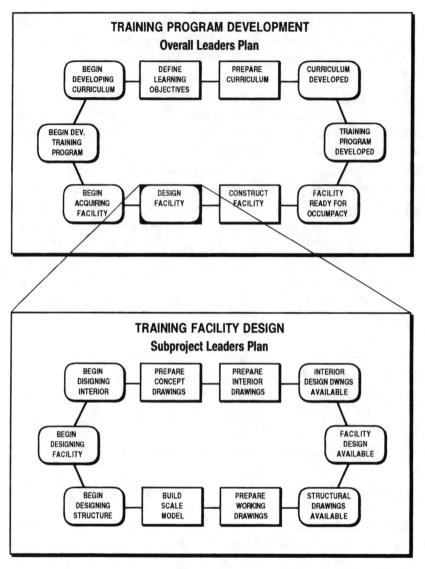

Figure B-49

## SUBPROJECT END ITEM TABLES

One of the most important systematic inputs to a Leaders Plan is in Step 2 that not only generates valuable creative ideas but also sorts out and organizes these random ideas into a hierarchy of categories. Each Subproject should be planned with the precision of the overall Leaders Plan. The Subproject Leaders Plan is developed from its own End Item table, as illustrated in Figure B-50. For very large programs, it is possible to plan more than one level of detailed Subprojects.

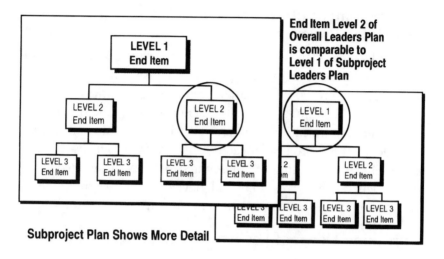

Figure B-50

# THE IMPORTANCE OF SUPERTASKS AND SUBPROJECTS

A Leaders Plans that features Supertasks offers an elegant way to create and comprehend many future programs and projects without the visual complexity of too many details. When much more detail is required, Subprojects should be created for one or more Supertasks in the plan. The following subsections discuss the reasons for considering this option.

## • Ensurance of an Adequate Amount of Task Detail

As we have already seen, one of the biggest charting problems is getting too much detail on one chart of any Leaders Plan or project management plan. This problem can usually be traced to a simplistic planning process which, if uncontrolled, can lead to thousands of tasks on one huge chart that may be technically correct but is of limited use. The procedure of creating Supertasks and Subprojects will more likely generate an adequate amount of detail because of the inherent sorting out and top-down planning process involved, similar to map making, where it must be determined just how many cities or towns should be included on a given map.

- ## Development of Leaders Plans for Complex Programs

The Leaders Plan for large complex programs, such as a major community development program, may consist of several interconnected Supertasks of research, engineering, business creation, education curriculum, a university, technical infrastructure, health care, and communication. Therefore it will be useful to develop a more detailed Subproject for each of these efforts. This is particularly useful for providing the planning capability at detailed technical levels, such as research and development, where there is always a great need for organizing and nurturing creativity.

- ## Breaking Down of Leaders Plans Into Cost Modules

In some instances, it may be advantageous to develop cost modules which reflect not only the work as defined in the Supertask but also the function on the organization chart, such as engineering, manufacturing or marketing. If a summarized Supertask combines these functions, the functions can be broken out as separate tasks in Subprojects to categorize costs in cost modules that reflect organizational functions or specific subcontractors who specialize in one type of activity. It is therefore easier to develop cost modules at the detailed level of a Subproject than if it is oversummarized.

- ## Representation of Typical Repetitive Sequences

In a construction project, such as erecting a twenty-one story high-rise office building, a Leaders Plan would summarize the entire project showing a separate Supertask for integrating the construction of the entire twenty-one story building. It would set the start and completion dates for the first floor, the second floor, and so on to the twenty-first floor. Rather than have an individual and separate detailed plan written for each floor, only one Subproject would have to be detailed. This one Subproject Leaders Plan can then be used as a template for the typical repetitive sequence for each floor. Twenty-one floors would require twenty-one separate Subprojects for setting start and finish dates. Each floor would be a clone of the template, except for the start and finish dates and and other information related to the needed resources.

## • Establishment of a Framework for Detailed Resource Allocation Analysis

In resolving conflicts due to overcommitted resources when two or more Supertasks in one project or from multiple projects are competing for the same limited resources, the resource allocation analysis works only at detailed levels. In many projects it is necessary to compromise by summarizing tasks, therefore losing the detail essential for resource allocation analysis.

If there is enough detail to perform resource allocation analysis, there may be just too much detail in the Leaders Plan. (The motion picture studio activation, described earlier, required 37,000 of these detailed tasks!) In many programs, particularly larger programs, where resource allocation analysis is desired, it will be necessary to establish eventually a framework for this by breaking down the Leaders Plan into more detailed Subprojects.

## • Development of Good Working Relationships Between Lateral Groups

In complex programs where several organizations or departments are working together, key people from each group often spend so much time trying to learn each other's specialty that there is not enough time to think about their own specialty. It is therefore not uncommon to see huge plans with hundreds and even thousands of tasks with an overzealous attempt to interconnect daily logic between everyone. This has been typical in aerospace programs and construction projects. Although this may be technically very accurate, the entire process fails miserably because managers, for whom the system has been designed, can no longer take the time to use the system.

Because Leaders Plans are designed to help team members perform their functions, it is imperative that all team members concentrate on their departmental work shown on their respective Subproject. The Leaders Plan interweaves the big picture at the highest level. Each Supertask is selected where departmental work begins and ends. The close working relationship is developed between departments or whole organizations.

## PLANNING METHODOLOGY FOR SUBPROJECTS

The planning methodology for Subprojects is really no different from that of the overall Leaders Plan. This means that the individual planner or the planning team is encouraged to evolve Subproject Supertasks as manageable segments of work. The guideline for producing the right amount of task detail in a Subproject is to produce its Supertasks from the Subproject End Item Table, for which the rationale is well established. Preparing the new End Item Table allows for as much detail as desired by anyone on the planning team during its preparation. All valid ideas, regardless of detail, are recorded without limitation. These End Items are then organized horizontally according to categories, then vertically in an outline hierarchy of headings and subheadings as levels 1, 2, 3, 4, and so on (forest, trees, branches, and twigs).

In the last analysis, developing a Subproject is really no different than developing an overall Leaders Plan. The cautionary suggestions are primarily to remember that the purpose of planning is to develop a tool for making better decisions now for improving the outcome in the future. The procedure for developing a Subproject should include the 5-Step leaders' planning process. Each Subproject should have its Overall Objective. Each member of the Subproject team should know the purpose and goal of the Subproject. Each should contribute to the Subproject End Item list. Each should help select key interim Milestones and the required Supertasks.

Supertasks on the overall Leaders Plan are primarily determined from level 2, but occasionally include level 3 End Items. Likewise, Supertasks for the Subproject are primarily determined from level 2 of the Subproject End Item Table. It is normal to use top-down planning when using Supertasks and Subprojects, although it is possible to create the detailed complex Subprojects first, then integrate them into an overall Leaders Plan. This might seem contrary to the concept of starting from the top with the major Overall Objective and proceed downward. However, when the Overall Objective of the Leaders Plan is extremely huge and long range, it is not unusual to develop a Leaders Plan for a Subproject first. When a Subproject is implemented first it should be in the context of the Overall Objective of the overall Leaders Plan.

## • Personnel Required to Develop Subprojects

It is imperative that the professionals in charge of a particular specialty get involved directly in developing Subprojects. However, because this is an exciting process that speaks the daily language of particular specialties, this sometimes leads to generating great amounts of detail at the technical level. It is a good idea to make sure that either these professionals understand the intent and procedure for creative planning (as differentiated from administrative scheduling) or they are supported by their department leaders and operating personnel for effective use of the Leaders Plan.

## • Conclusions About Using Subprojects

The 5-Step Leaders Plan provides a way to plan any type of endeavor such as a new product introduction program, a university campus, a construction project or the launching of a whole new business. This process has been proven effective on thousands of such applications.

As an option, the completed Leaders Plan can be supplemented with Subprojects, where additional detail is needed for one or more Supertasks in the plan. These Subprojects provide a framework for making equally detailed time/resource estimates and costs for the tasks. Just as in the rationale of map making, where a nation's map is broken down into state, province or city maps, the overall Leaders Plan can be broken down into Subprojects. The question is, When do you use the entire nation's map and when do you use a state or city map? It depends upon the specific focus and the details required.

The Leaders Plan provides copious amounts of detail in step 2, completely adequate to make the planning process thorough. Every Milestone is displayed. The only thing that is summarized is the logic diagram with its overall Supertasks. If, however, more intricate logic is required or if details are needed at the lowest task

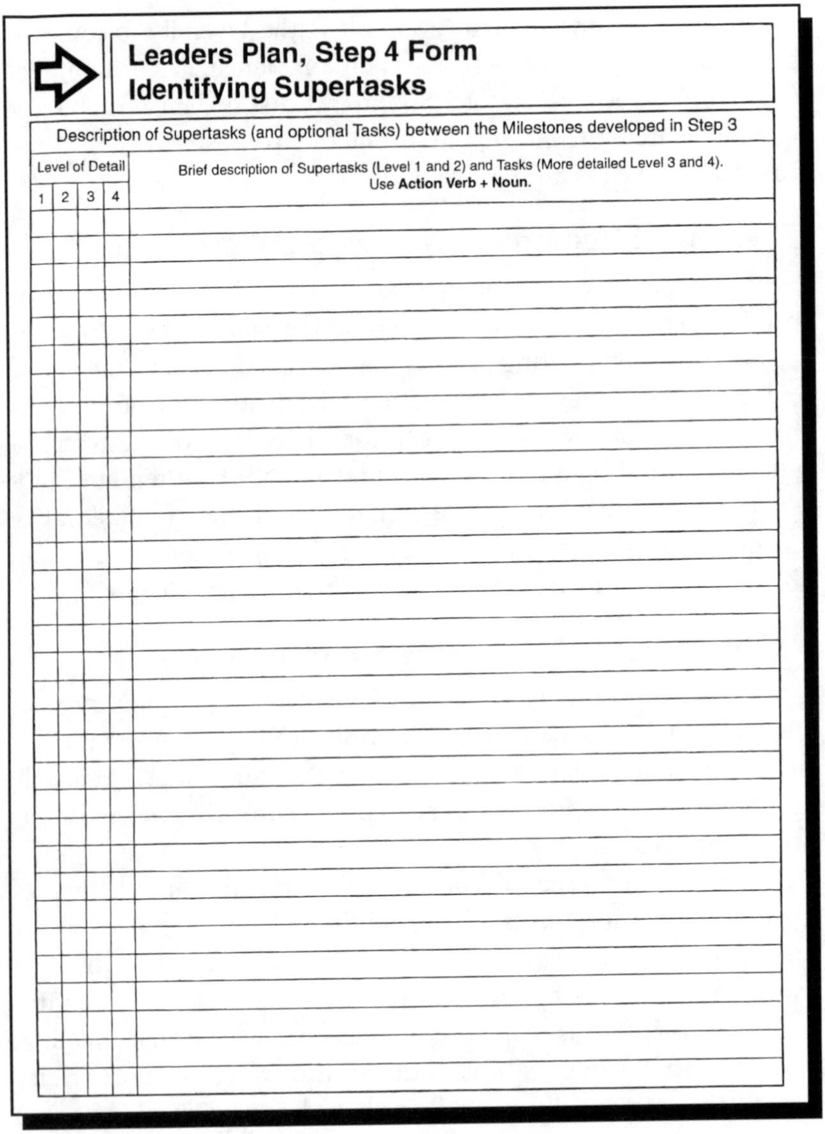

| Leaders Plan, Step 4 Form |
| :-- |
| **Identifying Supertasks** |

Description of Supertasks (and optional Tasks) between the Milestones developed in Step 3

| Level of Detail | | | | Brief description of Supertasks (Level 1 and 2) and Tasks (More detailed Level 3 and 4). Use **Action Verb + Noun.** |
| :-: | :-: | :-: | :-: | :-- |
| 1 | 2 | 3 | 4 | |
| | | | | |
| | | | | |
| | | | | |
| | | | | |
| | | | | |
| | | | | |
| | | | | |
| | | | | |
| | | | | |
| | | | | |
| | | | | |

**Figure B-51**

level where individual resources are itemized, the applicable Supertasks should be supplemented with equivalent Subprojects.

In planning Steps 1-3 we recommended using specific forms to help organize the information for the Overall Objective, End Items and Milestones. Similarly, a Step 4 Form, as shown in Figure B-51, can be helpful when recording Supertasks.

## CONCLUSION/SUMMARY

This chapter has provided you with a study of the concepts and purposes of Supertasks in authoring the Leaders Plan. You have learned how to create Supertasks and interconnect them logically with other Supertasks and Milestones. You have also learned who should develop Supertasks and how Supertasks link management leadership with professional involvement in the planning process. In the process, you have solved one of the most difficult problems in any program or project planning process—determining exactly how much task detail should be included in the plan. You have learned how to create Supertasks as manageable segments of work for making viable resource estimates during Step 5 in the next chapter.

We have considered the concept of Subprojects and how they enhance the leaders' planning process by providing additional levels of detail on the overall Milestone/Supertask Summary Chart. You have mastered the skills of defining Supertasks in the overall Leaders Plan, and learned how to link the Supertask to a new Subproject Leaders Plan with its own detailed End Items, Milestones, and Supertasks. You have learned the application guidelines of using Subprojects and why they are useful, particularly when additional details are needed and when a framework for making detailed estimates of needed resources is desired.

A brief example of using the Step 4 Form is shown in Figure B-52.

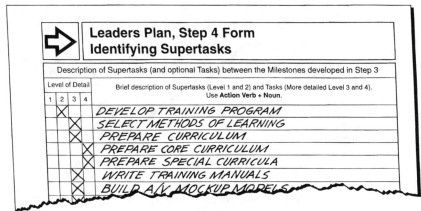

Figure B-52

159

# CHAPTER 9

# Planning Step 5— Evaluating Needed Resources and Critical Path

*"The people worked with all their heart"* (Nehemiah 4:6).

*"The LORD gives strength to his people; the LORD blesses his people with peace"* (Psalm 29:11).

*"Obey me, and I will be your God and you will be my people. Walk in all the ways I command you, that it may go well with you"* (Jeremiah 7:23).

*"Jesus Christ...gave himself for us to redeem us from all wickedness and to purify for himself a people that are his very own, eager to do what is good"* (Titus 2:14).

The right people are the most important resource for planning and implementing any project. Right from the beginning, we have emphasized the importance of the people (personnel) seeking the Lord so as to understand His will, His plan. In Step 1, people met together, and with the guidance of the Holy Spirit they created a clearly written statement of the plan's Overall Objective. People produced the innovative brainwriting of End Items in Step 2 and organized those God-inspired creative ideas of the planning team into the important End Item Table. People, in Step 3, determined and named the Milestones, those important strategic points along the way for reaching the Overall Objective, and produced the graphic Milestone Layout Chart. In Step 4, people identified the Supertasks that need to be completed to reach each Milestone, and produced the Milestone/Supertask Summary Chart. Now, in this final step of the Leaders Plan, the right people need to evaluate the resources needed and estimate the duration time for performing the Supertasks identified in Step 4. From this Step 5 information, the planning team can evaluate the critical path which provides a reliable estimate of the time-duration required to reach the Overall Objective.

In the subsequent Part C, the right people will be the major resource for implementing the Leaders Plan. Throughout the planning and the implementation phases, what happens to the people, to each individual, is important. Have the people been inspired, learned more of God's character, and grown closer to the Lord during the planning process and the implementation process? If the right things are done the right way both the process and the completed project will bring honor to our Lord.

In a biblical worldview no dichotomy exists between the visionary and the implementers. The leadership team works together to define the Overall Objective and all the End Items, Milestones, and Supertasks required to meet the Overall Objective. It also is responsible to see that all the necessary resources are available for accomplishing the Supertasks, reaching the Milestones, achieving the End Items, and thus fulfilling the Overall Objective. This is the point at which creativity, resourcefulness and faith go hand in hand so that the team can see the plan launched and be able to continue co-creating with God.

For the accomplishment of any project requires major categories of resources including personnel, time, information, finances, and materials. Without the necessary resources, the Overall Objective is unattainable. However the resources can be obtained in endlessly creative ways as the courageous leader walks closely with God and listens for His guidance.

As you master Step 5 of the Leaders Plan, you and your team will learn the concepts and principles for making reliable estimates of the resources required to complete the Supertasks you identified in Step 4. You will learn how to obtain estimates through information from the overall leadership team and the technical leaders, specialists, and other professionals who will be responsible and accountable for the use of resources in performing these Supertasks. For each Supertask you will enter and display a time-duration estimate which summarizes the estimates related to all the resources required to perform the Supertask. These time-duration estimates together with the names of the coordinators responsible for monitoring each Supertask are written in a cluster around each Supertask symbol displayed on the Leaders Plan.

## WHAT ARE NEEDED RESOURCES AND CRITICAL PATH?

As described in the chapter introduction, the right people (personnel) are the major needed resource for each Supertask. The availability of these people together with the other needed resources such as facilities, materials, finances, permits, spiritual refreshment and faith will influence the estimate of the time-duration required to complete the Supertasks of Step 4.

Steps 1 through 5 produce a progressive accumulation of planning information. Step 5 provides the realistic estimates of the resources that are summarized by estimates of the duration times for each Supertask. Also, Step 5 should include the names of lead persons who commit to each Supertask. Finally, evaluation of the critical path establishes the best estimate of the time-duration to reach the Overall Objective.

### • The Leaders Plan

When the Step 5 time estimates and personnel information are added to the Milestone/Supertask Summary Chart produced in Step 4, a complete planning document is produced for the first time, known as the Leaders Plan. Milestones, Supertasks, and their relationships are shown graphically in this document. Duration times for each Supertask are now included, along with the name of the person or team coordinator approving the time estimate, the one who is responsible and accountable for completing the Supertask within that committed duration time. No dates or imposed time frames are considered at all in Step 5. The time-duration for the Supertask is always recorded in terms of time required, never the time allowed.

## • The Critical Path

The critical path is simply the chain of Supertasks and Milestones that takes the longest to complete in the Leaders Plan. Because some Supertasks depend on one another and others are independent, a plan may end up with several parallel paths inter-linked at critical points. One of these paths—the critical path—will take longer to complete than any other in the plan. Occasionally, there are two or more equally critical paths.

The critical path is also defined as the unique sequence of Supertasks and Milestones taking the longest time to reach the final completion Milestone, the Overall Objective. A Leaders Plan can also have, along its most critical path, a sequence of the Supertasks and Milestones that lead to an interim Milestone, ahead of the completion Milestone. A subsequent segment of this chapter presents various concepts related to the critical path.

## • Evaluating Needed Resources

The main idea of Step 5 is to relate the availability and inspired use of resources to time in a Leaders Plan. Because the Supertasks cannot all be completed simultaneously, any estimate has to be structured so that you end up with an idea of their time-durations. By this means you can see how many Supertasks can be accomplished concurrently, given the available resources. A time-duration estimate indicates an assessment of the availability of the right people and other resources and how much time will be required to move from start to finish for a Supertask. The classical hourglass for measurement of time-duration is used as the symbol for Step 5, as shown in Figure B-53.

## •Reliable Estimates Are Thoughtful Commitments

Time-duration estimates should be commitments made by those responsible and accountable for Supertasks in the Leaders Plan. They are the fundamental elements of duration time units or

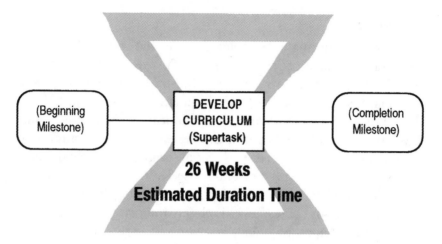

Figure B-53

costs within a contractual arrangement for future work, such as between a team member and team coordinator or between a customer and a supplier. An informal estimate for a car repair is different from a formal quote for a car repair. An estimate for a Supertask should normally be considered as a formal quote or a firm commitment by the leader or team coordinator who has made the estimate and is responsible for monitoring progress in implementing the Supertask. An estimate can also be a formal expression of the difficulty in accomplishing a Supertask, as in research and development planning. The estimating procedure can be used to statistically express the range of expected uncertainty by using optimistic and pessimistic estimates as well as the most likely estimates for this type of work activity.

## A BIBLICAL PERSPECTIVE ON NEEDED RESOURCES

From the Bible we learn that God often required projects to be started without all the needed resources available. Our own experience with God-inspired projects has shown that rarely does one have all the needed resources at the outset of any given project. The shortage of resources in one or more categories is not to be unexpected. Nor is it to be a source of discouragement, for the courageous leader will not *"despise the day of small beginnings"* (Zechariah 4:10). Rather he or she will take steps of faith in obedience to the Lord at this—as at every other—stage of the planning process.

## • People

Jesus, the ultimate example of leadership, realized what an important resource people are. Mark's Gospel very quickly established that the primary Supertasks of Jesus' earthly ministry were the dual tasks of preaching and healing/deliverance (Mark 1:38-39). But along with Mark's communication regarding Jesus' involvement in these Supertasks, we read of Jesus' purposeful selection of a team of colleagues whom Jesus recruited as the necessary personnel for the new enterprise He was launching (Mark 1:16-20; 2:13-14; 3:13-19). This last passage highlights how the selection of personnel resources is closely interwoven with the definition of the Supertasks. As Mark writes it, Jesus chose His team *"that they might be with him and that he might send them out to preach and to have authority to drive out demons"* (3:15).

Twelve may seem like a very small team to launch the kind of project that Jesus launched. But oftentimes it is possible with only a few people to make a significant impact in our world. Indeed, one of the Bible's courageous leaders, Jonathan, stated, *"Nothing can hinder the LORD from saving, whether by many or by few"* (1 Samuel 14:6) and proceeded to launch a battle, pitting himself and one colleague against a host of enemies—and won! We often overstaff a project because we have a false sense of security in having more than enough resources available. Gideon learned this when he was getting ready to launch a military campaign. He planned to gather a huge army, but God told him, *"You have too many men for me to deliver Midian into their hands"* (Judges 7:2). After cutting back his personnel resources to 300, Gideon proceeded to rout the vastly superior opposing army. The key was not in the quantity of men available, but the quality. When choosing a team, it is imperative to recruit people of like heart and mind whom with unity and faith will labor towards the accomplishment of the Overall Objective. This is so crucial that the courageous leader, following Jesus' example, dare not select a team without intense prayer (Luke 6:12-13), for this is perhaps the most crucial of all the resource decisions that a leader will make.

We see that Nehemiah spent a great deal of time on issues related to personnel. He carefully selected *"a few men"* (Nehemiah 2:12) who were completely reliable and trustworthy.

He then proceeded to pull together a larger leadership team. In Nehemiah chapter 3 nearly fifty leaders and leadership teams are mentioned by name. When the wall was finished and more permanent leadership positions were needed he selected Hananiah, *"because he was a man of integrity and feared God more than most men do"* (Nehemiah 7:2). Nehemiah was obviously concerned with the welfare and protection of the personnel involved with him in this project (Nehemiah 4:11-15; 5:1-13). People were important to him, and he gave much time to long lists of those who were a part of the reconstruction enterprise, highlighting the way in which he highly valued his co-workers (Nehemiah 7:6-68; 10:1-29; 11:3-24, etc.).

## • Time

A second resource with which courageous leaders must concern themselves is time. Jesus taught the value of time when He said, *"As long as it is day, we must do the work of him who sent me. Night is coming, when no one can work"* (John 9:4). Since time is a priceless commodity that once squandered can never be regained, the courageous leader must plan carefully how to utilize time to its fullest, maximizing the potential of every opportunity. Projects should be carried out with careful thought being given to time considerations. Time is of the essence, so much so that when Nehemiah presented his plan to the king, the king's first question was, *"How long will your journey take, and when will you get back?"* (Nehemiah 2:6). Because he had wisely planned, Nehemiah was able to give the king an accurate projection, thus gaining his approval for the project.

The capable leader will help the whole team move towards its Overall Objective in a timely manner. To do this, the courageous leader must proceed on a foundation of faith. The use of this resource—like the others of personnel and finances/materials— should not be planned in isolation from the Holy Spirit of God. Seemingly impossible scenarios can be accomplished if walked out in dependence upon God and careful communication with one another. Nehemiah accomplished the task of restoration of Jerusalem's walls in just fifty-two days because the *"work had been done with the help of our God"* (Nehemiah 6:15-16).

| Leaders Plan, Step 5 Form | | | | | | |
|---|---|---|---|---|---|---|
| **Evaluating Needed Resources** | | | | | | |

**Description of Supertasks/Tasks with Needed Resources**

| Level of Detail | | | | Brief Description of Supertasks/Tasks (Developed in Step 4) | Leader Responsible | Estimated Time (Weeks) | Estimated Costs |
|---|---|---|---|---|---|---|---|
| 1 | 2 | 3 | 4 | | | | |
| | | | | | | | |

**Figure B-54**

To help streamline and formalize the process of making time estimates, it is helpful to list the Supertasks on the Leaders Plan, Step 5 Form of the type in Figure B-54. The information on this form is used for evaluating the needed resources for the critical path. The form becomes a worksheet that helps organize the final information that will eventually appear on the Leaders Plan.

A brief description of each Supertask is entered, along with its level of detail. The Step 5 Form also has columns for the leader responsible, the estimated time in weeks and the estimated costs for each Supertask. The leader responsible may be a person's name or a title if that person has not yet been selected.

An example of a portion of the Leader's Plan, Step 5 Form with some information entered is shown in Figure B-55.

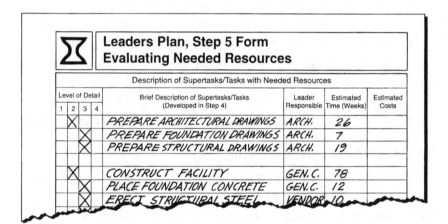

Figure B-55

## • Finances/Materials

A third area of needed resources for any plan is that of finances/materials. Nehemiah also planned for this as recorded in Nehemiah 2:8 and 10:31-39. Note that he employed different means of raising the needed resources to accomplish the task. Initially he used the king's provision; later he raised the resources from amidst the people. Whatever the method used for raising the financial and material resources, this is an area that the courageous leader must not neglect. The availability or lack thereof of this third category of resources is not the determining factor in a plan. Regrettably many projects do not get off the ground, because leaders view this resource as the necessary starting point. For the courageous leader, the Word of the Lord is the determining factor. The Word of the Lord, diligence, wise planning, and obedient execution of the God-given plan will open the way for resources to be released in a timely way.

## THE IMPORTANCE OF EVALUATING NEEDED RESOURCES

So far, we have explored how courageous leaders can plan for and then pull together the needed resources in order to see the Overall Objective accomplished. Many times the release of one or more of these resources is a point of arduous labor and spiritual warfare. It is the faith of the leadership team that will overcome the challenges and see the vision become implemented in reality.

Step 5 will take you to the point where you have a complete Leaders Plan. It provides viable time estimates, the final important step for providing the main inputs into the Leaders Plan. The following subsections discuss the importance of resource evaluation.

### • More Accurate Planning

If the individual Supertasks are estimated accurately and then analyzed properly, the overall duration of the Leaders Plan can be expected to be accurate. The GIGO principle applies: "garbage in...garbage out." Even though the Supertasks and the estimates that go into the plan are plagued with uncertainty, the overall computed date predictions will be accurate if the uncertainty is analyzed properly. Step 5 provides a rationale for estimating Supertasks and analyzing estimates that will produce overall accurate results.

### • Independent of Imposed Dates

It is typical to force the estimates of individual tasks to conform to unrealistically imposed deadlines. The inevitable results can range from disappointing to disastrous. Step 5 provides a way to isolate the individual task and time-estimating process so that it strictly observes the reality of what a task will require in terms of duration time units without the simultaneous influence of arbitrarily imposed dates. Later, more intelligent corrective decisions can be made if the impact of these independent estimates produces an incompatible situation.

## • Better Commitments from Responsible Team Members

Human nature favors a process whereby individuals on a given team make time estimates for their own work. Good planning practices of Step 4 have already provided that the right members of the planning team personally identify their tasks in the plan. These tasks are now ready for estimates in Step 5. Just imagine if someone else, no matter how qualified, identified the tasks and made the estimates. Later, the persons responsible and accountable would probably not go along with the estimates and might even tend to subconsciously sabotage those parts of the plan. The reason? The NIH (not invented here) factor. In Step 5, the original planners will provide the estimates. As a result, they genuinely buy into the plan and tend to stick to the estimates more closely because the numbers committed were theirs. Personal estimates, therefore, equate to personal commitment.

## • A Basis for Coping with Uncertainties

Within many plans, such as for research and development programs, tasks exist that are difficult to estimate. The estimating process used in Step 5 takes into account the experiential and statistical considerations of how long a task or series of tasks will take. This includes the optional use of various techniques and the likelihood of completing the overall sequence of tasks in the time period allotted. The effect of all of this is to make the law of averages work in favor of successful completion.

Another important benefit of this technique is that it provides an escape hatch for technical and scientific personnel who may be reluctant (and rightly so) to make estimates for difficult research and development types of tasks. No one likes to commit to a single time estimate for R&D work. The researcher needs a way to express the uncertainty inherent in this type of work, which understandably cannot always be expected to occur as planned.

Step 5 provides a way to express duration time estimates that anticipate this uncertainty. Then, even if disappointments occur, the plan will still have a high probability of succeeding, because it was developed with a backup strategy or extra time built into the plan. This process results in reality, understanding, and confidence

171

between the overall leadership and technical leaders in evolving and tracking work in the Leaders Plan.

## • Provision of a Method for Tradeoff of Time and Costs

Traditional budgeting systems usually call for an input method that is different from that of planning, and they generally fail to correlate time and cost estimates for any program. This can mean that the right hand of planning does not know what the left hand of accounting is doing, and vice versa. Step 5 bridges the two disciplines by providing a structure for making time-duration and cost estimates for the same manageable segments of work. Later the Leaders Plan can be tracked while you are analyzing the adherence to time and cost estimates separately or considering them together to make more intelligent trade-off decisions.

## • Step 5 Personnel

Personnel, time, and cost estimates should always be based on a commitment by those who are actually responsible and accountable for the Supertasks in the Leaders Plan. Great care should be taken in Step 4 to involve these key leaders in describing this work in the form of detailed task descriptions based on their manageable segments of work. These same key people should ideally make both the time and cost estimates. If they make estimates as commitments, they are fundamentally motivated to meet those commitments in carrying out their work later.

## WHAT IS CRITICAL PATH ANALYSIS?

The procedure called critical path analysis allows you to see at a glance which series of Supertasks will take the longest to complete—hence this path is called the critical path.

## • Planning Techniques and Methodology

The planning process can use either the deterministic or probabilistic approach to making time estimates. The deterministic approach relies upon historical records, memory or standard units. For example, the best estimate for how long it would take to paint a building is based on how long it took the last time it was painted.

It is reasonable to assume that under similar conditions it would take the same time to paint it again. This is the deterministic approach to estimating based on experience as validated from detailed records or from memory. On the other hand, the probabilistic approach can be used to estimate tasks for which little or no previous experience exists. For example, how long would it take to drill an exploratory oil well or invent a new product? Since this is a calculated risk, all you can do is gather the best information, and make a "most likely" time estimate.

If you were responsible and accountable for this estimate, it would be wise to bracket your estimate with an optimistic estimate (if all things went well) and a pessimistic estimate (if all things went wrong).

## • Critical Path Analysis Documents

After the Leaders Plan is thoughtfully created, you can generate time/date calculations, graphic charts and tables for studying ways to hasten completing the Overall Objective. When you enter a start date and properly set up the project calendar, you may use a manual method to generate a classic critical path schedule called the schedule chart. This is a logical sequence diagram with earliest and latest dates for each Milestone and Supertask start/finish. Heavy lines can be used around affected chart symbols to depict the critical path. A suitable computer program enables this computation to be accomplished more rapidly.

## THE IMPORTANCE OF CRITICAL PATH ANALYSIS

The following subsections discuss the reasons why the critical path analysis is so very important.

## • Accurate Determination of the Total Time of a Program

Critical path analysis computes the total elapsed time required to perform all the Supertasks in a program as originally planned. When this quantity is compared with imposed time limitations, if any, you can determine whether the entire program can be completed within this time period or by the completion date, or whether certain portions of the program can be completed earlier as may be required.

## • Identification of Tasks That Could Accelerate the Project

Critical path analysis identifies all Supertasks on the most critical path and sub-critical paths; that is, it shows which Supertasks are critical and which, if delayed, will delay successful completion. It also provides targets of opportunity for accelerating a program, if desired, by planning to shorten these critical Supertasks. You can determine "what if" simulations to determine whether steps can or cannot be accelerated by shortening Supertasks on the critical path, and whether such a decision would be cost effective.

## • Determination of Earliest and Latest Dates for Supertasks and Milestones

In addition to duration times, critical path analysis provides the earliest expected dates and latest allowable dates for every Supertask and Milestone in a program, both critical and non-critical, including the program completion Milestone. Normally, you would schedule all Supertask starts on their earliest dates; although, you can use the "schedulable limit" between the earliest and latest dates to make cost-effective decisions throughout the program.

Knowing the latest allowable dates for procurement cycles, for example, you can incorporate procedures such as JIT (just in time) to delay purposely the delivery (and payment) of costly purchased items until they are actually needed for installation. Instead of paying for flooring, you can reduce the costs of loans or the use of non-invested money until a reasonably delayed delivery time.

## • Increased Probability of Successful Completion

Imagine if every pilot puts exactly the same amount of fuel in the tank as required, without fuel reserve, for each flight. Half of all flights would crash short of the runway! Just as a pilot would never file a flight plan without a fuel reserve, you would probably never want to authorize a Leaders Plan without a built-in slack time reserve. This is accomplished by using the critical path analysis to reduce the time along the critical path, or to lengthen the overall time allowed. This decision, even if it requires overtime, will be cost effective because it will inevitably increase the chances of successful completion within the time allowed. When the time required (critical path) is less than the time allowed, the chance of success is greater than fifty percent. When the time required is more than the time allowed, the chance of success is less than fifty percent. Note that when the time required is *equal* to the time allowed, the probability of success is only fifty percent.

## CRITICAL PATH AND SLACK TIME

Leaders live with the reality of deadlines. When the logical planning is done, the leader must measure it by calendar deadlines. Suppose a Leaders Plan to construct a new training facility calls for twenty-six weeks of activity from the Beginning Milestone to the Completion Milestone. Well, if the advertised date for beginning classes in the new training facility is thirty weeks away, the leader has four weeks of cushion, which allow for some slack in the implementation of the plan. However if the Leaders Plan calls for twenty-six weeks and the opening day is only twenty-six weeks away, there is no slack. Everything must go according to schedule or the deadline won't be met. The leader would have a big problem to deal with if he or she had only twenty-two weeks left until classes were to begin. There's not enough time left to implement the plan as envisioned.

Time is a precious commodity and deadlines are inescapable. It's a part of life. Jesus recognized the constraints of time deadlines in His earthly ministry. He said, *"As long as it is day, we must do the work of him who sent me. Night is coming, when no one can work"* (John 9:4).

Slack time is the difference between the time period *required* and the time period *allowed* for a series of tasks for an entire program. The time required for the series is computed as the critical path. When the total required time (the critical path) is compared with the total time allowed, a figure of slack is computed.

Although commonly misconstrued as the path of zero slack, the amount of slack along the critical path can be positive, zero, or negative. Positive slack exists at any time when the critical path time is shorter than the allowed time, zero slack exists when they are equal, and negative slack exists when the critical path time is longer. Slack analysis is therefore very useful for making better decisions during the planning process and then afterwards when tracking the plan to successful completion. At all times, decisions should be made to maintain positive slack. As the Leaders Plan deteriorates into zero or negative slack, corrective decisions should be made immediately.

- ## "Non-Critical" Parallel Slack Paths off the Critical Path

By definition, the critical path is the path of least slack time (or greatest negative slack time) within any Leaders Plan. Critical path analysis determines and identifies not only the slack along the critical path sequence but also how "non-critical" is each of the other parallel sequences of Supertasks and Milestones. The amount of the non-critical path slack will always be greater than the slack along the critical path. Situations may exist where the non-critical path(s) are almost as critical as the main critical path. A better terminology would be to consider these paths sub-critical paths rather than non-critical paths. How non-critical are they? The seasoned decision-maker will refer to the figure for each of the lesser critical parallel paths.

- ## Methods for Computing the Critical Path and Slack Time

The critical path is the result of a mathematical procedure requiring one of several methods of computation. When PERT (program evaluation and review technique) and other critical path methods were first developed for space age projects, critical path analysis never became very popular as a practical business tool. The only way to perform a critical path analysis was to use tedious manual methods or complex mainframe computer systems available to only a few large companies or government agencies. The powerful critical path analysis seemed too complex or too expensive to be cost effective. The manual method of critical path analysis computes and identifies the longest time-duration path through the project using a simple adding machine. But because this procedure requires adding up each parallel path and selecting the longest sequence of tasks from start to finish of the project, the manual method can be time-consuming—especially for larger projects. It also tends to introduce errors unless every possible combination of paths is carefully totaled.

The calculation procedure used by various computer programs to determine the critical path does not involve adding up the many combinations of paths and taking the longest path per se, as does the manual approach. It is much simpler. The clever critical path algorithm consists of making only two basic calculations. The "forward pass" determines the earliest time or date when each Milestone or Supertask start/finish can be expected to occur. This is computed from the given start date of the project. The "backward pass" determines the latest time or date when each of these same Milestones or Supertasks can be allowed to occur. This is computed from a given date of project completion or from the computed earliest date. When the two sets of dates are compared for each Supertask and Milestone, the difference between them is slack time. The critical path traces the least amount of slack time from the beginning to the completion of the project.

## Conclusion/Summary

You are now able to predict the time it will take to achieve the Overall Objective through a practical estimating process. You have gained the knowledge and concepts for deriving accurate estimates and have learned a practical way to express usable information about uncertainties in the Supertasks of a Leaders Plan. A biblical perspective on making estimates of resources provides you with important insight. You have also learned effective ways to obtain and display estimates, resources and other task information through techniques that ensure that technical coordinators and other professionals who make these estimates will consider them commitments. Samples of complete Leaders Plans may be viewed on the internet by going to www.courageousleaders.com.

In Chapter 9, you have learned a significant approach to display and analyze the Leaders Plan called critical path analysis, which is based on two of the most powerful management techniques ever developed: PERT (program evaluation and review technique) and CPM (critical path method). You have learned how to create positive slack to increase the probability of success by overcoming the realistic expectation of occasional delays. You have, for the first time, completed the Leaders Plan to the point where it is compatible with imposed time constraints. You have used the critical path analysis to provide information for the leaders to make wise decisions about allocating resources so as to meet critical time constraints.

By prayerfully following God's guidance throughout the planning process of Steps 1-5, including the critical path analysis, you have learned how to co-create a Leaders Plan that can bring honor and glory to God. We can say with Moses *"Oh praise the greatness of our God! He is the Rock, his works are perfect, and all his ways are just. A faithful God who does no wrong, upright and just is He"* (Deuteronomy 32:3-4). You will continue to see God's rock-solid faithfulness if you now use His plan to move obediently into implementation of the Leaders Plan. As described in Part C, you will need to persevere and use inspired and courageous leadership to move from the Leaders Plan into the action which will make the Overall Objective a reality.

# God-Motivated Action— Doing the Right Things Right

# God's Plans Implemented In God's Ways

*"Jesus replied, 'What is impossible with men is possible with God'"* (Luke 18:27).

**P**lans: God-inspired plans for reaching the lost in a megacity with the gospel; plans to provide employment for five hundred persons in a poor community by a new company to be started by a group of Christian servant leaders; plans to manufacture and distribute water purifiers in Asian areas that have contaminated water supplies; plans to develop a mission-oriented cell church in the inner city; plans to emulate the great reformers of the past, like William Carey, Hans Hauge, and Abraham Kuyper, and to transform a nation to the glory of God; plans to bring hope and a future.

With the right plan in hand we must be prepared to move into action and do the right things right—to make a seamless transition from plan to action. God's plans done in God's ways give us exciting opportunities to co-create with Him. However, we have found that there are often long and disappointing delays between preparing and implementing the plans. Subtle temptations arise to do things in our own ways—actions that pattern the world's ways and not the Master's ways. We have seen it happen over and over again. The road map is right, but drivers often ignore the map and follow their own path. This happens when God's ways are not paramount, and His Overall Objective is not accomplished.

Part C reviews and considers the many leadership principles, skills, and related resources that are essential and must not be ignored if one is to move from a God-inspired plan into God-motivated action that leads to the mission being accomplished.

Chapters 10 and 11 emphasize the importance of seeking God's strategies every step of the way and of moving into action with Him. Leaders often fail to implement plans in God's ways for several reasons. God-led plans sometimes involve more complex projects than the leaders have experienced. The required resources are overwhelming. These factors cause some Christian leaders to wait for the big breakthrough and accumulation of major resources before taking the first action. Although this could be God's instruction, often, as discussed in Chapters 10 and 11, He expects the leaders to start small, to use what they have in hand and step out in faith, to sow seeds along the way, build a team, and trust for resources. Committing to the "impossible" and doing the possible is an exciting paradox under which Christian leaders are often called to operate.

Chapter 12 recognizes that in a major project the leaders make many daily decisions that can have long-range implications. Leaders must therefore foresee the future consequences of today's decisions in dealing with present realities. Foresight is an essential leadership skill. Procedures for tracking, updating, and reporting the status of a plan that provides a reality check of the present situation are presented in this chapter.

As discussed in Chapter 13, it is important to stand firm in God's ways throughout the plan's implementation, including equipping for battle, overcoming obstacles, seeing the forest *and* the trees, and persisting as servant leaders. Chapter 14 concludes the book with reaching your goal—mission accomplished. The focus here is on being a transformational leader, fighting the good fight, understanding victory in God's terms, and giving honor and praise to Him. We trust that Part C will encourage leaders to review and act upon God's ways at the beginning, in the midst of, and to the end of the battle so as to see the mission accomplished.

# CHAPTER 10

## Moving Into Action With God

A Spanish proverb says, "Even the longest journey begins with a small step." Similarly, even the largest projects and the greatest of endeavors begin with small first steps. The prophet warns against despising *"the day of small things"* (Zechariah 4:10). Life starts small and grows. One does not look on a newborn baby and despise it for its smallness, but rather celebrates the possibilities of new life and nurtures it so as to enable it to reach its potential. So it is with the courageous leader who has a God-inspired vision in his or her heart and a God-led plan in hand. Such a leader values and guards this small beginning and nurtures it through God-motivated action into its full potential.

History is full of small steps that led to great events. For the courageous leader, these small steps are decisive acts of faith made in obedience to God. Such was the case with Moses, who grew up with the awareness that the fact that he was alive was a miracle and his upbringing was providential. Moses understood that God had raised him up to be a deliverer of his people. But although he had a God-inspired vision, he did not pursue God-motivated action. He tried to do God's work in his own ways—not in God's ways. Once he had understood what God was calling him to do he failed to wait on Him to understand how he was to do it. He followed his own course of action rather than God's and ended up murdering another human being (Exodus 2:11-15). He spent the next forty years in hope-destroying exile. The one-time prince of Egypt became a nomad shepherd. All sense of destiny would have long been blown away by the hot, searing desert sandstorms. The vision of freedom was lost. The plan of deliverance was forgotten. Until Moses met with God.

It is neither the vision nor the plan alone that enables the courageous leader to act, but the leader's relationship with God. As Moses and God conversed at the burning bush, Moses had many questions for God. He felt ill-equipped and ill-prepared for the task God was calling him to. He posed many questions to the Lord, seeking to understand what course of action he should take. As their time drew to an end, God asked Moses a question: *"What is that in your hand?"* (Exodus 4:2). God was expecting Moses to begin acting not with what he did not have but with what he did in fact have in his hand. All Moses had was a staff, but that, along with the word of the Lord, was sufficient to begin the process of liberating a whole people from their oppressors. When Moses did with his staff what God asked him to do, one of the greatest and most courageous exploits in history began to unfold.

## BEGINNING WITH WHAT IS AT HAND

*"What is that in your hand?"* God often asks this question. His great works begin with our obedient use of the resources available to us. So it was with David, who used what he had at hand—his slingshot—to fulfill the God-inspired vision. With it he killed the bear and the lion and ultimately brought down the Philistine giant (1 Samuel 17:1-54). So it was with Jonathan, who also used what he had at hand—one sword and the help of his armor bearer—to defeat a mighty army (1 Samuel 14:1-23). So it was with the widow of Zarephath who used what she had at hand—*"a handful of flour in a jar and a little oil in a jug"*—and in so doing saw the miraculous provision of God (1 Kings 17:8-16). So it was with the little boy who offered up what he had at hand—his two loaves and five fish—to Jesus and saw a multitude of five thousand fed (John 6:5-13). All these, and many others, began simply with

what they had at hand, and as they walked in obedience to the word of the Lord, they saw great things happen.

*"What is that in your hand?"* God continues to ask this question of today's would-be courageous leaders. Do not underestimate the potential of small beginnings. As a young man, Loren Cunningham had a vision from God. He saw, as it were, a map become animated before his eyes. The waves of the sea began to crash upon the shores of the continents, and as they did so he saw the faces of young people—waves and waves of young people—going to all the nations of the earth. With hardly anything more than a persevering commitment to this vision, Loren launched what in time would become one of the largest mission organizations on earth, Youth With A Mission. That vision became a reality as young people ministered in every country and territory on the globe. Small beginnings give birth to great accomplishments when obedience to the word of the Lord is paramount in the life of the courageous leader.

## FLEXIBLE TENACITY

As the courageous leader endeavors to put the God-led plan into God-motivated action, he or she must cultivate a lifestyle of flexible tenacity. Those who desire to make a transforming difference in their world must be able to persistently stick to their dream and determinedly hold on to the vision. This quality of tenacity is indispensable for all courageous leaders. It is the determination to always, in every circumstance, and against all difficulties hold on to the God-inspired vision. The courageous leader must relentlessly develop a bulldog's mentality. This unbecoming little canine has a stellar virtue: Once it bites into something it locks its jaws and will, under no circumstances, let go. Beatings and floggings go unheeded as it clamps onto its prey. The great courageous leaders of history have all had a bulldog mentality.

Elisha was determined to obtain Elijah's anointing. Although the elder prophet repeatedly tried to dissuade the young disciple from following him, Elisha could not be put off. *"As surely as the LORD lives and as you live, I will not leave you,"* he said time and again to his reluctant mentor in his persistent pursuit of the prophetic anointing (2 Kings 2:1-15).

Ruth was determined to be a part of the people of God. The sufferings caused by the severe famine and her early widowhood would not deter her from her objective. When her mother-in-law repeatedly encouraged her to return to her own people, Ruth replied, *"Don't urge me to leave you or to turn back from you. Where you go I will go, and where you stay I will stay. Your people will be my people and your God my God. Where you die I will die, and there I will be buried"* (Ruth 1:16-17). Ruth's persistence went against all cultural mores but opened the door for her to play an historic role among the Jewish people.

Eleazar, one of David's three mighty men, accomplished exploits on the basis of his undeterred tenacity in the midst of great adversity. We are told that when all his colleagues fled in the face of the oncoming foe, *"he stood his ground and struck down the Philistines till his hand grew tired and froze to the sword. The LORD brought about a great victory that day"* (2 Samuel 23:10). This kind of determined perseverance is the stuff of which victories are made.

How does one develop such tenacity? By walking in close, intimate fellowship with God. It is said of Moses, *"By faith he left Egypt, not fearing the king's anger; he persevered because he saw him who is invisible"* (Hebrews 11:27). As we continue to grow in our knowledge of God, His character marks us. So it was with David, who *"found strength in the LORD his God"* to persevere in one of the darkest hours of his life (1 Samuel 30:1-20). When his home was destroyed, his family was taken captive, and his men were talking of stoning him, the mettle of David's leadership was being tested. Persevering in the midst of adversity through fellowship with God prepared him for greatness. As Daniel says, *"The people that do know their God shall be strong, and do exploits"* (Daniel 11:32 KJV).

As you encounter the *"God who takes hold of your right hand"* (Isaiah 41:13), you learn to persevere even as He has persevered with you. Tenacity in the task is birthed out of a tenacity in our relationship with God. Indeed, our unyielding commitment to Him and His ways is birthed out of His undying commitment to us. The psalmist says, *"My soul clings to you; your right hand upholds me"* (Psalm 63:9). Paul, writing of his life's call, describes such tenacity:

*Not that I have already obtained all this, or have already been made perfect, but I press on to take hold of that for which Christ Jesus took hold of me. Brothers, I do not consider myself yet to have taken hold of it. But one thing I do: Forgetting what is behind and straining toward what is ahead, I press on toward the goal to win the prize for which God has called me heavenward in Christ Jesus. All of us who are mature should take such a view of things* (Philippians 3:12-15).

This pressing-on attitude, this taking-hold-of lifestyle, characterizes the courageous leader.

Such tenacity does not imply that the leader will not err. Rather, it speaks of the determined ability to bounce back on track as soon as one realizes that one has gotten off course. The righteous man is not the one who never falls; rather, he is the one who although he *"falls seven times, he rises again."* In contrast, *"the wicked are brought down by calamity,"* unable to rise again, for they lack the buoyant tenacity that comes from walking in a close, committed relationship with God (Proverbs 24:16). This buoyant tenacity is a hallmark of the courageous leader.

Some may associate such tenacity with inflexibility. However, the bulldog mentality of which we speak here has nothing to do with pigheaded stubbornness. The difference lies in the courageous leader's ability to distinguish between the desired End Items and Overall Objective on one hand and the means of achieving them on the other. Changing circumstances, unexpected obstacles, and unanticipated developments may require creative modifications of Supertasks, Milestones, and the allocation of needed resources. The courageous leader adjusts the strategies to lay hold unwaveringly to the unchanging Overall Objective. True tenacity requires creative flexibility because the courageous leader works in a complex world with many variables. One of the factors that the courageous leader must always consider is the plans of the opposition. Like a chess player, the courageous leader has an unchanging Overall Objective: to checkmate the opponent. However, the means by which he or she achieves that objective must be modified to rightly counter the opponent's emerging strategies. There is no one fixed road to victory. There are many strategies and many options, and the courageous leader will creatively and skillfully employ as many as possible to reach the desired goal of victory.

At times, less-experienced leaders confuse the means with the end, the process with the Overall Objective. At other times, they fail to recognize the hierarchy of importance of various activities, not distinguishing between the importance of Supertasks and that of other, less important tasks. Because of this, they fixate a misplaced tenacity on the "minors" rather than on the "majors," on the means rather than on the end. This can produce a counterproductive rigidity that hinders the team from accomplishing the Overall Objective. Whereas unswerving tenacity must be cultivated with regard to the Overall Objective, a creative flexibility should be pursued with regard to the means and the methods employed in achieving that end. The courageous leader blends unyielding tenacity in moving toward the Overall Objective with creative flexibility in the means employed.

This lifestyle of flexible tenacity keeps leaders walking in daily dependence upon God, for it requires the courageous leader to regularly check in with God as well as with his or her team. The Leaders Plan is neither an inflexible blueprint nor a substitute for the daily seeking of God as various challenges emerge. Rather, it is a means to help leaders continually evaluate their progress toward the Overall Objective and lead them back into the presence of Him who gave them the vision in the first place. Courageous leaders must learn to listen well, and as they do so, they will become equipped to make the necessary course corrections and implement the creative solutions to stay on track for the accomplishing of the overall objective.

President Reagan declared 1983 as "The Year of the Bible" in the United States. Loren Cunningham was asked to chair the Hawaii State Committee for the Year of the Bible, which was to become part of the state's 25th Silver Jubilee celebration. The Overall Objective was to place a Commemorative New Testament in every home in Hawaii in the primary language spoken by each household. To distribute the Scriptures in the required seventeen major languages spoken in Hawaii, finances had to be raised, the churches had to be motivated and mobilized, distribution strategies had to be established, and the public had to be made aware of the key role the Bible had played in the history of the state. In the course of moving toward the Overall Objective, Loren encountered many hindrances. When Plan A didn't work, Loren worked with his staff to develop Plan B. When that was only a partial success, Plan C was created. And when the Overall Objective still was not reached, Plans D, E, and F were each, in turn, implemented. Loren's unquenchable blend of creative flexibility in the means and tenacious persistence toward the end made it possible for this historic Overall Objective to be accomplished. Loren's courageous leadership demonstrated that where there is a will there is a way, especially when our will is submitted to the will of God.

This kind of flexible tenacity in the courageous leader breeds a contagious commitment among the team members. This is evidenced in the story of the battle that was launched by Jonathan and his armor bearer. When everyone else had given up hope of beating the enemy and had fled from the powerful Philistines, Jonathan tenaciously held on to the overall objective of victory. This he did in spite of the terribly lopsided military odds against him. On the one hand, the Philistines numbered *"three thousand chariots, six thousand charioteers, and soldiers as numerous as the sand on the seashore"* (1 Samuel 13:5). On the other hand, the Israelites *"were about six hundred men"* (1 Samuel 14:2)—with only two swords among them, one in Saul's possession and one in Jonathan's. Conventional military strategies did not apply in this situation, which would seem to be hopeless but for the fact that Jonathan trusted God. Jonathan was tenacious in his commitment to the goal and was willing to use any God-motivated action possible. Since normal military plans and procedures were not applicable, Jonathan developed a creative new strategy based on his understanding of the character of God. *"Jonathan said to his young armor-bearer, 'Come, let's go over to the outpost of those uncircumcised fellows. Perhaps the LORD will act in our behalf. Nothing can hinder the LORD from saving, whether by many or by few'"* (1 Samuel 14:6). Such courageous commitment, such flexible tenacity, is contagious. *"'Do all that you have in mind,' his armor-bearer said. 'Go ahead; I am with you heart and soul'"* (1 Samuel 14:7). As Jonathan and his armor bearer took the first steps to implement their plan, they obtained a small but significant victory, which ultimately led to the overwhelming defeat of the enemy. Though they killed but twenty men—a drop in the bucket of this vast host—the whole army panicked and fled in total confusion. The Scriptures state, *"It was a panic sent by God"* (1 Samuel 14:15). Jonathan's courageous leadership not only motivated his armor bearer to action and released the power of God, but also turned all the cowards into heroes. *"When all the Israelites who had hidden in the hill country of Ephraim heard that the Philistines were on the run, they joined the battle in hot pursuit"* (1 Samuel 14:22). What immense motivational power is released by a courageous leader when flexible tenacity is embraced as the fruit of a practical faith in God.

During World War II the newly appointed Prime Minister of England, Winston Churchill, exemplified the power of courageous, flexible tenacity. He addressed Parliament on May 13, 1940:

> I say to the House...I have nothing to offer but blood, toil, tears, and sweat. We have before us many, many months of struggle and suffering. You ask, what is our policy? I say it is to wage war by land, sea, and air. War with all our might and with all the strength God has given us, and to wage war against a monstrous tyranny never surpassed in the dark and lamentable catalogue of human crime. That is our policy. You ask, what is our aim? I can answer in one word. It is victory. Victory at all costs—victory in spite of all terrors—victory, however long and hard the road may be...I take up my task in buoyancy and hope...I feel entitled at this juncture, at this time, to claim the aid of all and say, come then let us go forward together with our united strength.

Churchill's battle plan was for victory using every available means and creative strategy.

As a courageous leader seeking to implement a God-inspired vision and a God-led plan into God-motivated action, you can do nothing less, no matter the scope of your project, no matter the magnitude of your endeavor. If your vision originated in the heart of God, it will not come to pass without being contested by the enemy. You, too, must have the tenacity to never surrender and the flexibility to employ any and all means possible that God provides to ensure the victory.

## FOSTERING CREATIVITY

Earlier we compared the development of the Leaders Plan to the filing of a flight plan by a pilot preparing for a trip. The pilot does not fill out his flight plan in isolation; rather, he consults with the airport dispatch office. Once in the air, the pilot may encounter unforeseen circumstances, such as stronger head winds than anticipated or greater turbulence at certain altitudes. The pilot may need to make various adjustments to the flight plan to arrive safely at the desired airport. Whether or not changes are in order, the pilot remains in regular contact with nearby control towers confirming speed, altitude, location, direction, fuel endurance, etc. Not only does the pilot give information, but he also receives information from the various towers regarding other craft in the area, radio frequencies to employ, and other data. The communication between pilot and towers is both frequent and regular.

Likewise, communication with God and with one another must be frequent and regular as the team begins to implement the Leaders Plan. While formulating the Leaders Plan, the leadership team worked together to understand God's heart for the project. Once the team begins to move into action, their reliance upon and communication with God must not diminish. Even as the pilot is always in touch with the control tower, so also the courageous leader must keep in close contact with God. Courageous leaders seek to remain open to God's leading throughout the implementation stage.

Great leaders discipline themselves to depend upon God. Consulting with God is not an exceptional event but is the standard modus operandi. In the heat of battle, David *"inquired of the Lord"* (1 Samuel 23:1,4). Nehemiah checked in with God even while being interviewed by the king (Nehemiah 2:4). Daniel set time aside at crucial, decisive moments to pray and hear from God (Daniel 2:16023). The regularity and constancy of this practice were so much a part of his life that the practice was common knowledge to both friends and foes (Daniel 6:1-13). Jesus habitually paused amidst public ministry to pray to His Father (John 11:41-42). Regular prayer must become a way of life for the courageous leader. The result of this regular communication with God should be heightened creativity. Conversing with the Creator should be designed to purposefully keep the leader asking the questions that will enable him or her to exercise creativity to its maximum.

One of the advantages that a leader gains over the years is experience. However, although experience can be a useful instructor, teaching much to the attentive pupil, it can be a short-sighted strategist, ill-equipped to lead you into the challenges of the future. New situations cannot always be faced merely on the basis of experience previously gained. Therefore, though one must learn from experience, one should not depend on it. Dependency is to be placed only on God. As He most clearly understands past issues, present challenges, and future concerns, He and He alone can rightly guide us in all circumstances, both old and new, through the familiar and into the unknown.

The courageous leader frequently faces new situations for which experience alone is an insufficient reference point. God alone has the needed wisdom to guide the leader into these uncharted waters. Even situations that seem familiar may contain unexpected and unusual elements that require fresh strategies and creative approaches. That is why Jesus said that we are to be *"like the owner of a house who brings out of his storeroom new treasures as well as old"* (Matthew 13:52). Fresh creativity is as valuable as proven experience. It is here that the diligent seeking of God is paramount.

Joshua learned this lesson the hard way. Flush with the victory over the great city of Jericho (which he was able to conquer not because of the great military strategy he employed but because he listened to the word of the Lord in detail), he turned his attention to the small, insignificant town of Ai. He sent his spies to do their reconnaissance work, and based upon their evaluation of the situation, he launched what should have been a more than sufficient host against the seemingly defenseless city. But because he failed to consult with God prior to launching this military campaign, his research was in vain and the attack resulted in a horrifying defeat. Joshua's spies had provided him with accurate but insufficient information. The missing data could be obtained only from God. Had Joshua consulted with God earlier, the defeat in Ai could have been avoided. After the defeat, Joshua did indeed consult with God, and when he obeyed God's word in detail, he was able to rout his enemies in Ai (Joshua 6:2–8:29).

It is so easy to forget this lesson of needing to consult God diligently in every situation. This, in fact, happened again to Joshua. Shortly after the conquest of Ai, the Gibeonites, who were fearful of being overrun by Joshua and his army, *"resorted to a ruse: They went as a delegation whose donkeys were loaded with worn-out sacks and old wineskins, cracked and mended. The men put worn and patched sandals on their feet and wore old clothes. All the bread of their food supply was dry and moldy. Then they went to Joshua in the camp at Gilgal and said to him and the men of Israel, 'We have come from a distant country; make a treaty with us'"* (Joshua 9:4-6). Joshua and his leadership team examined and cross-examined the Gibeonite delegation. They were convinced by their story and based their decision on their reason alone. Though they thought they were making the best decision based on the empirical data they had before them, they were, in fact, deceived. Their decision proved to be unwise because they *"did not inquire of the LORD"* (Joshua 9:14). How unwise we are when we rely only upon our own limited intellectual resources to make life-impacting decisions. For this very reason, Proverbs admonishes us to *"trust in the LORD with all your heart and lean not on your own understanding; in all your ways acknowledge him, and he will make your paths straight. Do not be wise in your own eyes; fear the LORD and shun evil"* (Proverbs 3:5-7).

Notice what tremendous creativity Joshua demonstrated as a leader when he did seek God. To conquer Jericho, he marched his army around the city walls for six days in silence. Then on the seventh day, the army circled the city seven times, and on the seventh time, the people shouted and blew the trumpets until the walls fell down and the city was taken (Joshua 5:1–6:20). To conquer Ai, Joshua divided his forces in two. One battalion hid out of sight of the city. The other made a frontal attack on the city and feigned a retreat so as to draw out the forces of Ai into the open plain. This enabled the men in ambush to rise from hiding and enter the city and capture it (Joshua 8:1-26). The next battle that Joshua won, he did so by means of a surprise attack after a long, hurried all-night march. As the enemy fled in panic, Joshua's army was running out of daylight hours to finish off its job, so Joshua cried to the Lord, and the sun stopped in its normal course for a time (Joshua 10:1-21). What incredible diversity of strategies Joshua employed as he sought and obeyed the leading of the Lord. The resulting God-given creativity greatly enhanced the natural military expertise of Joshua and his men and gained for them extraordinary victories.

Even so, how easy it is to forget to seek the Lord! Such was the case of Asa, third king of Judah. Asa began his reign well. His leadership was exemplary. *"Asa did what was good and right in the eyes of the LORD his God...He commanded Judah to seek the LORD, the God of their fathers, and to obey his laws and commands"* (2 Chronicles 14:2,4). Because he diligently sought God and actively depended upon Him, Asa was able to defeat a powerful Cushite invasion (2 Chronicles 14:8-15). After this great victory, a prophet encouraged Asa by putting into words the principles he had learned through practice. He told him, *"Listen to me, Asa and all Judah and Benjamin. The LORD is with you when you are with him. If you seek him, he will be found by you, but if you forsake him, he will forsake you"* (2 Chronicles 15:2). Asa *"took courage"* from these words (2 Chronicles 15:8), and because he lived a lifestyle of seeking God, the kingdom of Judah experienced peace until the thirty-fifth year of his reign. At that time, the advancing forces of the kingdom of Israel again threatened his kingdom, but instead of seeking God, he sought out the help of the king of Aram. Surely this military treaty must have been seen as reasonable and sensible in his day, but it turned out to be most unwise. Once again a prophet spoke with Asa, but this time the words were not nearly so encouraging:

> *"Because you relied on the king of Aram and not on the LORD your God, the army of the king of Aram has escaped from your hand. Were not the Cushites and Libyans a mighty army with great numbers of chariots and horsemen? Yet when you relied on the LORD, he delivered them into your hand. For the eyes of the LORD range throughout the earth to strengthen those whose hearts are fully committed to him. You have done a foolish thing, and from now on you will be at war"* (2 Chronicles 16:7-9).

Sadly, Asa did not repent at this admonition and ended his days tragically. He forgot the lessons learned in his youth, and even when he became terminally ill, *"he did not seek help from the LORD, but only from the physicians"* (2 Chronicles 16:12). How different an ending there might have been to his life had he only persevered in an attitude of reliance upon God, seeking Him diligently in every situation, drawing on His resources. There is no greater loss than that of opportunities lost because leaders have chosen to rely upon themselves and their own finite resources rather than on God and His unlimited resources!

Jehoshaphat, Asa's son, learned from his father's error. He counseled another king, saying, *"First seek the counsel of the LORD"* (1 Kings 22:5). This should be the first thing a courageous leader does in any circumstance. We are promised that if *"you seek the LORD your God, you will find him if you look for him with all your heart and with all your soul"* (Deuteronomy 4:29). Therefore, we are to *"look to the LORD and his strength; seek his face always,"* (Psalm 105:4) for *"those who seek the LORD lack no good thing"* (Psalm 34:10).

Among the "good things" that we will not lack is the enhanced creativity that comes from not relying only on one's own limited experience and wisdom. We should steer clear of the jaded comments of the cynical old king who said, *"What has been will be again, what has been done will be done again; there is nothing new under the sun. Is there anything of which one can say, 'Look! This is something new'?"* (Ecclesiastes 1:9-10). God Himself tells us, *"See, I am doing a new thing! Now it springs up; do you not perceive it?"* (Isaiah 43:19). He declares, *"See, the former things have taken place, and new things I declare; before they spring into being I announce them to you"* (Isaiah 42:9). He therefore encourages us, *"Call to me and I will answer you and tell you great and unsearchable things you do not know"* (Jeremiah 33:3). And He promises us, *"From now on I will tell you of new things, of hidden things unknown to you"* (Isaiah 48:6) because our God *"will create a new thing on earth"* (Jeremiah 31:22). It is only as we deliberately seek the Creator God and listen to His word that our creativity will be maximized as we seek to live as courageous leaders.

## GOD'S GOALS, GOD'S WAYS

Courageous leaders who want to transform their world must be committed not only to God's goals but also to the accomplishing of these goals in God's ways. Great harm can be done when good things are targeted but the means for achieving them do not reflect the good, just, and loving character of God. Integrity, servanthood, humility, faith, perseverance, and self-sacrifice are the ways of the courageous leader. Jesus is our ultimate paradigm. He not only did what God wanted Him to do but also did it how God wanted Him to do it. There is no leadership model greater than His. Nor is there a leadership model that requires greater sacrifice than His. Paul instructs that we should imitate Jesus: *"Your attitude should be the same as that of Christ Jesus: who, being in very nature God, did not consider equality with God something to be grasped, but made himself nothing, taking the very nature of a servant, being made in human likeness. And being found in appearance as a man, he humbled himself and became obedient to death—even death on a cross!"* (Philippians 2:5-8). Jesus himself tells us that there is no way to follow Him other than by adopting this self-sacrificing lifestyle: *"Anyone who does not carry his cross and follow me cannot be my disciple"* (Luke 14:27). Peter declares, *"To this you were called, because Christ suffered for you, leaving you an example, that you should follow in his steps"* (1 Peter 2:21).

No genuine, permanent, life-giving transformation can take place without taking up the cross, even as there can be no redemption without renunciation, no salvation without sacrifice. This way of the cross cannot be followed by the fainthearted. Like Jehoshaphat, we must learn to be *"courageous in the ways of the LORD"* (2 Chronicles 17:6 RSV) and be willing to pay the price of Christlike service, laying our life down for others out of love. Let us imitate Christ, for in both word and deed He has shown us God's way. *"He has showed you, O man, what is good. And what does the LORD require of you? To act justly and to love mercy and to walk humbly with your God"* (Micah 6:8).

## CHAPTER 11

# Embracing the Impossible, Doing the Possible

**W**hen courageous leaders take on projects shaped by God-inspired vision, faithful diligence on their part alone will not be sufficient cause for success. Such leaders will need to see God act powerfully on their behalf. If the project is truly of God, then God Himself will be at work. When the challenges seem too great, God is providing an opportunity to prove Himself great. Such was the case for Moses, who, in obedience to God, led over four million Jewish slaves out of Egypt into the desert. Already Moses had seen God do many prodigious miracles on their behalf. Imagine how powerful a torrent of water must have gushed from the rock to quench the thirst of such an immense multitude! Imagine what imposing quantities of manna this awesome God supernaturally provided every day to feed such a host of hungry people! Moses was learning that where God guides, He provides. Reflecting on God's amazing provision and great deliverance, Moses in awe declared, *"O Sovereign LORD, you have begun to show to your servant your greatness and your strong hand. For what god is there in heaven or on earth who can do the deeds and mighty works you do?"* (Deuteronomy 3:24). And yet God had only *"begun to show"* His greatness.

One day, the people began to complain, *"If only we had meat to eat!"* (Numbers 11:4). Moses could not believe their ingratitude and went to God to complain about the complaining people he had to lead. God cut him off in the midst of his complaint to say what seemed to Moses the most ludicrous thing possible. Instead of rebuking the people for their culinary desires, God tells Moses that He is going to provide the people with meat not *"for just one day, or two days, or five, ten or twenty days, but for a whole month"* (Numbers 11:19-20). Moses can't believe what he has just heard. Surely God must be mistaken. Imagine how much meat four million hungry people could eat if they had limitless quantities available to them breakfast, lunch, and supper day after day for a full month? To Moses this seemed to be too tall an order to fill—even for God, so he proceeded to explain to God why this could not be. Incredulously he asked God, *"Would they have enough if flocks and herds were slaughtered for them? Would they have enough if all the fish in the sea were caught for them?"* (Numbers 11:22). Moses stood in need of a fresh revelation of the greatness of God, who simply said, *"Is the LORD's arm too short? You will now see whether or not what I say will come true for you"* (Numbers 11:23). The Scriptures recount the amazing thing that then occurred: *"Now a wind went out from the LORD and drove quail in from the sea. It brought them down all around the camp to about three feet above the ground, as far as a day's walk in any direction"* (Numbers 11:31). If one pauses to do the math, this matter-of-fact record of God's greatness documents an outstanding provision. For a nomadic people a day's walk would be—very conservatively—at least twenty-five miles (forty kilometers). The picture the Scriptures paint is of the Israelite camp at the center of a circle of quail with a radius of at least twenty-five miles. If we compute out the area of this circle we discover that the amount of meat God provided on that single occasion covered an area of nearly two thousand square miles (five thousand square kilometers)—all three feet (one meter) deep! Wow! How big is your God?

## EMBRACING THE IMPOSSIBLE

Paul writes, *"These things happened to them as examples"* (1 Corinthians 10:11). Even as in days of old, God wants to show Himself great to courageous leaders committed to God-inspired vision, God-led plans, and God-motivated action. For each one, the question remains: How big is your God? We're looking not for the right catechism response but for a practical revelation that is proved amidst the challenges of life. Is your God big enough to help you handle the challenges and difficulties—including the financial ones—of leadership? Is He the powerful God of Moses, able to intervene in spectacular ways? Either you have a big God or you will have big problems. Oftentimes, our challenges become problems because we lose perspective of the greatness of God.

One can take a coin, say, a silver dollar, and hold it before one's eyes. If the beholder draws the coin closer and closer to the eye, soon this small round object can fill the totality of one's vision, blocking from view objects of much greater dimension, such as the sun. Similarly, some people focus so much on financial or other challenges that all the attention of their gaze is drawn to the problem, and before they know it, the problem permeates their whole view of the world. Nothing else can be seen. The problem is so big that even God is hidden from view. The courageous leader can't afford to have this skewed perspective of reality. If he or she is to see the problem, financial or otherwise, for what it really is, then he or she must first look toward heaven. Only when He is looked to for the solution do we most truly see the reality of the circumstances around us. In light of His greatness, our problems shrink to a manageable size.

The psalmist knew the importance of gaining such heavenward perspective to be able to deal rightly with earth's challenges: *"I lift up my eyes to the hills—where does my help come from? My help comes from the LORD, the Maker of heaven and earth"* (Psalm 121:1-2). The courageous leader lives daily with the conscious awareness that *"God is our refuge and strength, an ever-present help in trouble. Therefore we will not fear, though the earth give way and the mountains fall into the heart of the sea, though its waters roar and foam and the mountains quake with their surging"* (Psalm 46:1-3). Through gaining a fresh perspective of God's greatness, courageous leaders are able to draw not only upon their own resources but also, and most importantly, upon God's.

Jesus' disciples were taught this lesson when Jesus asked them to feed the listening multitudes that had been following them. They were flabbergasted. How could He possibly ask such a thing of them! They were shocked. *"We have only five loaves of bread and two fish—unless we go and buy food for all this crowd"* (Luke 9:13). Then Philip, having quickly done the math in his head, declared, *"Eight months' wages would not buy enough bread for each one to have a bite!"* (John 6:7). It is interesting to note that when Jesus spoke to the disciples of feeding the crowd, they immediately thought of money. He spoke to them of the desired End Item ("multitude fed") to counter the undesirable situation ("multitude hungry"), and they began thinking of the Supertasks ("buy food") and the resources needed ("eight months' wages"). It did not cross their minds that Jesus might want to reach the desired End Item by some other means.

The disciples assumed that money was the answer, the means to feed the people. However, that was not the case. Money was not then—and never should be—the focus. Money may at times be one of the means of reaching the goal, but it is certainly not the only means. God is more creative than that. He does not limit Himself to only one way of providing. Our dependency should be placed not on the finances but in God's creative and loving character. The disciples erred because they lost focus, not only of the character of God but also of the goal, and concentrated only on one means of achieving the goal. Because they could envision only one way of obtaining the food to feed the multitude (purchasing it with money), they were caught completely off-guard by Jesus' miraculous multiplication of the loaves and fish. Some time later, another miraculous multiplication of food took place to feed a crowd of four thousand, as if to underscore the fact that they were to expect God to provide in unexpected ways.

Sometime after these two events, Jesus reminded the disciples of what had occurred: *"'When I broke the five loaves for the five thousand, how many basketfuls of pieces did you pick up?' 'Twelve,' they replied. 'And when I broke the seven loaves for the four thousand, how many basketfuls of pieces did you pick up?' They answered, 'Seven'"*(Mark 8:19-20). Consider these figures carefully. In the second episode there was 40 percent more food available to begin with and the crowd was 20 percent smaller. This situation was less impossible than the former one. However, the miraculous provision was greater in the first event not only in that more people were fed on less but also in that more basketfuls (70 percent more) were left over when all was said and done. Go figure! It seems that God relishes the more impossible situations and displays His greatness even more when the opposing odds are the greatest. For the courageous leader who understands these things, when the situation gets more difficult, it is time not for greater discouragement but for greater anticipation of the greater acts of God. Do the possible and expect God to do the impossible!

## AVOIDING THE MONEY PITFALL

"If we only had the money..." is an oft-repeated lament. Many have allowed their dreams to die because of lack of financial resources. Many God-inspired visions have failed because those responsible for moving into God-motivated action simply did not do so. Their forward movement was dependent not upon the ability of God so much as it was upon the availability of finances. God-led plans have been shelved because those responsible for implementing those plans, upon encountering financial adversity, have sadly shrugged their shoulders, declaring, "If we only had the money..." This hopeless, "poor me," fatalistic attitude toward resources stifles true creativity. It serves only to create impotent excuses that become a deadly shoal upon which many projects unfortunately run aground, founder, and die.

Financial shortages should not be a detriment to advancing a God-led endeavor if we have the attitude of a co-creator. Financial resources are not a fixed commodity within a closed economic system that hopelessly keeps the haves as haves and the have-nots as have-nots and in which the increase of one person's wealth necessitates the decrease of another's resources. Such unbiblical determinism should be rejected, and the poverty mentality should be broken. Our God is not limited to act within the confines of the current balance of our bank account. He's bigger than that! If we are co-creating with Him, new financial resources can be generated, fresh wealth can be created, current income can grow, and innovative sources of revenue can be developed. When cash flow stops, creativity needn't stop. And if God-led creativity continues, the project will continue even amidst financial adversity. It is the lack of God-led creativity—not the apparent lack of finances—that is, in fact, the true killer of God-led plans. The success of the plan is dependent not so much on external circumstances as on internal convictions.

The best-laid plans can be thwarted by a fearful, restrictive, can't-do, miserly perspective—best described as a poverty mentality—that stifles God-given creativity. In contrast to this fatalism is a faith-filled, confident, can-do, opportunity-creating possibility mentality that cultivates God-given creativity. It is not the amount of one's income that determines whether a person has a poverty mentality or a possibility mentality. It is an issue of the heart. It is more than just a personality trait. It is a determined attitude of the will. Both rich and poor alike can live in bondage to a poverty mentality. Likewise, both rich and poor can be liberated to live with a possibility mentality. Jesus praised the exemplary life of an extremely poor widow who lived free from a poverty mentality and gave generously in the midst of her need (Mark 12:41-44). At the same time, Jesus warned us not to be like a wealthy man who lived as a prisoner to this poverty mentality, selfishly hoarding his wealth to the detriment both of himself and of others (Luke 12:16-21).

Like the widow commended by Jesus, we must develop the lifestyle of a giver to break the poverty mentality. The Scriptures teach us this. *"A generous man will prosper; he who refreshes others will himself be refreshed"* (Proverbs 11:25). On the other hand, *"a stingy man is eager to get rich and is unaware that poverty awaits him"* (Proverbs 28:22). The former is willing to take the risk of giving; the latter is not. *"One man gives freely, yet gains even more; another withholds unduly, but comes to poverty"* (Proverbs 11:24).

Some people never have enough to launch their project. Fear immobilizes them from taking risks. They state, "We can't do it because we don't have enough." This deadly attitude kills projects before they are born and aborts visions that otherwise would have lived. If you feel like there's never enough to embark on any venture, you are keeping company with a lifeless lot: *"There are three things that are never satisfied, four that never say, 'Enough!': the grave, the barren womb, land, which is never satisfied with water, and fire, which never says, 'Enough!'"* (Proverbs 30:15-16). Notice the barrenness, drought, and devastation that accompany the attitude of "I don't have enough." This attitude is a recipe for death and destruction.

The reality is, you always have enough to begin. Two loaves and five fish were enough to begin feeding a hungry multitude (John 6:5-13). Jonathan's one sword and one armor bearer were enough to begin conquering the mighty Philistines (1 Samuel 14:1-23). The widow's last jar of oil was enough to begin to see the abundant provision of God (1 King's 17:8-16). If you have the word of the Lord, you have enough to begin. The bottom line cannot be the annual financial statement but must be the daily obedience record. Are we doing what God asked us to do? His word to us (and our obedient response to it!)—and not the present status of our financial resources—must be the primary factor in shaping the course of our projects. More money won't win the battle for you! More obedience will!

## DOING THE POSSIBLE

You have been doing the possible. You responded to a God-inspired vision. You and your team worked intensely and prayerfully to co-create the Leaders Plan with the Creator of the universe. You have in hand specific plans that show the Milestones and Supertasks that must be implemented to reach your Overall Objective. You have an awesome sense of responsibility and excitement as you realize that the mission can be accomplished if you and your team continue to do the possible while God does the impossible. Now you must seek His strategies and move into God-motivated action.

How will you move ahead? You are at a critical point in your leadership. It is crucial that the implementation of the vision as expressed in the Leaders Plan is built on a solid foundation. What are some of the major keys that contribute to this? First, as a courageous leader, you must continually communicate the vision to your team and others. Second, you need to be prepared to begin small and see the vision's implementation grow progressively.

Third, you should be ready to embrace new challenges that will keep you on the cutting edge. Fourth, you must walk in God's way of integrity in order to build the trust needed to complete the task and see the mission accomplished. We will consider each of these steps in turn, *"confident of this, that he who began a good work in you wil carry it on to completion until the day of Christ Jesus"* (Philippians 1:6).

## • Communicating the Vision

Chapter 3 emphasized that leaders must be communicators of the vision and the plan. For example, assume that you now have a Leaders Plan that provides economical water purification systems to areas with badly contaminated water. Availability of the systems in these areas can prevent hundreds of deaths each day. Implementation of this plan will also provide opportunities for you to share the gospel and demonstrate the love of Jesus. Your project becomes a vehicle for evangelism to communicate the good news of salvation. In fact, the project is part of the good news. It is the "two-handed" gospel that meets both physical and spiritual needs. The news is so tremendous that you are excited and enthusiastic about sharing it with others. Now you as a leader need to take the lead and see that the communication of the vision results in the resources necessary to implement your plan and that spiritual as well as physical needs are met.

Countless other projects and programs have been inspired by God and have the potential of opening channels for communicating the good news of salvation to the unreached. Each God-led project or cause becomes a vehicle for evangelism. Each requires commitment to God-motivated action. The interest for each project creates opportunities for many seeds to be sown. Jesus spoke to a large crowd assembled on the shores of Galilee, saying:

> *"A farmer went out to sow his seed. As he was scattering the seed, some fell along the path, and the birds came and ate it up. Some fell on rocky places, where it did not have much soil. It sprang up quickly, because the soil was shallow. But when the sun came up, the plants were scorched, and they withered because they*

*had no root. Other seed fell among thorns, which grew up and choked the plants. Still other seed fell on good soil, where it produced a crop—a hundred, sixty or thirty times what was sown"* (Matthew 13:3-8).

Note that a God-inspired project provides opportunities to sow many seeds. Only some of those seeds become fruitful. But those that do bear fruit yield a great increase compared to what was sown. The project leader must sow as many seeds as possible so as to increase the potential harvest. More and more people become interested and want to be part of a project team with a truly God-inspired vision and plan. As in the parable of the sower, some of those who join your team will bear much fruit. They are readily discipled and become evangelists who sow more seeds that yield a bumper crop of resources to implement the project. When the project leader does the possible and encourages the sowing of many seeds, the Lord continues to provide the right personnel and other resources at the right time.

It has been exciting to be a part of the founding and development of YWAM's University of the Nations (U of N). The Lord provided a God-inspired vision for a mission-oriented university. He led in developing plans for an international university that would have colleges/faculties, schools, and centres for equipping men and women spiritually, culturally, intellectually, and professionally and inspiring them to use their God-given abilities to communicate and demonstrate the good news in all nations and in all areas of society.

The team began building the first prototype campus in Kona, Hawaii, in 1978. Unique new schools were developed. Many seeds were sown. Many people, young and old, caught the vision. The Lord continued to lead people from nations worldwide to join in the U of N development and to attend U of N schools. Many came with the necessary skills to build, teach, lead outreaches, and administer major programs. The U of N schools are now given in over 110 nations and 250 locations worldwide. The early pioneers of the U of N did the possible while God did the impossible. The planting of seeds for the U of N vision continues throughout the world. One-on-one testimonies by students and staff are the most effective way of sowing seeds. Small-group meetings and conferences are also effective. Information can be provided by the Internet, brochures, catalogues, and other media that help in cultivating the seeds. A God-inspired vision and God-led plan continue to be implemented with God-motivated action.

The following excerpt from the U of N founding principles gives some perspective of the vision. Everyone involved in the project has been blessed to see the vision being implemented throughout the world.

> The University of the Nations sees the world as its classroom. It is committed to develop Christian men and women who are called to reach those who do not know Christ. Special attention is given to nations, cities and people groups who are without the Gospel. Evangelism and concern for the poor are presented as ways of life.
>
> The university seeks to broaden the scope of evangelism by equipping students to serve worldwide in the various domains of life. Opportunities are provided for students to grow and learn in their area of calling in order to serve effectively in the profession or vocation to which they are called. Believing that the command of Jesus to be salt and light in the world means Christian service and witness in all walks of life, the University of the Nations endeavors to equip students to take the Gospel to their profession by learning to think Biblically, discern spiritually and act humbly.
>
> The University of the Nations' approach to education is based on 2 Peter 1:5-8 which stresses balanced development in every area of life—in faith, virtue (character), knowledge, self-control, perseverance, godliness, brotherly kindness and love. By God's grace and surrounded by the love of Christ, students increase in their faith and worship of God. They are fortified with knowledge, turned toward wisdom, and inspired to be obedient to God's calling on their lives.
>
> While the University of the Nations is committed to educational excellence in every aspect, its aims are

206

achieved through knowing and loving God and seeking His revelation and guidance. Intercession, worship and praise are integrated into every course. The living out of God's ways is to be apparent in student and staff relationships—in forgiveness, openness, repentance, honoring the gifts and abilities of each person, unity, teamwork, hospitality, servant leadership and loving one another as commanded by Jesus.

As more seeds are planted daily, we trust that the U of N will continue to grow as it seeks to fulfill its commitment to Christ's great commission: *"Therefore go and make disciples of all nations, baptizing them in the name of the Father and of he Son and of the Holy Spirit, and teaching them to obey everything I have commanded you. And surely I am with you always, to the very end of the age"* (Matthew 28:19-20).

## • Beginning Small

Near the end of the book of Proverbs you'll find an interesting prayer: *"give me neither poverty nor riches, but give me only my daily bread. Otherwise, I may have too much and disown you and say, 'Who is the LORD?' Or I may become poor and steal, and so dishonor the name of my God"* (Proverbs 30:8-9).

We often hear people grumble because they have not enough. But how often have you heard someone complain because he or she has too much? Actually too much can be as disadvantageous—if not more so—to a new project as not enough. The children's story of Goldilocks and the Three Bears tells of the importance of finding that which is not too much or too little but that which is "just right." What is the "just-right" amount of resources to launch a project? Oftentimes it is less than we in our insecurity would like to have.

When God led the children of Israel into the promised land, He realized that if He gave them too much too quickly it would actually do them a disservice. He explained to them, *"I will not drive them out in a single year, because the land would become desolate and the wild animals too numerous for you. Little by little I will drive them out before you, until you have increased enough to take possession of the land"* (Exodus 23:29-30). God knew that they would need time to grow into the rights and responsibilities of possessing the land. Too quick of an inheritance would bring undue pressures to bear upon them. Having to work hard for each victory would progressively develop within them the capacity to live rightly with the rewards of victory. Proverbs distills the principle behind God's dealings with His people: *"An inheritance quickly gained at the beginning will not be blessed at the end"* (Proverbs 20:21).

Likewise, we see in the story of Gideon how God kept him from the error of too much. God had called Gideon to deliver His people from the oppressive rule of the Midianites. Gideon, in his youthful zeal, mustered a huge army of thirty-two thousand. "The more the better," he naturally thought. God thought otherwise and told him, *"You have too many men for me to deliver Midian into their hands"* (Judges 7:2). God then proceeded to teach Gideon that it is not sheer numbers that guarantee victory but having the right team: a team that has godly values, a common objective, and a shared commitment to a courageous, faith-filled life. So God led Gideon through a process of screening out those who would be detrimental to the team. Gideon, following God's instructions, whittled the team down to ten thousand. What did God think? He told Gideon, *"There are still too many men"* (Judges 7:4) and continued with the selection process until only three hundred were left (Judges 7:4-8). This was the "just right" number, and through these people, God and Gideon won a decisive victory.

Most projects require fewer resources in hand to get under way than what we would generally prefer or consider necessary. For the sake of security, we often like to stockpile our resources—both human and financial—in advance, but this is often not the best allocation and utilization of resources. There are many benefits of obtaining the resources JIT (just in time). Stockpiled resources are underutilized, and underutilized team members will become demotivated and lower their expectations of what they can accomplish. Like underutilized muscles, the team becomes "flabby" and inefficient. Its effectiveness is likewise diminished. Because of the habitual lack of challenge, when its full capacity is required, it will not be able to respond as it should in the moment of need. Imagine what would have happened to Gideon's three hundred had they not been the whole army but had been only three percent of a host of ten thousand? Their full potential would not have been maximized. They would never have known their own capacity to rise to the challenge. They would have placed lower expectations upon themselves and throughout life would most likely have lived as underachievers. But because of the magnitude of the challenge, they rose to it and discovered a previously untapped fortitude within themselves when their faith was placed in the living God. They learned that lean and mean is better than fat and flabby. In God-motivated projects, "just right" is often far less than what we would expect. Do not be tempted to have too much, for too much can destroy a team more subtly but more surely than too little. It can destroy the inner faith and fortitude that are necessary for victory.

Beginning small has other advantages. It enables leadership to develop and mature as progressive challenges—both financial and otherwise—are met and overcome. We are told that *"he who gathers money little by little makes it grow"* (Proverbs 13:11). "Little" is the best training ground for "more." In the parable of the talents, Jesus is speaking about financial management and stresses the importance of being *"faithful with over a little* (Matthew 25:21,23 RSV). He teaches us, *"Whoever can be trusted with very little can also be trusted with much"* (Luke 16:10). Because of faithfulness, the accomplishments of the servants were *"well done"* (Matthew 25:21,23). Without faithfulness, without consistency of character, without integrity, you cannot do a job well. But since you learn these qualities in the small, unseen chores of life, it is best to learn them when the pressures and challenges are small. If they are not learned then, the reliability that comes from tested faithfulness and the constancy that is born of moral integrity will not be available in the moments of great public pressure and challenge. When such moments arise, it is best that the leader has previously been trained in the disciplined ways of trustworthiness. Beginning small and growing faithfully into increasing responsibilities will be of great benefit to this leader in those times when the world requires truly courageous leaders.

## • Accepting Challenges

Courageous leaders who seek to transform their world accept challenges beyond their capacity. They aim for a goal that requires resources above and beyond themselves. To do anything less would be to aim too low. If the project is something you can easily manage given your current resources, you should consider whether or not you are pursuing a diminished dream, a vision of your own making rather than of God's. When you aim beyond the reach of your capabilities, God has room to act. If you leave God room and diligently do your part, you can expect Him to intervene in extraordinary ways.

How do you accept just enough challenge into your project to keep you from mediocrity, but not so much that you are left with something unattainable? What degree of impossibility is "just right"—not too much and not too little? We can take lessons from avid mountain climbers. On each outing they push themselves a little harder, a little higher. They know their physical capabilities and prepare themselves so that on each successive occasion they are able to slightly exceed their capacity. A committed mountain climber may begin training by rapelling down a small cliff, but as experience and skills increase, the mountain climber always aims higher. Though he does not begin with Mount Everest, he's expanding his abilities in hopes of someday being able to climb Everest. Each challenge is greater than the previous one, and in this way, the mountain climber develops his capacities to the maximum. So also with courageous leaders. They accept challenges that push them to new levels of ability, stretching themselves to take challenges that can be accomplished only as they exercise their faith and see God work in the situation. They aim to do something that lies between the manageably possible and the unmanageably impossible. They aim to do the manageably impossible.

This kind of leadership requires not only buoyant faith in God but also diligent, indeed sacrificial, hard work. We have all been inspired by stories of people like Horatio Alger who went from rags to riches on the basis of their sacrificial effort, persevering diligence, and creative resourcefulness. We may be motivated by the "riches" part of the stories, but we should in fact learn from the "to" part of the rags-to-riches sagas. It is in the process of progress that the key lessons of life are learned. One does not leave Egypt and immediately enter the promised land. One must first traverse the desert, where, in the crucible of trials, one has the opportunity to acquire the needed skills and character to enter the promised land successfully. Similarly, it is not without great struggle and extreme effort that a butterfly breaks out of the cocoon and begins to develop its wings for a life of unimpeded flight. It is well-known that if external help is given to the butterfly at this difficult stage of its development as it emerges from the cocoon, its wings will never develop properly and it will never be able to fly. Overcoming the adversity of escaping the cocoon prepares the butterfly for a future of flight. There is benefit in the struggle itself, for it shapes the courageous leader—as certainly as it shapes the butterfly—for the future. For this reason, the courageous leader can willingly embrace adversity while resisting the adversary.

Great financial challenges often have the same effect on us that the cocoon has for the butterfly. Financial need can be a major stimulus for cultivating an industrious lifestyle. The challenges posed by financial needs are not to be avoided but are to be embraced. Responsibility for such pressures is not to be shirked but is to be welcomed, as the courageous leader sees it as an opportunity for personal and organizational growth. Proverbs insightfully informs us that *"the laborer's appetite works for him; his hunger drives him on"* (Proverbs 16:26). Hunger is a great motivator. What are you hungry for? What are you trying to accomplish? If it's worth doing, it's worth doing diligently. When hunger is met by diligence, great things can be accomplished. Through diligence, want turns into provision, as these verses make clear:

> *Lazy hands make a man poor, but diligent hands bring wealth* (Proverbs 10:4).

> *All hard work brings a profit, but mere talk leads only to poverty* (Proverbs 14:23).

> *The plans of the diligent lead to profit as surely as haste leads to poverty* (Proverbs 21:5).

## • Building Trust

The character of courageous leaders is tested in times of pressure. Oftentimes such pressure is related to financial areas of need. Consistency of integrity and continued commitment to living according to the ways of God when under pressure are signs of true greatness. It is easy to be godly when the pressure is off. But how about when it's on? Are you steady when the storms begin to rage around you? Do you faithfully persevere in godly values or succumb to the temptation to take the shortcuts of expediency? Many pressures will tempt the courageous leader to compromise in areas of integrity, financial and otherwise. In this regard, we can be encouraged by the record of the life of King Jehoshaphat, of whom it was said that he *"was courageous in the ways of the Lord"* (2 Chronicles 17:3 RSV). Indeed it takes courage to resist ungodly peer pressure and circumstantial temptation. Whereas some leaders capitulate to their own lack of self-control, courageous leaders persist in faithful management of their lives and of the vision that has been commended to them. They will choose godly values over facile expediency.

This was not the case with Esau, who sold his birthright for a bowl of stew (Genesis 25:29–34). Esau despised a future inheritance in exchange for immediate gratification. Present needs took precedence over principled behavior. Every leader has to choose between these two, not only once but on repeated occasions. Anything less than an uncompromising determination to walk in integrity will lead to a subtle drift into unethical compromise. How many leaders who, having begun well, did not give due attention to character issues and their leadership authority was eroded by their lack of integrity?

One such leader was Solomon, who allowed himself to be seduced by inappropriate use of power, sex, and money. Moses had warned future kings about the potential pitfalls these three areas pose for leaders. He therefore admonished them not to multiply horses, wives, and gold. He wrote:

> *"The king, moreover, must not acquire great numbers*
> *of horses for himself or make the people return to*
> *Egypt to get more of them, for the LORD has told you,*

*'You are not to go back that way again.' He must not take many wives, or his heart will be led astray. He must not accumulate large amounts of silver and gold. When he takes the throne of his kingdom, he is to write for himself on a scroll a copy of this law, taken from that of the priests, who are Levites. It is to be with him, and he is to read it all the days of his life so that he may learn to revere the LORD his God and follow carefully all the words of this law and these decrees and not consider himself better than his brothers and turn from the law to the right or to the left. Then he and his descendants will reign a long time over his kingdom in Israel"* (Deuteronomy 17:16-20).

In spite of these clear and wise instructions, Solomon's leadership, which began so auspiciously, ended disastrously. Oftentimes Solomon is remembered only for the immoral way in which he multiplied his wives: He did acquire *"seven hundred wives of royal birth and three hundred concubines"* (1 Kings 11:3). However, this was only part of his downfall. His other major leadership errors were also the result of a lack of self-control. Not only did Solomon multiply wives, but he also multiplied gold (1 Kings 10:14-22) and chariots and horses (1 Kings 10:26-29) in direct contradiction to the leadership principles laid down by Moses. His unparalleled wisdom gave way to unbridled idolatry. He had so much going for him, but he squandered it away through lack of self-control. Greatness was swallowed up by idolatry, not in one great moment of national crisis but in countless progressively unethical private decisions in which pleasure was picked over principle. His great power and wealth meant nothing in light of his crumbling character. He should have more carefully heeded the wise words of his earlier years:

*Ill-gotten treasures are of no value, but righteousness delivers from death* (Proverbs 10:2).

*Wealth is worthless in the day of wrath, but righteousness delivers from death* (Proverbs 11:4).

213

The legacy of one's life is best seen by looking at the effects it has on subsequent generations. Solomon was praised in his day by the queen of Sheba, who said:

> *"The report I heard in my own country about your achievements and your wisdom is true. But I did not believe these things until I came and saw with my own eyes. Indeed, not even half was told me; in wisdom and wealth you have far exceeded the report I heard. How happy your men must be! How happy your officials, who continually stand before you and hear your wisdom! Praise be to the LORD your God, who has delighted in you and placed you on the throne of Israel. Because of the LORD's eternal love for Israel, he has made you king, to maintain justice and righteousness"* (1 Kings 10:6-9).

Subsequent generations would give a different report. During the reign of Solomon's son, the kingdom was divided and much of the former glory lost. Why? Because the people sought relief from the harsh taxation imposed by Solomon. They made their request to Solomon's son Rehoboam: *"Your father put a heavy yoke on us, but now lighten the harsh labor and the heavy yoke he put on us, and we will serve you"* (1 Kings 12:4). Rehoboam did not heed their request and, in the same spirit of greed that he had observed in his father, vowed to increase the taxes. The people rebelled and unleashed a whole sequence of tragic episodes that eventually brought about the total downfall of Israel. This devastating sequence of events was the result of a lack of self-control in financial areas by the nation's leadership. It is not without reason that the Scriptures declare, *"For the love of money is a root of all kinds of evil. Some people, eager for money, have wandered from the faith and pierced themselves with many griefs"* (1 Timothy 6:10).

## REMAINING FOCUSED ON GOD'S WAYS

Jesus said, *"No one can serve two masters. Either he will hate the one and love the other, or he will be devoted to the one and despise the other. You cannot serve both God and Money"*

214

(Matthew 6:24). Many people err in this regard. The major decisions in their lives are shaped not by a passion to love God but by what will enable them to make more money. Finances—and not the ways of God—become the driving force of their lives. They end up serving money instead of letting money serve them as they seek to serve God. What a tragic waste of life this is, as reflected in Jesus' insightful question: *"What good is it for a man to gain the whole world, yet forfeit his soul? Or what can a man give in exchange for his soul?"* (Mark 8:36-37). The true value of an individual so far exceeds the maximum net worth that can be earned by an individual that to spend your life for money is a very poor business deal indeed. Nothing but the advancement of the kingdom of God in all of its multifaceted implications is a worthy investment of a human life. For this reason Jesus declares:

> *"Therefore I tell you, do not worry about your life, what you will eat or drink; or about your body, what you will wear. Is not life more important than food, and the body more important than clothes? Look at the birds of the air; they do not sow or reap or store away in barns, and yet your heavenly Father feeds them. Are you not much more valuable than they? Who of you by worrying can add a single hour to his life? And why do you worry about clothes? See how the lilies of the field grow. They do not labor or spin. Yet I tell you that not even Solomon in all his splendor was dressed like one of these. If that is how God clothes the grass of the field, which is here today and tomorrow is thrown into the fire, will he not much more clothe you, O you of little faith? So do not worry, saying, 'What shall we eat?' or 'What shall we drink?' or 'What shall we wear?' For the pagans run after all these things, and your heavenly Father knows that you need them. But seek first his kingdom and his righteousness, and all these things will be given to you as well"* (Matthew 6:25-33).

Limited financial or other resources are no reason to disobey the word of the Lord and not follow the God-inspired vision. Paul, after decades of courageous leadership and even amidst the most adverse of circumstances, was able to declare, *"I was not disobedient to the vision from heaven"* (Acts 26:19). Elsewhere he describes some of the hardships he faced—many of which imply financial challenges: *"I have labored and toiled and have often gone without sleep; I have known hunger and thirst and have often gone without food; I have been cold and naked"* (2 Corinthians 11:27). He also tells us that he was often *"poor, yet making many rich; having nothing, and yet possessing everything"* (2 Corinthians 6:10). This is not inspirational poetry but down-to-earth, where-the-rubber-meets-the-road, autobiographical transparency. Many times Paul did not have the financial resources to do what he was endeavoring to do. How could he continue exercising his world-impacting leadership in such harsh circumstances without what many would consider the minimal financial resources? It had to do with his perspective of the character of God and his passion for the God-inspired vision. We are urged to have the same attitude: *"Therefore, holy brothers, who share in the heavenly calling, fix your thoughts on Jesus, the apostle and high priest whom we confess"* (Hebrews 3:1). In this way, obedience to God is always possible, no matter what the difficulties of our circumstances—financial or otherwise.

Some would argue that you should not launch a project prior to having all the needed financial resources at hand for the completion of the project. Some even appeal to Jesus' words in Luke 14:28-29: *"Suppose one of you wants to build a tower. Will he not first sit down and estimate the cost to see if he has enough money to complete it? For if he lays the foundation and is not able to finish it, everyone who sees it will ridicule him, saying, 'This fellow began to build and was not able to finish.'"* Note here that in this parable Jesus employed—as was His custom—an ordinary, everyday event that illustrated a deeper truth.

The ordinary event (a commonplace construction project) shows that Jesus presupposed that people would plan projects (*"Will he not first sit down and estimate the cost"*). Planning, in Jesus' view, is normative and expected; it is to be integrated into the way we live our lives as naturally as eating and sleeping.

The deeper truth is that discipleship requires wholehearted commitment. Total obedience to the leading of God is the outstanding characteristic of the Christian disciple. Indeed, three times in this passage, Jesus states that one cannot be His disciple if one seeks to follow Him with anything less than unconditional commitment to His will. No circumstances—financial or otherwise—will dissuade the true disciple from obedience. Jesus says:

> *"If anyone comes to me and does not hate his father and mother, his wife and children, his brothers and sisters—yes, even his own life—he cannot be my disciple.... And anyone who does not carry his cross and follow me cannot be my disciple.... In the same way, any of you who does not give up everything he has cannot be my disciple"* (Luke 14:26-27,33).

Partial dedication and halfhearted commitments are unacceptable standards for Christian discipleship. If you are going to follow Jesus, you must be willing to go all the way and pay the price—whatever it may be. You must be willing to finish what you begin, even if it costs you all you hold most near and most dear—even if it costs you your life. It's an all-or-nothing radical obedience that Jesus is looking for in His followers. Total obedience to Jesus and His word, not circumstances, should characterize the life of the courageous leader. What we do is dependent not upon family relationships, personal ambition, financial means, or anything else other than the word of the Lord, the God-inspired vision, so that we might fully follow Him. Unconditional obedience to His leading is the bottom line. When total obedience to the God-inspired vision is coupled with unrelenting faith in the character of God, the courageous leader can face and overcome any difficulty.

CHAPTER 12

# Foreseeing the Future, Dealing in the Present

The ability to foresee or discern the impact of a decision today on the future of a specific project, group, or institution is an essential leadership characteristic. Robert K. Greenleaf, in his classic book *The Servant as Leader*, said, "Foresight is the central ethic of leadership." He added, "Serious ethical compromises are often attributed to yesterday's failure to foresee today and take the right actions yesterday. This is a failure of leadership... Leadership thus degenerates into command, the power to issue orders. The result may be ethically bad choices because the lee-way within which to initiate action has been narrowed and only bad choices remain."

In his book *Leadership Is an Art*, Max Depree stated, "The art of leadership dwells a good deal in the future, providing for the future of the organization, in planting and growing other leaders who will look to the future beyond their own." This need to fore-see and dwell in the future and also deal with the present realities generally requires two basic types of leadership, often referred to as leading and managing. It is important to recognize the differences between the two types and ensure that one's projects, programs, and institutions are being led and managed effectively.

# LEADERS AND MANAGERS

In this book, vision is described as the broad perspective or the big picture of what you believe God has shown you—a glimpse of what could be in the future. Often the vision is a mental picture of a situation that brings joy to the Lord's heart or a solution to a situation that breaks God's heart. In any case, the vision is a look into what could be in the future. The Overall Objective encompasses all or a part of the vision that a leadership team believes it is called to accomplish within a specified time frame. Therefore, the Overall Objective is a declaration of foresight. It describes the mission to be accomplished; it is the target or final goal to be reached within an estimated time frame.

Leaders are expected to lead by ensuring that their groups understand the vision and the Overall Objective. They must lead by guiding, influencing, and providing an environment for members of the group to experience being part of a team aiming for a God-inspired goal while accomplishing the necessary Supertasks to reach the Milestones and the ultimate End Item, the Overall Objective. They should regularly remind their teams and the public of the vision and the present status of the project. If a leader fails to do this in a refreshing and interesting way, the project tends to lose the dynamic of enthusiasm and creative input by the team members.

Leaders are also expected to ensure that the daily tasks and overall programs are managed reliably. They must therefore understand management responsibilities. Generally, these tasks require managers who can deal effectively with the present. The managers must know how to get things done and ensure that all segments of the team are smoothly synchronized.

Managers are leaders who deal primarily with the present realities. They manage the personnel and other resources necessary to perform the daily operations. This is a significant leadership responsibility that has a broad impact and requires key skills. The manager must be capable of giving leadership to the recruitment and training of skilled personnel, the aquisition of the necessary equipment and services, the establishment of a healthy working environment, the oversight of a reliable cash flow, the anticipation and prevention of potential delay, and the preparation of the other contingencies required to achieve intermediate Milestones and the ultimate Overall Objective.

The manager's responsibilities require considerable experience, good judgement, and ability to foresee not only the need for the tangible items but also personnel attitudes and the felt needs beyond their work. Although managers require many leadership skills, the general functions of visionary leaders and managerial leaders are different but complementary. Both should be strong and courageous leaders. Both must develop implicational thinking skills and the ability to foresee the impact of their decisions today on the future as related to their specific responsibilities. It is generally a mistake for one person to attempt to fill the roles of both leader and manager unless the project is quite small.

## GAINING FORESIGHT

Foresight involves both the attitude of the heart and the latitude of the mind. It has to do with both the availability to serve long-range purposes and the ability to understand long-range implications. It requires both a commitment to do and a discernment to know. It has to do with both dedication and intuition. As a result, it will make you, at one time, both more daring and more prudent.

Foresight understands future implications of present actions. It presupposes that how you live your life today is important because it can have multigenerational implications. Therefore foresight begins with a commitment to live today for tomorrow. An attitude of forward-looking servanthood will enable the courageous leader to begin to have insight into the possibilities of the future. Foresight is birthed out of a commitment to such a multigenerational servanthood. Courageous leaders do not merely live for their generation but carry out the God-inspired visions in the light of eternity.

God is a God with multigenerational commitments. When He met Moses at the burning bush, He introduced Himself as *"the God of Abraham, the God of Isaac and the God of Jacob"* (Exodus 3:6), a designation of the divine that is often repeated throughout Scripture. His multigenerational commitment to Abraham and his descendants resulted in the most world-transforming project of all time.

God likewise instructs His people to have a multigenerational perspective. Time and again He reminds His people that their actions—for good or for ill—have consequences not only to the third and fourth generation (Exodus 20:5, 34:7; Numbers 14:18; Deuteronomy 5:9) but also beyond. What we think and do today does indeed impact tomorrow. *"Be very careful, then, how you live—not as unwise but as wise, making the most of every opportunity, because the days are evil. Therefore do not be foolish, but understand what the Lord's will is"* (Ephesians 5:15-17).

What happens when we fail to live and think multigenerationally? We see a graphic example in the life of Hezekiah, one of Israel's greatest leaders. In many respects, Hezekiah was a wonderful paradigm of a courageous leader. We are told, *"Hezekiah trusted in the LORD, the God of Israel. There was no one like him among all the kings of Judah, either before him or after him. He held fast to the LORD and did not cease to follow him; he kept the commands the LORD had given Moses. And the LORD was with him; he was successful in whatever he undertook"* (2 Kings 18:5-7). However, this good man had a serious flaw: he lacked foresight. Though Hezekiah served God *"faithfully and with wholehearted devotion"* (2 Kings 20:3), he was shortsighted in his commitments. He lived only for his own generation. Toward the end of his reign he acted unwisely and proudly showed off all his wealth to emissaries from Babylon, at that time a small but growing power on the world scene. He was not paying attention to the signs of the times and made a serious error in judgement. Consequently, Isaiah came to him and prophesied of Babylon's rise and Judah's fall. It was a horrible prediction of death and destruction. But Hezekiah's response was one of indifferent shortsightedness. His callous lack of concern for subsequent generations is one of the saddest passages in the Bible. *"'The word of the LORD you have spoken is good,' Hezekiah replied. For he thought, 'Will there not be peace and security in my lifetime?'"* (2 Kings 20:16-19). He cared not for the future as long as his present was secure. Tragedy ensued, for good leaders usher in devastation when they fail to live for the next generation. Good leaders welcome destruction when they fail to walk in the counsel of foresight.

How did this story end? Hezekiah's son Manasseh became the worst king of Judah's history, deliberately undoing all the good that his father had done. He even sacrificed his son, Hezekiah's grandson, in a fiery offering to the pagan god Moloch (2 Kings 21:2-6). Things went from bad to worse, and within eighty years of Isaiah's words, all the horror that had been prophesied had come to pass.

How do we avoid errors like that of Hezekiah? We make a commitment to the next generation (Psalms 48:13; 71:18; 78:4,6) and seek to develop implicational thinking skills. We can do the latter by considering how God instructed the descendants of Abraham.

The heart of God's revelation to the Jews was the Ten Commandments (Exodus 20:1-17; Deuteronomy 5:6-21). Now, when we think of the Ten Commandments we tend to think of them only as moral law and judicial decrees. But for the Jewish people, they were the very foundation of the Torah, which means that though they had legal implications, their primary purpose was didactic in nature. The Ten Commandments were designed to disciple a nation in foresight. They are not just a bunch of good rules thrown together but are a deliberate instruction in the principles of implicational thinking so that the Jews would be *"a wise and understanding people"* (Deuteronomy 4:6). They're words not to be passively accepted through mindless familiarity but to be purposefully embraced through thoughtful reflection.

Through the Ten Commandments, God the Master Teacher trains His people how to think, leading them from practice to precept, from the concrete to the abstract. The Ten Commandments are organized to lead us through a thinking process, pressing us to follow a train of thought through to its ultimate conclusion and application. To train oneself in implicational thinking, one must learn to skillfully ask the question, Why? Let's consider the final six commandments—the ones that have to do with our horizontal relationships with other human beings—to illustrate this point.

The fifth commandment instructs us to *"honor father and mother."* Why? Because they are the begetters of life and life is to be valued. For this reason, lifegivers are to be honored.

The sixth commandment logically follows on this. It tells us, *"You shall not murder."* Why? Again, if life is valuable, to take someone's life is to destroy something of immense worth. If you love your neighbor, you could not rob him or her of life.

The seventh commandment continues this line of thought. It instructs us, "*You shall not commit adultery.*" Why? At this point, one has to think a bit harder. If taking another's life is wrong, then taking that which is precious in another's life, that which is intimately connected to another's life—the person's spouse—is wrong. It destroys life, not as graphically as murder but just as surely.

The eighth commandment presses us one step further. It teaches us, "*You shall not steal.*" Why not? Things are inanimate objects and have no life in them. How does this follow the implication from the earlier commandments? Objects represent life. Consider, for example, what is required to buy a television. A person must pay a certain sum of money. That money represents (depending on one's income) perhaps two weeks or possibly four months of one's life spent working to earn enough to buy the television. The thief who steals the television is in fact stealing a portion of the victim's life, those many weeks or months of labor. It is a difference of degree but not of kind with the former laws. If life in its entirety is not to be destroyed through murder, it follows that no part of life should be destroyed through theft. If that which is most precious to one's life is not to be destroyed through adultery, it follows that anything of value to one's life should likewise not be destroyed through theft. If the axiom is accepted as a true presupposition, its corollary must likewise be embraced as a necessary consequence. Each commandment has already been implied in the truth contained in the preceding commandments.

The ninth commandment takes us even further, pushing the implications of what has been learned in the world of concrete objects into the world of abstract concepts. It tells us, "*You shall not give false testimony.*" Why is this wrong? When a person lies about another person, the other's reputation is stolen, adulterated, perhaps even destroyed. Even though you can't put it in a test tube, a reputation is very real. "*A good name is more desirable than great riches; to be esteemed is better than silver or gold*" (Proverbs 22:1). If thievery of goods is wrong, the thievery of a good name through deceitful or dishonest words is likewise wrong. The process of implicational thinking has taken us to a new level of understanding and insight. It will shape how we lead our lives.

Now, although all of the preceding commandments can be found in the law books of nearly every nation, the next and final commandment is found in no nation's judicial system. It is the culminating apex of the revelatory process, the climax of the teaching, the ultimate insight of implicational thinking. It says, *"You shall not covet."* Why? Because this internal, spiritual attitude is the seed that produces the external, physical fruit of lying, theft, adultery, and murder. *"For out of the heart come evil thoughts, murder, adultery, sexual immorality, theft, false testimony, slander"* (Matthew 15:19). The culminating revelation of the Ten Commandments is that if you truly value life, you cannot willingly harbor a thought that, if it were to be acted out, would lead to the destruction of life.

This kind of implicational insight is the foundation of applicational foresight. It was because He had implicational understanding that Jesus was able to teach as He did in the Sermon on the Mount. Jesus continued the process of walking out the implications of seed truths planted at an earlier time. He trained His disciples to think in terms of truth's corollaries: "If this be true...then that is consequently true..." by saying time and again, *"You have heard that it was said... But I tell you..."* (Matthew 5:21f, 27f,31f, 33f, 38f, 43f). Jesus takes the seed truths of the Old Testament to their ultimate conclusion and applies them in totally fresh, life-transforming ways.

Persistent, clear, implicational thinking built upon God's revealed truth is foundational for foresight. Courageous leaders seek to cultivate this skill daily. They pray the prayer of Moses, *"Teach us to number our days aright, that we may gain a heart of wisdom"* (Psalm 90:12), for foresight is the fruit of a heart trained in the discipline of God's wisdom. Therefore, *"Buy the truth and do not sell it; get wisdom, discipline and understanding"* (Proverbs 23:23). Again, *"Get wisdom, get understanding....do not forget my words or swerve from them. Do not forsake wisdom, and she will protect you; love her, and she will watch over you. Wisdom is supreme; therefore, get wisdom. Though it cost all you have, get understanding"* (Proverbs 4:5-7). *"How much better to get wisdom* than gold, to choose understanding rather than silver!" (Proverbs 16:16). And how is this wisdom obtained? Proverbs again instructs us, *"The fear of the LORD is the beginning of wisdom, and knowledge of the Holy One is understanding"* (Proverbs 9:10). Once again we are reminded that wise and courageous leadership begins with a right relationship with God.

Foresight builds upon revealed wisdom, considering actions and motives, following them through to their ultimate implications. It understands that *"a man reaps what he sows"* (Galatians 6:7). Understanding the implications of today's choices on tomorrow's reality helps us make wise decisions today. This kind of foresight is at the heart of many biblical statements, such as these final words of Moses:

> *"See, I set before you today life and prosperity, death and destruction. For I command you today to love the LORD your God, to walk in his ways, and to keep his commands, decrees and laws; then you will live and increase, and the LORD your God will bless you in the land you are entering to possess. But if your heart turns away and you are not obedient, and if you are drawn away to bow down to other gods and worship them, I declare to you this day that you will certainly be destroyed. You will not live long in the land you are crossing the Jordan to enter and possess. This day I call heaven and earth as witnesses against you that I have set before you life and death, blessings and curses. Now choose life, so that you and your children may live and that you may love the LORD your God, listen to his voice, and hold fast to him. For the LORD is your life, and he will give you many years in the land he swore to give to your fathers, Abraham, Isaac and Jacob"* (Deuteronomy 30:15-20).

Time and again the Scriptures help us gain foresight by contrasting the way of the righteous with the way of the wicked. Many such examples are found in Proverbs. That is why one of the great courageous leaders of our time, Billy Graham, has disciplined himself to read a chapter of Proverbs every day of his life since his youth. Without being trained in such foresight as that found in Proverbs, one can easily misjudge events and respond incorrectly to a situation. Psalm 73 is a case in point. The author says he had bitterly complained of the success and prosperity of the wicked *"till I entered the sanctuary of God; then I understood their final destiny"* (Psalm 73:17). A fresh encounter with God gave him a new perspective of the future that enabled him to live his life more wisely in the present.

This psalm illustrates an important truth. Though foresight is built upon implicational thinking and deliberate consideration of future consequences of present actions, human reasoning processes alone are not sufficient for the task. Even when you train yourself to think implicationally, you will find yourself in situations that *"you cannot foresee"* (Isaiah 47:11), for the future holds many unknown variables. Herein lies the perennial problem. *"Since no man knows the future, who can tell him what is to come?"* (Ecclesiastes 8:7). Gazing into a crystal ball will not help. Looking to the stars and reading a horoscope will not help. No medium or guru can help. We need to hear from the living God. He is the only one who can *"make known the end from the beginning, from ancient times, what is still to come"* (Isaiah 46:10).

Once again, this reality drives courageous leaders to deliberately seek God. Appropriate humility in the face of the future rightly leads us to press in to God. Dependency on Him and His revelation is key to foresight. It is necessary to rightly interpret the signs of the times. Without His insight, all the data we amass, all the megatrends that we ponder, all the information whirling around us will serve only to confuse. Are you not sure of the way ahead? Cry out to God. *"How gracious he will be when you cry for help! As soon as he hears, he will answer you....Whether you turn to the right or to the left, your ears will hear a voice behind you, saying, 'This is the way; walk in it'"* (Isaiah 30:19,21).

Prayer is key to foresight. Many have commented on Jesus' incredible foresight in the selection of the twelve apostles. How did He see in those rustic, uneducated fishermen future courageous leaders? How did He see in a wily tax collector one who could be a world changer? The key lay in the fact that even though

He was the Son of God, He made this decision not on His own but in intimate consultation with His Father. We are told that *"one of those days Jesus went out to a mountainside to pray, and spent the night praying to God. When morning came, he called his disciples to him and chose twelve of them, whom he also designated apostles"* (Luke 6:12-13). In fact, on another occasion when Jesus was praying, He said to the Father regarding the apostles, *"You gave them to me"* (John 17:6). He was acutely aware that the foresight He had had to select the twelve had originated not in Himself but in the Father. If this was true for Jesus, how much more so for us! Intimacy with God through prayer is indispensable for foresight to be formed.

Indeed, the truest foresight is formed in God's presence. When we are before His throne we can glimpse His view of the future. It is as we come before His throne that we can gain a proper perspective of eternity. It is only then that we have sufficient foresight to live today rightly. Courageous leaders need to have a vision of the coming kingdom of God, for no other vision is a true picture of that which is to come. They must live with a throne room perspective. Any other way of living is not in keeping with reality, for God indeed is seated on the throne. Courageous leaders must live in the light of His eternal reign. Any other way of living is inadequate for the demands of the day, because God *"has also set eternity in the hearts of men"* (Ecclesiastes 3:11). And when courageous leaders look to that eternal throne, what do they see? John tells us what he saw: *"After this I looked and there before me was a great multitude that no one could count, from every nation, tribe, people and language, standing before the throne and in front of the Lamb. They were wearing white robes and were holding palm branches in their hands. And they cried out in a loud voice: 'Salvation belongs to our God, who sits on the throne, and to the Lamb'"* (Revelation 7:9-10).

This is the ultimate vision that must motivate and drive every courageous leader. This perspective provides the overarching foresight to live life courageously today. In light of this ultimate vision, the leader's task is to pull the future into the present, to make the foreseen vision a seen reality. When leaders have clearly foreseen the future, they can do nothing less than live their lives in such a way as to see the Lord's prayer fully realized: *"Your kingdom come, your will be done on earth as it is in heaven"* (Matthew 6:10).

## TRACKING THE PROJECT STATUS

Luke's Gospel begins, *"Many have undertaken to draw up an account of the things that have been fulfilled among us, just as they were handed down to us by those who from the first were eye-witnesses and servants of the word. Therefore, since I myself have carefully investigated everything from the beginning, it seemed good also to me to write an orderly account for you"* (Luke 1:1-3). Luke has carefully researched the life and acts of Jesus from His birth to His resurrection, and has prepared an accurate report to communicate the information to others.

In some respects, the purpose of tracking a project's progress is similar. That is, everyone involved wants a careful investigation of the project activities plus an accurate and orderly report of what has been accomplished. The tracking report must show the project's progress at regular intervals, often weekly or monthly. A regular tracking and review of the project status accomplishes many things. The leaders, managers, and entire team have an up-to-date and accurate account of whether or not the project is on schedule. When the project status is posted and made readily available, it provides incentive, encouragement, and recognition of the results of the collective effort. When the project is on schedule, the team has reason to rejoice. When it is not on schedule, the entire team has reason to put forth extra effort and send up specific prayers. The tracking report can be made attractive and challenging and become a focal point, reminding the workers that they are a team working in unity to reach the Overall Objective. Regardless of each person's regular project role, all team members should *"consider how we may spur one another on toward love and good deeds. Let us not give up meeting together, as some are in the habit of doing, but let us encourage one another"* (Hebrews 10:24-25).

As the team deals with the present realities of a project, it behooves everyone to model servant leadership, as Paul wrote, *"Each of you should look not only to your own interests, but also to the interests of others. Your attitude should be the same as that of Christ Jesus"* (Philippians 2:4-5).

## REPORTING AND MANAGING

During the construction of the huge Alaska Pipeline, the president of the company stated that his office received about six hundred pounds of traditional management reports daily! This generated far too much reporting information and was in the wrong format to be useful to the leadership team. Dozens of prime contractors and hundreds of subcontractors in this multibillion-dollar project needed useful project reports So, a reporting system based on management-by-exception displays for the Leaders Plan was successfully established. What is a management-by-exception display? A good example is found on the dashboard of every car. You know that your car's engine is too hot or that the alternator is not working when the the red light on the dash comes on. This kind of management-by-exception display works not only in cars, but also in huge power stations that use flashing lights to show when a subsytem is malfunctioning, as illustrated in Figure C-1:

**Figure C-1**

In a similar way, management-by-exception displays can be used to oversee any project. With this system of reporting, the Leaders Plan becomes the standard to which actual progress is compared and reported. Decision makers are alerted only when something goes wrong.

Persons who are responsible and accountable for their segments of work track the progress on the Leaders Plan. The leadership team illustrates the progress on the Leaders Plan by symbolic marking for the Supertask completions, Milestone occurrences, and impacts of delays using a code that is easily recognized. The team can use an interpretive set of colors, shapes, and symbols to determine whether progress is being made according to the approved plan.

In the accounting discipline, many scheduling and budgeting systems rely on a two-color system. The program is either in the black or in the red, indicating that it is either ahead of or behind schedule, or it is either within the budget or in an overrun condition. Under such a system, only two conditions are indicated. The disadvantage with this system is that there are no warnings that something is about to go into a red status. For this reason, a more effective approach is to use a three-color system of reporting, with an interim warning alert condition between the two extremes. This same three-color system is used for many types of control systems, including traffic control, and is readily understood worldwide. Green means "normal/go," yellow means "caution/slow," and red means "danger/stop." The three-color indicators form the basis of updating and reporting progress on the Leaders Plan as in Figure C-2.

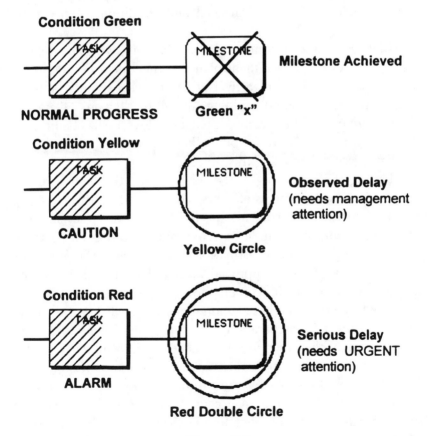

Figure C-2

Condition green (normal), condition yellow (caution), and condition red (danger) always apply. This makes it very easy for key people to see trouble spots, even when they view dozens of Supertasks and Milestones displayed in printed reports or on wall charts in an office or strategy room environment.

The Leaders Plan can also feature special unambiguous symbols in conjunction with green, yellow, and red so that compatible copies of the updated plan can be made on an office copier that uses only black ink when a color copier is not available, as illustrated in Figure C-2.

Ideally, it is possible to avoid condition red altogether by making timely corrective decisions when condition yellow problems first occur. If unchecked, these would result in a nonrecoverable condition red situation. However, with proper reporting and follow through, they can be checked and condition green can be restored.

Management leadership can be compared to flying an airplane. First the pilot prepares a flight plan and then identifies and computes estimated times of arrival at several checkpoints between departure and destination, adding enough fuel for proper reserve. This entire process has been adopted as an FAA flight planning/air traffic control procedure for pilots. For this reason, relatively few mishaps occur when using this procedure.

During the actual flight, the pilot follows the flight plan by using a navigation process of course correction for drift, changing power adjustments for an unexpected headwind, or revising the plan to circumnavigate an unexpected thunderstorm so as to safely reach the predetermined destination. Like the pilot, the project or program leader uses an approved Leaders Plan to "navigate" the program to its successful completion.

The Leaders Plan is based upon the best knowledge of the facts revealed during its preparation. When progress begins to deviate from the plan, the program leader makes thoughtful decisions for taking corrective actions; otherwise, the success of the program may be jeopardized. A deviation from the original Leaders Plan might, however, be required because of unexpected factors. The program leadership must therefore be flexible enough to consider that the Leaders Plan be modified to implement corrective action.

A revised Leaders Plan reflects new knowledge or discoveries that have become apparent while tracking the plan. The destination is still the same. The Overall Objective does not change, but modified Supertasks and Milestones might be required. *"Do not move an ancient boundary stone"* (Proverbs 23:10). Tenaciously hold to the Overall Objective, while creatively adjusting the means to the end. Because a whole team worked together on developing the Leaders Plan, it is important to formalize the replanning process with the same care and thorough communication among the team members as used for the original plan.

Many management methods are presented in dozens of books that can facilitate navigating the Leaders Plan to successful completion. Only a few reflect servant leadership. We hope that the Christlike characteristics of a strong and courageous leader presented in the chapters of this book become the standard with which management procedures and methods are compared. Again Paul's words ring out: *"Each of you should look not only to your own interests, but also to the interests of others. Your attitude should be the same as that of Christ Jesus"* (Philippians 2:4-5).

# CHAPTER 13

# Standing Firm in God's Ways

We are at war. Courageous leaders are aware that their endeavors to bring a God-inspired transformation to their world will be met with opposition. They have entered a spiritual battle that has been going on since long before our time. It is a battle for the allegiance of the hearts and minds of men and women. It is a battle that pits the ways of God against the ways of Satan. It is a battle that is being waged both in heaven and on earth. It is a battle in which we must take an active role, loosing the power of God to be at work in heaven and on earth and binding the efforts of all those who oppose Him (Matthew 18:18). It is a battle that can be won only when we resist the temptation to resort to the enemy's dirty tactics and persist in the higher way of the cross. It is a battle that is won not only by our God-motivated action but also by our God-directed prayer. It is a battle both private and public, for it has to do with the internal attitudes that reflect the character of God and the outward actions that exhibit the ways of God. It is a battle of righteousness over corruption, of faith over fear, of integrity over dishonesty, of humility over pride, and of servanthood over manipulation.

Earth's history is more intertwined with heaven's activities than most of us can begin to imagine. Most of us live our lives in light of the physical dimension, responding to life primarily through the signals picked up by our five physical senses. But there is a spiritual dimension that is just as real as the physical dimension. This spiritual reality is not otherworldly; indeed it is very much part of this world's daily reality. The courageous leader must cultivate a deliberate awareness of this spiritual reality if he or she is going to successfully engage in the spiritual battle.

The Scriptures give us a few insightful glimpses into the spiritual dimension of the battle in which we are immersed. In the book of Job we see that behind the scenes of Job's earthly struggles lies a cosmic contest between Satan and God. Job's struggles are not understandable in a world where only physical reality exists. But in a world where physical and spiritual dimensions daily interact, each influencing the other, the story carries strategic insights into life.

We get another helpful glimpse into this other aspect of reality from Elisha's life. Elisha's cool demeanor and confident faith were baffling to his servant Gehazi when the city in which they lived was surrounded by enemy troops intent on killing the prophet. Gehazi, like most of us, had only a partial view of reality—that which he perceived with the five physical senses. However, Elisha had a complete view of reality, seeing not only the physical but also the spiritual armies that were camped around the city. So when Gehazi asked Elisha, *"Oh, my lord, what shall we do?"* the prophet's response simply reflected the bigger picture. *"'Don't be afraid,' the prophet answered. 'Those who are with us are more than those who are with them.' And Elisha prayed, 'O LORD, open his eyes so he may see.' Then the LORD opened the servant's eyes, and he looked and saw the hills full of horses and chariots of fire all around Elisha"* (2 Kings 6:15-17). May God open our eyes as He did Gehazi's so that we might see the *"chariots of fire"* that are on our side and thus be able to do battle in light of heaven's resources.

This heavenly perspective gave Elisha a distinct edge in the battle, and he was able to act creatively to overcome the enemy. The whole of the attacking army was struck with blindness, and Elisha led them by hand to the courts of the Israelite king in the capital city of Samaria. Instead of killing or abusing his prisoners, he prayed for them so that their sight was restored and lavished hospitality upon them. Elisha *"prepared a great feast for them, and after they had finished eating and drinking, he sent them away, and they returned to their master. So the bands from Aram stopped raiding Israel's territory"* (2 Kings 6:23). What an extraordinarily creative and gracious way to win a battle and stop the designs of the enemy! No military strategy was ever more successful!

## EQUIPPING FOR BATTLE

The story of Elisha shows us our need for divine revelation. We must ask God to allow us to see the challenges we face as He sees them, not limiting ourselves to only our physical perceptions. This story also illustrates for us the principle of the "opposite spirit." In the world's way of doing battle, when one is attacked, one attacks back. Force is met with force. Blows are countered with more blows, quickly leading to an escalating cycle of retaliation and counterretaliation. When persons succumb to the temptation of getting even, they relinquish their leadership role. The other party is now in control, setting the agenda, establishing the terms of engagement. This vicious circle of reprisals is not a scenario in which the courageous leader participates. Instead of reacting in like manner, the courageous leader learns to respond in the opposite spirit. This is Christ's way of doing battle. He taught us to turn the other cheek and to love our enemies (Matthew 5:37-48). Paul builds on Christ's teaching of responding in the opposite spirit when he writes, *"Do not repay anyone evil for evil....Do not be overcome by evil, but overcome evil with good"* (Romans 12:17,21).

The famous prayer known as the prayer of Saint Francis reflects the principle of responding in the opposite spirit. This is how the spiritual battle is to be conducted:

Lord, make me an instrument of your peace.
Where there is hatred let me sow love;
Where there is injury, pardon;
Where there is doubt, faith;
Where there is despair, hope;
Where there is darkness, light;
And where there is sadness, joy.

Lord, let me not so much seek
To be consoled as to console,
To be understood as to understand,
To be loved as to love,
For it is in giving that we receive;
It is in pardoning that we are pardoned;
And it is in dying that we are born into eternal life.
Amen.

Along these lines, Paul writes, *"For though we live in the world, we do not wage war as the world does. The weapons we fight with are not the weapons of the world. On the contrary, they have divine power to demolish strongholds. We demolish arguments and every pretension that sets itself up against the knowledge of God, and we take captive every thought to make it obedient to Christ"* (2 Corinthians 10:3-5).

Because our warfare is born out of the knowledge of God and obedience to Christ, it has a most distinctive quality to it. It does violence to Satan's kingdom of darkness precisely because we refuse to follow Satan's violent ways, because we have determined to *"put aside the deeds of darkness and put on the armor of light"* (Romans 13:12). Paul, in another passage, describes this *"armor of light."* He exhorts us:

> *"Finally, be strong in the Lord and in his mighty power. Put on the full armor of God so that you can take your stand against the devil's schemes. For our struggle is not against flesh and blood, but against the rulers, against the authorities, against the powers of this dark world and against the spiritual forces of evil in the heavenly realms. Therefore put on the full armor of God, so that when the day of evil comes, you may be able to stand your ground, and after you have done everything, to stand. Stand firm then,*
> - *with the belt of truth buckled around your waist,*
> - *with the breastplate of righteousness in place,*
> - *and with your feet fitted with the readiness that comes from the gospel of peace.*

- *In addition to all this, take up the shield of faith, with which you can extinguish all the flaming arrows of the evil one.*
- *Take the helmet of salvation*
- *and the sword of the Spirit, which is the word of God. And pray in the Spirit on all occasions with all kinds of prayers and requests. With this in mind, be alert and always keep on praying for all the saints"* (Ephesians 6:10-18).

This "armor" is nothing less than a life lived in the ways of God. It is a life that demonstrates the fruit of the Spirit: *"love, joy, peace, patience, kindness, goodness, faithfulness, gentleness and self-control"* (Galatians 5:22-23). It is a life committed to walking in obedience to the word of God. It is a life of aggressive, persistent prayer because it is a life lived in active dependence upon God. Saint Patrick of Ireland lived such a life. He knew that he could not be victorious in this battle apart from a life of concerted prayer in the Spirit. Daily he prayed a prayer that has come to be known as "Saint Patrick's Breastplate," for with it he clothed himself for the spiritual battles of each day. The prayer reflects an approach to life that is indispensable if the courageous leader is going to win life's spiritual battles. An excerpt of this prayer follows:

I arise today
Through God's strength to pilot me:
God's might to uphold me,
God's wisdom to guide me,
God's eye to look before me,
God's ear to hear me,
God's word to speak for me,
God's hand to guard me,
God's way to lie before me,
God's shield to protect me,
God's host to save me
From snares of devils,
From temptations of vices,
From everyone who shall wish me ill,

Afar and anear,
Alone and in multitude.

## OVERCOMING OBSTACLES

When Nehemiah began his project of rebuilding the wall and restoring the people of Jerusalem, he encountered persistent opposition. Sanballat, Tobiah, Geshem, and others set themselves against Nehemiah because *"they were very much disturbed that someone had come to promote the welfare of the Israelites"* (Nehemiah 2:10). The biblical account tells us that time and again these enemies tried to stop and destroy Nehemiah's project (Nehemiah 2:19-20, 4:1-15, 6:1-14). Intimidation, manipulation, false accusations, fear, division, ridicule, doubt, gossip, discouragement as well as frontal armed assault were all part of the enemy's tactics to grind the work to a halt. But whatever the enemy threw at him, Nehemiah would always pray and keep on working. Prayer was an integral part of Nehemiah's life and battle plan, fully interwoven into the way he faced life's challenges. Nehemiah's prayers are given a prominent place throughout the book (1:5-11; 2:4; 4:4-5; 5:19; 6:9,14; 13:14,22,29,31). In a similar way, prayer is to have a prominent place in the life of the courageous leader. It is key to overcoming obstacles.

Nehemiah didn't get bent out of shape with the enemy's constant onslaughts. Because he regularly took his burdens to the Lord in prayer, he was able to take it in stride. He understood that opposition came with the territory. His calm in the face of adversity was remarkable. It was not that he was nonchalant about it, but he was prepared. His prayers were coupled with action. *"We prayed to our God and posted a guard day and night to meet this threat"* (Nehemiah 4:9). We are told that those building the wall *"did their work with one hand and held a weapon in the other"* (Nehemiah 4:17). Work and warfare went together. Battle preparedness should be normative for those engaged in God-motivated action. Opposition should not take us by surprise, and like Nehemiah's construction crew, we should be ready for it.

Nehemiah's wonderful blend of prayerful reliance upon God and practical, down-to-earth action is a model for every courageous leader to imitate. Ponder on the wisdom of his tactics when under attack in chapter 4. Nehemiah understood the nature of the attack, laid a foundation of prayer, motivated the people to work *"with all their heart"* (Nehemiah 4:6), took preventive measures against the threats, listened to the concerns of his team, adjusted strategies to protect the most vulnerable parts of the project, built up people's confidence by reminding them of the *"great and awesome"* (Nehemiah 4:14) character of God, equipped them with the necessary weapons to fight the enemy and defend themselves, set up an alarm system to maximize communication among all the parts of the team so that all necessary resources could be quickly directed to any major problem area, promoted unity and solidarity among all the members of the team, and inspired all to their utmost in the way he led by example, he himself being fully involved hands-on in the defense and the direction of the work. How integrated his leadership was! The strategies he employed in the midst of opposition were spiritual...practical...spiritual...practical...There was no dichotomy in his leadership—nor should there be in ours.

One of the remarkable lessons to be learned from Nehemiah's life is how he did not let the constant opposition of the enemy absorb all of his attention and keep him from his priorities. He kept things in perspective and did not go chasing after every problem that arose. On one occasion his enemies called a meeting to discuss their differences with him. He tells us, *"I sent messengers to them with this reply: 'I am carrying on a great project and cannot go down. Why should the work stop while I leave it and go down to you?' Four times they sent me the same message, and each time I gave them the same answer"* (Nehemiah 6:3-4). Though he took action against the opposition when it was in the interest of the work, he did not let the enemy set his agenda and dictate his priorities. He had a God-led plan to carry out and would not be distracted from it.

In a similar way, Nehemiah urged his team to keep focused and not succumb to an excessive preoccupation with the enemy. In an embattled situation one can easily lose perspective. Because Nehemiah realized this, he spoke to his team about the enemy: *"Don't be afraid of them. Remember the Lord, who is great and awesome"* (Nehemiah 4:14). Nehemiah wasn't impressed with the enemy in the least, but he was very much impressed with God.

Though it is of some benefit to know our enemies so as to be aware of the forces that are pitted against us, it is of much greater value to know our God so that we can draw on the divine resources He makes available to us. Paul wrote, *"If God is for us, who can be against us?"* (Romans 8:31). After all, even though Satan may be more powerful than we are, he is nevertheless a finite creature— and a defeated one at that! Jesus conquered the enemy's hosts through His life laid down: *"And having disarmed the powers and authorities, he made a public spectacle of them, triumphing over them by the cross"* (Colossians 2:15). The powers of darkness do not stand a chance against the infinite Creator. No enemy can begin to compare with Him. No obstacle can thwart Him. No opposition can overcome Him. And you, too, can overcome the powers of darkness *"because the one who is in you is greater than the one who is in the world"* (1 John 4:4).

The reason we can live in such confidence, impressed with God and unintimidated by the enemy, is that we can be sure of God's ultimate victory. Instead of feeling beleaguered, the courageous leader can rejoice in the midst of adversity. Because God is who He is, the courageous leader can face difficulties and obstacles with a song. Confident praise befits the one engaged in a battle to see a God-inspired vision established (Psalm 149:6). Therefore, *"because you are my help, I sing in the shadow of your wings. My soul clings to you; your right hand upholds me"* (Psalm 63:7-8). *"I will sing of your strength, in the morning I will sing of your love; for you are my fortress, my refuge in times of trouble. O my Strength, I sing praise to you; you, O God, are my fortress, my loving God"* (Psalm 59:16-17). In anticipation of the final victory we can fervently join the multitudes who have sung the words written by John and made popular by Handel: *"Hallelujah! For our Lord God Almighty reigns....The kingdom of the world has become the kingdom of our Lord and of his Christ, and he will reign for ever and ever"* (Revelation 19:6; 11:15). Hallelujah!

## PERSISTING IN SERVANTHOOD

One of the keys to Nehemiah's overcoming success in his battles is that he considered himself to be a servant (Nehemiah 1:6,11; 2:5,20). A courageous leader needs to learn how to persist in servanthood. This is how the battle is ultimately won. This is achieved by, among other things, learning to relinquish rights, embrace diversity, love excellence, and practice generosity.

## • Relinquish Rights

Servanthood begins by learning to relinquish rights. Oftentimes, people in today's world demand their rights and try to avoid their responsibilities. Never have you seen a public protest of people marching through the streets carrying placards emblazoned with the slogan "We demand our responsibilities!" No, people generally are more concerned with what they are getting out of life than with what they are giving to the lives of those around them. This is not so with courageous leaders. For them, servanthood is adopted as a lifestyle. This means that responsibilities aren't avoided; they're embraced. Rights and privileges aren't tenaciously held on to; they are relinquished in order to serve. The focus is not to gain but to give.

## • Embrace Diversity

Paul wrote to Titus, a young leader whom he was mentoring. In his writings he instructs Titus as to the qualifications for leadership. In a few words he details what he considers the characteristics of paramount importance for a leader. Though the passage is brief, it is a distillation of wisdom that requires much careful meditation. In Titus 1:6-8, Paul repeats only one word: "*blameless.*" This word sums up for him the high standard of integrity to which the courageous leader must aspire. Paul details three areas in which this standard of excellence must evidence itself. It must be seen in:

the leader's family relationships (Titus 1:6),
the leader's personal character (Titus 1:7-8), and
the leader's skills and abilities (Titus 1:9).

The central section on character is the one to which he gives the most attention. Paul gives five negative commands related to what the leader should not be, followed by six positive commands that highlight what the leader should be. If you were asked to make such a list, what would you include? If you could make a list of fewer than a dozen items that would serve as an inerrant guide for all leaders of all time, what would be on your list? We've asked this question of people in seminars all around the world and are astounded at how different their lists tend to be from Paul's. It would behoove us to ponder especially on those things that Paul includes on his list that are absent from ours. Let's look now at his list. The five things that he says leaders must not be are:

overbearing
quick-tempered
given to drunkenness
violent
pursuing dishonest gain

The six things that Paul says leaders must be are:

hospitable
a lover of what is good
self-controlled
upright
holy
disciplined

Each of these points merits lengthy consideration, but for now let us reflect only on the first of these positive qualities. What a surprising, unexpected thing it would seem to be to find "hospitable" on a leadership list, let alone to find it at the top of the list. Not many would give this characteristic such a prominent place. Why does Paul? Does he only mean that a leader should know how to serve tea and cookies to his or her guests? Or is there something more we are to learn from this?

The Greek word from which the word *hospitable* is translated is *philoxenos*. It is the opposite of *xenophobia*, the fear of strangers/foreigners. It is a compound word that literally means "to love strangers/foreigners." Of course, this is what one does when one shows hospitality to outsiders and welcomes them into one's life and home. But there is much more to the word than a gracious welcome and a kind reception. In order to be able to demonstrate love toward a stranger, the courageous leader must have a sufficient breadth of perspective that allows him or her to gladly embrace diversity. Many people feel comfortable only when surrounded by people of like kind, with similar backgrounds, with common tastes, with a shared culture, and with mutual likes and dislikes. Differences can be seen as uncomfortable, diversity as threatening. But one who is able to embrace only that which is similar to one-self will lead a shallow, dull, monochromatic existence.

God is obviously a lover of diversity. Consider the world He has made. It is anything but shallow, dull, and monochromatic. He could well have made it a black-and-white world and we would have been none the wiser. However, He made it a polychromatic world and beautifully filled it with every imaginable hue and color. He could have made one kind of tree or flower, but He decorated our planet with thousands of varieties of richly diverse flora. Perhaps one animal species would have sufficed for another god. But not so with the true God who left the imprint of His creativ-ity on innumerable species of mammals, birds, fish, amphibians, reptiles, insects, etc. Every unique snowflake and each baby's sin-gular smile bear testimony to the fact that He is not a God of cookie-cutter mass production. In His magnificent artistry He's filled the whole earth with life-enhancing diversity.

Similarly, truly courageous leaders will be lovers of diversity. They are not ones who merely accept diversity. They are not ones who have learned to put up with the inconvenience of differences. They are not ones who endure diversity with a sense of resignation. No! They embrace diversity with passionate enthusiasm. In their presence, people with divergent opinions, unique gifts, different per-sonalities, unconventional suggestions, and dissimilar backgrounds all feel welcome. This is hospitality at its leadership best. Therefore, courageous leaders do not surround themselves with look-alike "yes" men. Instead, they recognize both the gifts they have and those they don't have and deliberately staff their weaknesses, welcoming onto the team those who will act in a complementary way, not just in a compliant way to "the boss." Because they espouse diversity, courageous leaders will spot and champion the differing gifts of God in their teammates, enthusiastically making room for the unique contribution each one has to give. This will add great strength to and invigorate the team.

## • Love Excellence

It seems that Paul had much in mind when he urged that leaders be *"philoxenos,"* lovers of strangers/foreigners and embracers of diversity. Interestingly enough, the next characteristic Paul lists in his instructions to Titus has to do with another point of passion in the leader's life. Courageous leaders should be *philagathos*—lovers of that which is good. They should be lovers of the good life, not in the crass, materialistic way that that term is most commonly employed but in the most noble, all-encompassing way possible. They are to love excellence in all its multifaceted dimensions. Indeed, *"whatever is true, whatever is noble, whatever is right, whatever is pure, whatever is lovely, whatever is admirable—if anything is excellent or praiseworthy"* (Philippians 4:8), it is to be the object of their passion, filling their thoughts, shaping their conduct.

God clearly loves excellence. He's a doer of excellent things. Everything He created *"was very good"* (Genesis 1:31). Indeed, He's the unparalleled Master Craftsman who has accomplished all His work with incredible care and exquisite elegance. The hosts of heaven declare to Him, *"Great and marvelous are your deeds, Lord God Almighty. Just and true are your ways, King of the ages"* (Revelation 15:3). Likewise, it was said of Jesus, *"He has done everything well"* (Mark 7:37). Excellence is forever His hallmark. He therefore hopes to be able to say to each one of us, *"Well done, good and faithful servant!"* (Matthew 25:21,23), for indeed *"we are God's workmanship, created in Christ Jesus to do good works"* (Ephesians 2:10).

For this reason, the courageous leader's love of excellence must be evidenced in the commitment to integrity of character and in *"the quality of each man's work"* (1 Corinthians 3:13). Organizational elegance will be the result of making excellence the standard of both personal conduct and corporate endeavors. This can be accomplished only when something more than the next paycheck is the primary motivation for all on the team. Paul encourages his colleagues on toward excellence by reminding them, *"Whatever you do, work at it with all your heart, as working for the Lord, not for men, since you know that you will receive an inheritance from the Lord as a reward. It is the Lord Christ you are serving"* (Colossians 3:23-24).

How can such excellence be promoted in the workplace? Paul says, *"I will show you the most excellent way"* (1 Corinthians 12:31)—and he proceeds to speak of the way of love. A courageous leader will foster a corporate environment in which love is the standard ethos for team members to relate to one another. This is not some mushy sentimentalism or an unattainable utopian ideal. Love is the necessary condition for maximizing corporate excellence. This becomes clearer as Paul defines love:

> *"Love is patient, love is kind. It does not envy, it does not boast, it is not proud. It is not rude, it is not self-seeking, it is not easily angered, it keeps no record of wrongs. Love does not delight in evil but rejoices with the truth. It always protects, always trusts, always hopes, always perseveres. Love never fails"* (1 Corinthians 13:4-8).

Love is excellence in action. Leaders who lead with this kind of love and who foster an environment of love enable all on their team to excel.

## • Practice Generosity

The courageous leader who has learned to relinquish rights, embrace diversity, and love excellence must also be committed to practicing generosity. Leadership is a servant role that requires giving, giving, giving. You give of your time, of your resources, of your expertise, of yourself. You give and keep giving, when you feel like it and when you don't. There is no genuine leadership without a lifestyle of generosity. God is the ultimate leader, and He is the most extravagant, superlative, generous giver of all. *"He who did not spare his own Son, but gave him up for us all—how will he not also, along with him, graciously give us all things?"* (Romans 8:32). Giving is the mark of true servanthood. Therefore, courageous leader, *"just as you excel in everything—in faith, in speech, in knowledge, in complete earnestness and in your love for us—see that you also excel in this grace of giving"* (2 Corinthians 8:7).

## SEEING THE FOREST AND THE TREES

Some people, as the saying goes, "can't see the forest for the trees." Others see only the big picture of the forest and never even notice the individual trees. Within these extremes lie many different ways of looking at reality. Of course, every person has his or her own unique perspective drawn from his or her God-given gifts and personality traits. It's as if everyone was born with a different set of glasses. Some seem to have a built-in wide-angle lens: They tend to see the big picture. Others seem to have a built-in microscope: They tend to see the details. It is possible, however, to learn to use a different set of lenses from the ones you naturally have before you. The courageous leader seeks to increase the capacity of his or her perspective so that he or she can see both with a wide-angle lens and with a microscope, as the need arises. The courageous leader must always keep in view the big picture of the project as well as the project's significant details. If the leader loses sight of the big picture, the whole team will tend to get off course and lose their way.

The courageous leader must always keep the big picture before the team. At the same time, the leader must pay attention to significant details: those that can jeopardize progress along the plan's critical path, those that can affect team morale and destroy unity, those that can compromise the corporate ethos and integrity. The leader should be aware that excessive absorption with details could result in unwise micromanagement and strategic blindness resulting from myopic absorption with minutiae. However, total indifference to the details will lead to a detached unreality and lack of connectedness that will hinder both team dynamics and progress toward the Overall Objective.

To achieve this balanced perspective, courageous leaders need to staff their weakness. As has already been noted, this means that they surround themselves with people who see differently than they do and learn to draw on the expertise of others so that together both the forest and the trees are kept in perspective. Teamwork and deliberate communication are essential for this to happen.

Now, the role of the leader requires that the leader major on the majors. This means that the most important things—not necessarily the most pressing and urgent things—are given major attention. Jesus chastised the religious leaders of His day because they allowed themselves to be sidetracked by the trivial and insignificant issues while failing to focus on the major matters. He said, *"Woe to you, teachers of the law and Pharisees, you hypocrites! You give a tenth of your spices—mint, dill and cummin. But you have neglected the more important matters of the law—justice, mercy and faithfulness. You should have practiced the latter, without neglecting the former"* (Matthew 23:23).

At the same time that the leader majors on the majors, he or she must watch out for *"the little foxes that ruin the vineyards"* (Song of Songs 2:15). Some "little" problems prove to be not so little over time. If the "little foxes" are not caught in time, the whole harvest can be spoiled. It's a case of "a stitch in time saves nine." The problem is not "little" if it creates a hole in the dike. If that is the case, it behooves you to immediately plug the hole by any means possible and begin devising a permanent solution to the problem. In this case, the urgent becomes important and it is important to take care of it urgently.

The key to discerning whether or not a "little" problem is of the hole-in-the-dike type is to consider the long-term implications. What will happen to the team, to the project, to the organization, to the vision if this little problem continues to develop unchecked? If it will produce no critical effect in the long run, it is genuinely a little problem and can be dispensed with. However, if it is indicative of a drift toward that which can destroy the God-inspired vision, frustrate the God-led plan, and render ineffective the God-motivated action, it is no longer a little problem and should be dealt with accordingly. Many of the most destructive trends begin as a subtle, nearly imperceptible drift. Drift can be avoided only as we pay *"careful attention"* (Hebrews 2:1), rightly anchoring our actions to the God-given vision by daily seeking God. He can give the necessary foresight and the sensitivity to observe situations and understand the long-term implications so that problems can be nipped in the bud.

As the courageous leader seeks to live with a balanced perspective of the forest and the trees—majoring on the majors while not ignoring the little foxes—it is helpful to apply the "teeter-totter principle." The teeter-totter is a playground game through which children learn the art of balance. The courageous leader must hone this art to its fullest. Therefore, the leader must develop an awareness of organizational direction. If everyone in the organization is beginning to teeter, the leader must totter. If everyone is tottering, the leader must teeter. In this way, the team's equilibrium remains balanced and the project is able to stay on course.

Similarly, some have learned that it is at times hard to stay on course when driving in snow. The road conditions can be treacherous, and with little warning, the car can be thrown into a spin. The alert driver knows that by driving into the spin he or she can pull the car out of the spin and keep it safely on the road. When the leader is sensitively guiding the project he or she will make mid-course adjustments so that the car will never spin out of control. By serving the team in this way, tragedy can be averted and the ultimate destination will be safely reached. Together the team will celebrate a job well done and rejoice in a mission accomplished.

# CHAPTER 14

# Reaching the Goal— Mission Accomplished

**W**e are reaching the goal, our Overall Objective. Soon we may say that *the mission is accomplished*. Will it be true? We do know that we've used powerful planning procedures that have proven very effective for completing thousands of projects worldwide. Multibillion-dollar projects involving thousands of personnel, such as putting a man on the moon and bringing him back safely to earth, have been guided by these planning procedures. Similar methods have been used for planning new churches, universities, educational curricula, industries, and mission bases and for the discipling of nations. Yes, the powerful 5-step procedure for developing the Leaders Plan provides a very dependable guide for reaching our Overall Objective. However, it is not enough to plan well. A good plan that is not based on a God-inspired vision or is not implemented through God-motivated action can be very dangerous. Even though our desire in writing this book was to give people tools to lead well as courageous leaders, we are keenly aware that isolating the planning methods in Part B from the other scriptural truths presented throughout this book can be destructive. Therefore, we believe it is important for Christian leaders to consider each project as a seamless transition from a God-inspired vision to the development of a God-led plan and on into God-motivated action. This can result in a God-honoring mission accomplished. The project is thus accomplished by God's involvement every step of the way, with His inspiration, wisdom, protection, and guidance and by His strength and grace. He has allowed us to co-create with Him. Imagine being an intern on a project with the Creator of the world! Such a project brings glory to God.

As we close Part C, let us touch briefly on the significance of being a transformational leader, gaining victory, and bringing glory to God.

## BEING A TRANSFORMATIONAL LEADER

In the early part of the twentieth century, Abraham Kuyper was prime minister of Holland and brought glory to God by transforming the nation. In *The Crown of Christian Heritage*, Kuyper said that he had a passion to "carve as it were into the conscience of the nation the ordinances of the Lord, to which the Bible and Creation bear witness, until the nation pays homage again to God." His actions were spurred by the burning conviction that Jesus Christ rules by a living power. Kuyper wrote:

> The fellowship of being near unto God must become reality in the full and vigorous prosecution of our life. It must permeate and give color to our feeling, our perceptions, our sensations, our thinking, our imagining, our willing, our acting, and our speaking. It must not stand as a foreign factor in our life, but it must be a passion throughout our whole existence.

Others like Kuyper have transformed their worlds by living in close fellowship with God, embracing God-inspired visions, and following through with God-led plans and implementing them in God's ways. They gave their lives to Him as living sacrifices, holy and pleasing to God. They did not conform to the patterns of this world. They were transformed by the renewing of their minds and were able to do God's will and collaborate with Him (Romans 12:1-2). Being transformed themselves they became transformational leaders.

In an inspiring talk at a leadership conference, Dr. Tom Bloomer (University of the Nations associate provost) built on the transformational leadership concepts introduced by James MacGregor Burns in his 1978 book on leadership. Tom contrasted transformational and transactional leadership styles, demonstrating that Jesus is our ideal model of a transformational leader. Jesus gave His life that we might be saved. Satan is a transactional leader. He gives dubious promises only in return for strict obedience to him.

A group or institution led by a transformational leader is characterized as being visionary, creative, and joyful. It cultivates an environment that embraces diversity, enhances unity, facilitates good communication, and enables a dynamic work environment in which team members share harmoniously with each other. A group led by a transactional leader is characterized as being hierarchical, authoritarian, and manipulative. It is dichotomized into compartments and departments, and regulated by many rules. Loyalty is valued over truth, and major decisions are announced to the group, not processed by the group. A small number of leaders hold tightly to all information, and relationships between members of the group are based on jealous competitiveness.

It behooves all Christian leaders to be alert to the dangers of becoming transactional leaders rather than transformational leaders. Jesus called His disciples together and described these two types of leadership: *"You know that the rulers of the Gentiles lord it over them, and their high officials exercise authority over them. Not so with you. Instead, whoever wants to become great among you must be your servant...just as the Son of Man did not come to be served, but to serve, and to give his life as a ransom for many"* (Matthew 20:25-28). The Christian leader is not called to serve by leading but is called to lead by serving. Paul wrote, *"And we, who with unveiled faces all reflect the Lord's glory, are being transformed into his likeness with ever-increasing glory, which comes from the Lord, who is the Spirit"* (2 Corinthians 3:18). Jesus is committed to transform us into His likeness if we seek Him.

## GAINING VICTORY

During World War II, the prime minister of England, Winston Churchill, gave a stirring and inspiring speech during some of the darkest days of the war.

> We shall defend our island whatever the cost may be; we shall fight on the beaches, we shall fight in the fields; we shall fight in the streets; and we shall fight on the hill. We shall never surrender and if this island were subjugated and starving, our empire on the seas would carry on the struggle until in God's good time the New World with all its power and might steps forth to the rescue and liberation of the old.

Churchill communicated to everyone that the nation was determined to continue to fight, and his faith gave others the hope and confidence that their nation would ultimately gain the victory. Many brave men and women died and did not witness the promised victory that their sacrifice helped win.

Near the end of his life, Paul expressed a great sense of victory, even as he faced death. He said, *"I have fought the good fight, I have finished the race, I have kept the faith. Now there is in store for me the crown of righteousness, which the Lord, the righteous Judge, will award to me on that day—and not only to me, but also to all who have longed for his appearing"* (2 Timothy 4:7-8).

The powerful chapter in Hebrews on faith emphasizes that *"...without faith it is impossbile to please God, because anyone who comes to him must believe that he exists and that he rewards those who earnestly seek him. By faith Noah, when warned about things not yet seen, in holy fear built an ark to save his family. By faith he condemned the world and became heir of the rightousness that comes with faith"* (Hebrews 11:6-7). The writer continues to tell about the faith shown by Abraham, Isaac, Jacob, Joseph, Moses, and Rahab and then says:

> *I do not have time to tell about Gideon, Barak, Samson, Jephthah, David, Samuel and the prophets, who through faith conquered kingdoms, administered justice, and gained what was promised; who shut the mouths of lions, quenched the fury of the flames, and escaped the edge of the sword; whose weakness was turned to strength, and who became powerful in battle....still others were chained and put in prison. They were stoned;*

*they were sawed in two; they were put to death by the sword....the world was not worthy of them....These were all commended for their faith, yet none of them received what had been promised. God had planned something better for us so that only together with us would they be made perfect* (Hebrews 11:32-40).

Through this faith, the saints of old gained some fulfilling earthly victories, but only in life eternal with their Creator God did they experience the ultimate victory. The same is true for those who go to be with the Lord before completion of a God-motivated project. The day-by-day intimate relationship with God and the project team can be the source of daily victories, but these people do not experience the celebration of an earthly victory when the goal is reached and the mission is accomplished. Their reward must be found in gaining the ultimate victory, for God had planned something better for them, too.

## BRINGING GLORY TO GOD

Shortly before His crucifixion and resurrection, Jesus looked toward heaven and prayed to the Father, *"I have brought you glory on earth by completing the work you gave me to do"* (John 17:4). When we reach the goal, complete the project, and can say that the mission is accomplished, we have an overwhelming sense of joy and thankfulness. The project was accomplished by God's involvement and guidance every step of the way. The glory goes to Him. Jesus said, *"If you remain in me and my words remain in you, ask whatever you wish, and it will be given you. This is to my Father's glory, that you bear much fruit, showing yourselves to be my disciples"* (John 15:7-8).

At the beginning of this book we included an acknowledgment to our Creator God who gives us opportunities to collaborate with Him. It seems right to close the book with a portion of this same acknowledgment that gives glory to Him. "We bow down and give praise, honor, and heartfelt thanks to our God, the God who is so very personal and yet infinite, the God who millennia ago initiated an awesome, life-changing, world-transforming project through His courageous Son, Jesus Christ. We thank You, Father, Son, and

Holy Spirit, for Your life-transforming work, which continues through the ages and has impacted our lives. We pray that those who read this book will be inspired to be courageous leaders who will collaborate with You to transform their worlds and bring honor and glory to You."

# References and
# Recommended Reading

*Carey, Christ and Cultural Transformation.* The Life and Influence of William Carey; by Ruth and Vishal Mangalwadi; OM Publishing, 1997.

*Leadership is an Art,* by Max De Pree, Dell Publishers, 1989.

*Lend Me Your Ears: Great Speeches in History;* Selected by William Saffire; N.W. Norton, Inc. Publisher, N.Y., London, 1992.

*The Crown of Christian Heritage;* Abraham Kuyper's famous L. T. Stone lectures at Princeton University. Nivedit Good Books, Distributor, Pvt. LTD Publisher, India, 1994. It contains an excellent introduction by Vishal Mangalwadi about Kuyper's life.

*Lincoln at Gettysburg—The Words That Remade America;* by Gary Wells, Simon and Shuster Pub. 1992.

*How the Irish Saved Western Civilization;* by Thomas Cahill; Anchor Books, Doubleday Pub. 1995. Includes the prayer known as "St. Patrick's Breastplate."

*Great Souls—Six Who Changed the Century,* by David Aikman, former Senior Correspondent for *Time* Magazine; Word Publishing, 1998; contains outstanding biographical information including Aleksandr Soltzhenitsyn and Mother Teresa.

*Dimensions for Living;* great prayers including the Prayer of Saint Francis; Lion Publishing, Nashville, TN, 1998.

*Christian Growth Study Bible;* New International Version contains the YWAM 30-Path Study Guide; Zondervan Publishing House, 1997.

*My Utmost for His Highest;* Oswald Chambers, published by Barbour and Company, Inc., New Jersey; Copyright by Dodd, Mead & Company Inc. 1935.

*Contemporary Black Biography, Vol. 4;* B.C. Bigelow Ed.; pub. Gale Research Inc., 1993. Includes a brief biography of George Washington Carver.

*Economic Effects of Revival;* by Alv Magnus; in Proceedings of the University of the Nations Bi-Annual Leadership Workshop, 1995; Restenas, Sweden. Presents the impact of Hans Hauge ministry which led to transformation of a nation.

*A Treasury of the World's Great Speeches;* Houston Peterson; Pub. Simon and Schuster, Inc., N.Y. 1954, 1965; includes Sir Winston Churchill's famous speech "This was their finest hour" in June 1940, and the "Blood, Toil, Tears and Sweat" speech to Parliament, May 13, 1940.

*The Leader of the Future;* F. Hesselbein, M. Goldsmith, R. Beckhard, Editors; The Peter F. Drucker Foundation, N.Y., 1996.

*Reflections on Leadership;* How Robert K. Greenleaf's Theory of Servant-Leadership Influenced Today's Top Management Thinkers; edited by Larry C. Spears; Pub. John Wiley & Sons, Inc., 1995.

*Let the Nations Be Glad! The Supremacy of God in Missions;* by John Piper; Pub. by Baker Books, MI, 1973.

*Knowing God;* by J.I. Packer; printed by InterVarsity Press, Illinois, with permission of Holder and Sloughton, Ltd., England, 1973.

*Selling the Dream;* by Guy Kawasaki; published by Harper Collins Publishers, NY, 1991.

*University of the Nations Catalogue;* published by U of N 1999; includes the Foundational Principles.

*Transformational Vs Transactional Leadership;* by Thomas Bloomer; a talk to an international Leadership Training School in South Africa, 1998, via the GENESIS network.

*Management: A Biblical Approach;* by Myron Rush; published by Victor Books, a division of SP Publication, Inc. 1988.

# ABOUT THE AUTHORS

## Howard V. Malmstadt

Howard V. Malmstadt is the International Provost and Vice President of Academic Affairs for the University of the Nations (U of N). Together with YWAM's president, Loren Cunningham, and a team of courageous leaders, Howard co-founded the U of N in 1978. YWAM's University now has branches in over 100 nations.

Howard Malmstadt has poured his life into that fledgling university with the same zest that he gave to his scientific teaching, research and administration for nearly 3 decades as a professor at the University of Illinois. Through the U of N, Dr. Malmstadt has continued to pursue academic excellence. His top priority is still the same—excellence in serving Jesus. He believes his experiences in the military, university teaching, research and administration, and industrial/governmental consulting have prepared him for a time such as this—a time to develop programs, enthusiastic teams, and courageous leaders who will meet the felt needs of people worldwide while also communicating the Good News of Jesus Christ.

Dr. Malmstadt was born in Marinette, Wisconsin in 1922. After receiving a BS degree at University of Wisconsin and specialized Naval radar training at Princeton and MIT, he served as a Naval Officer aboard destroyers in the Pacific during World War II. Following the war, he received a Ph.D. in chemistry from the University of Wisconsin, and joined the faculty of the University of Illinois in 1951.

At Illinois, he and his research team pioneered several areas of science and technology, including applied spectroscopy, automated chemical measurement systems, clinical methods, kinetic methods of analysis, and instrumentation for scientists. He has received several national and international awards for these developments. More than 60 research students did their doctoral theses under his direction. He has authored or co-authored over 150 journal publications, books, and patents.

His first books, co-authored with Dr. C.G Enke were *Electronics for Scientists*, published in 1961, *Digital Electronics for Scientists* (1969), and *Computer Logic* (1970), followed by several others between 1970 and 1995. These books were the bases for many new courses and were used in hundreds of universities and laboratories worldwide. Malmstadt's latest book, co-authored with James L. Halcomb and David Joel Hamilton, is entitled *Courageous Leaders Transforming Their World* (2000). This book is largely the result of important leadership observations and participant feedback from the U of N Project Development Leadership school, started and led yearly by Dr. Malmstadt since 1986. The importance of a seamless transition from Vision to Plan to Action to Mission Accomplished became increasingly clear to him over the years, and thus became a major topic for the book.

# David Joel Hamilton

David Joel Hamilton, the son of United Methodist missionaries who served in Bolivia, was born in the United States, born again in Mexico, baptized in the Spirit in Peru, received a mission call in Holland, and served God for nearly 24 years in YWAM. Raised in a bilingual and bi-cultural context, he developed intuitive cross-cultural sensitivity and a deep desire to see people from developing nations released into leadership.

Upon completing his BA in Political Science at Cornell College, David attended the first YWAM School of Evangelism in Heidebeek, Holland in May 1977. In January, 1978, his fiance, Christine, also attended an SOE. They were married a year later and moved to Santiago, Chile to help pioneer the work of YWAM and lead Discipleship Training Schools. In 1987, David pioneered the first School of Biblical Studies in South America in the Spanish language. He received a Masters in Biblical Studies from the University of the Nations. He recently served as one of the senior content editors for the *Christian Growth Study Bible*, which was published by Zondervan in conjunction with YWAM.

David currently serves as an International Associate Provost for the University of the Nations, and also as Assistant to the President. he is in the process of co-authoring a book with Loren Cunningham on women in ministry. For a period of three years, David and his family will be traveling to some 150 YWAM/U of N training locations in more than 100 nations to assist in school staff and leadership development, course and curriculum development, and campus development, spearheading the U of N Global On-site Development Program. Last year, David and his family spent eleven months visiting 57 YWAM and U of N locations in 38 nations throughout Africa.

Over his past 23 years with YWAM David has worked eleven years in Chile, three and one half years in Hawaii, five years in Virginia, one year in Amsterdam, six months in Spain, and short periods of time in some 102 countries. David and Christine have four children: Jonathan (16), Timothy (14), Sarah (12), and Matthew (10).

# James Halcomb

James Halcomb is a pioneer and author in leadership planning and management systems, having served many churches and Christian ministries as well as Fortune 500 companies from his headquarters in Silicon Valley California.

He designed the "war room" management information center in Anchorage for history's largest non-government project, the Trans Alaska Pipeline project. He has popularized using computers in conjunction with large screen projection systems in conference rooms for leadership planning. He developed the widely used 5-step leadership planning process of how to set the Overall Objective, to creatively evolve a leader's strategic plan, and to successfully reach the Overall Objective.

Halcomb developed the PERT-O-GRAPH System of simplified math and emphasis on management charts while at Lockheed Aircraft at the time the Navy instituted PERT (Program Evaluation and Review Technique) for effectively speeding up the Polaris missile project.

As director of his consulting firm, Halcomb has trained many business executives and government leaders and has assisted in planning key projects and new product introductions at CBS, XEROX, U.S. Air Force, AT&T, NASA, RCA, Bank of America, Hughes Aircraft, ARCO, KFC Corporation, and B. F. Goodrich.

James Halcomb is the author of the McGraw-Hill book, *PLANNING BIG with MacProject*, with a foreword by John Sculley, former Chairman and CEO, Apple Computer, Inc. The book shows how to interactively speed up the Halcomb 5-step planning process in a typical conference setting through the use of a computer-driven large screen display. Halcomb based this system on the biblical principles of Proverbs 15:22: *"Plans fail for of lack of counsel, but with many advisors they succeed."*

In his desire to be a businessman in the Lord's service, he has helped pastors plan at his own church, Peninsula Bible Church in Palo Alto, and many other pastors and leaders of Christian ministries, including Christian and Missionary Alliance, Campus Crusade for Christ, FamilyLife, Louis Palau Evangelistic Association, Focus on the Family, Walk Thru the Bible, Point Man Leadership Ministries, and World Vision. He is a member of the U of N's International Advisory Board and a seminar speaker at several of YWAM's worldwide training activities including the University of the Nations, Island Breeze, and GENESIS.

With a BS degree in physics, Halcomb has a background as an engineer and manager at ITT, Lockheed, and Varian, before forming Halcomb Associates in 1962. He is currently an instrument-rated pilot of multi-engine aircraft, and served in the U.S. Navy in WWII as an electronics technician and as an officer in the U.S. Army Signal Corps in Korea.

James Halcomb is very supportive of the divine institution of Christian marriage and of the family ministries which emphasize it. He is very devoted to his precious wife, Konda, whom he considers a special gift from the Lord. They have four sons in their thirties and forties who all love the Lord, and are very grateful that their seven grandchildren are being raised in the nurture and admonition of the Lord.